D0073136

A
27-1051   LA217   87-19887 CIP
Siegel, Harvey. ✓Educating reason: rationality, critical thinking, and
education. (Philosophy of education research library, 1) Routledge, 1988.
191p   bibl index   ISBN 0-415-00175-7, $25.00
   Siegel (philosophy, University of Miami) reopens inquiry into the aims of education. Here critical thinking is construed as the fundamental educational ideal.
The author takes issue with three important interpreters of critical thinking: Robert H. Ennis, Richard W. Paul, and John McPeck. Siegel claims that a critical
thinker is one who is appropriately moved by reasons and who believes and acts
on the basis of good reasons. Morality and respect for persons, self-sufficiency and
preparation for adulthood, initiation into the rational traditions, and the requirements of democratic living are offered as justifications for establishing critical
thinking as the fundamental educational ideal. Siegel defends his position against
objections based on ideology or indoctrination. He argues for a pluralistic science
education as an instance of curricular support that favors critical thinking. Minimum competency testing is judged not to be a defensible educational practice
since it is not aimed at critical thinking goals. Siegel's style is clear but often unnec-
essarily repetitious. For advanced students.—*D. A. Haney, Marywood College*

Educating
Reason

Philosophy of Education Research Library
Edited by
Dr Vernon Howard and Dr Israel Scheffler
Harvard Graduate School of Education

Recent decades have witnessed the decline of distinctively philosophical thinking about education. Practitioners and the public alike have increasingly turned rather to psychology, the social sciences and to technology in search of basic knowledge and direction. However, philosophical problems continue to surface at the center of educational concerns, confronting educators and citizens as well with inescapable questions of value, meaning, purpose, and justification.

PERL will publish works addressed to teachers, school administrators and researchers in every branch of education, as well as to philosophers and the reflective public. The series will illuminate the philosophical and historical bases of educational practice, and assess new educational trends as they emerge.

Educating Reason

Rationality, Critical Thinking, and Education

Harvey Siegel
Associate Professor of Philosophy
University of Miami

ROUTLEDGE
NEW YORK AND LONDON

First published in 1988 by
Routledge Inc.
in association with Methuen Inc.
29 West 35th Street, New York, NY 10001
Published in Great Britain by
Routledge
11 New Fetter Lane, London EC4P 4EE

Set in 10/11 point Times
by Witwell Ltd, Liverpool
and printed in Great Britain
by Billings, Worcester

Library of Congress Cataloging in Publication Data

Siegel, Harvey, 1952–
Educating reason: rationality, critical thinking, and education/
Harvey Siegel.
p.   cm.–(Philosophy of education research library: 1)
Bibliography: p.
Includes index.
1. Education–United States–Aims and objectives. 2. Critical
thinking–United States, 3. Reasoning. I. Title. II. Series.
LA217.S52 1988
370'.973–dc19   87–19887
                                                        CIP

British Library CIP Data also available
ISBN 0 415 00175 7

For Nancy
With love, gratitude and sorrow

Contents

Preface   ix

Acknowledgments   xii

Introduction: Rationality, critical thinking
and education   1

1 Three conceptions of critical thinking   5

2 The reasons conception   32

3 The justification of critical thinking as an educational ideal   48

4 The ideology objection   62

5 The indoctrination objection   78

6 Science education   91

7 Minimum competency testing   116

Postscript: Towards a theory of rationality   127

Notes   138

Bibliography   177

Index   187

Critical thought is of the first importance in the conception and organization of educational activities.

Israel Scheffler

Mankind in the main has always regarded reason as a bit of a joke.

G.K. Chesterton

Preface

Three considerations have conspired to bring about this book. First, there is the hue and cry — from a number of national commissions on education and from a variety of educationists — concerning the need to move away from rote memorization and an emphasis on information acquisition, and to incorporate critical thinking (or analytical thinking, or logical thinking, or reasoning) into the curriculum. Second, there is the growing "Informal Logic Movement," a movement which emphasizes the alleged weaknesses of formal logic, and the alleged strengths of informal logic and critical thinking, for the curriculum. Finally, there is the widely shared conviction, which I strongly endorse, that contemporary philosophy of education suffers from a stultifying misconception of "analysis" according to which deep philosophical questions concerning values and the aims of education are somehow off-limits. This misconception is seen, by me and many others, to have bred a barren and boring corpus of work in contemporary analytic philosophy of education. To escape the misconception is to re-open the possibility of conducting a worthwhile, technically competent philosophical inquiry into the aims of education. This is the task taken on in what follows.

Which aims, though, are to be considered? The first two considerations suggest a candidate. For both philosophers and educationists have suggested, in their various ways and for their various reasons, that critical thinking be regarded as an educational aim. So too, for that matter, have the vast majority of historical figures in philosophy of education, from Plato to Dewey. But what critical thinking is, and how it is to be justified as an educational aim or ideal, are questions which demand explicit attention. Likewise demanding attention are questions concerning the ramifications of this aim for the curriculum and for educational policy and practice. Additional questions raised concern the relationship between critical thinking and rationality, the nature of rationality, and the status of the latter as an intellectual idea.

All of this is the subject of the present effort. (A more detailed guide is offered in the following Introduction.) This work has been developed over several years; much of it has already been published in the form of journal articles. I beg the reader's indulgence for this. My justification for reworking older material is the hope that it might prove useful to highlight the thread—rationality and critical thinking—running through these earlier efforts.

In the course of developing and articulating my views and my arguments, I have incurred the intellectual debt of many, and it is a pleasure to acknowledge that debt here. Harold Alderman, Barbara Arnstine, Don Arnstine, Robin Barrow, John Biro, J. Anthony Blair, Brad Bowen, Nick Burbules, Robert Ennis, Robert Floden, Sophie Haroutunian-Gordon, Ralph Johnson, John McPeck, Edward Mooney, David Moshman, Stephen Norris, Richard Paul, Emily Robertson, Al Spangler, Bruce Suttle, Jeffrey Tlumak, Fletcher Watson, and Perry Weddle have all read and helpfully commented on at least one chapter (or journal article on which a chapter has been based), and in many cases on several. Dennis Rohatyn has provided lively, detailed and insightful commentary on the entire manuscript—as is his wont, in a variety of communicative media. Audiences at meetings of the Association for Informal Logic and Critical Thinking, of the Philosophy of Education Society, and at several conferences at Sonoma State University and elsewhere have helpfully criticized earlier versions of some of the ideas presented below. Members of the California Association for Philosophy of Education have heard and usefully commented on several presentations whose substance can be found in these chapters. One of their number, Denis Phillips, has also provided extensive written commentary on several draft chapters, the importance of which has been overshadowed only by his philosophical colleagueship and friendship over the years. Students in my philosophy of education courses at the University of Nebraska, Sonoma State University, and Northern Arizona University have contributed enormously to my thinking on the matters considered below. To all these students, colleagues and friends I am most grateful.

My greatest debt, however, is to Israel Scheffler. It was my good fortune to study with Professor Scheffler, and he has been, since our earliest acquaintance, a constant source of knowledge, wisdom, good sense, good cheer, and a rare human decency. As the reader will soon discover, many of my own ideas are inspired by, or simply taken from his; indeed the work to follow is perhaps best seen as an extension and exploration of Scheffler's insistence that "critical thought is of the first importance in the conception and organization of educational activities." My debt to Scheffler is one that can never be repaid; it nevertheless gives me great pleasure to acknowledge it here, and to have this book appear in a series co-edited by him.

I am also most grateful to Michigan Technological University for support of this work in the form of a creativity grant, and especially to the John Dewey Foundation and the Center for Dewey Studies for support in the form of a John Dewey Senior Research Fellowship. Without the generous financial support of these two institutions, the present volume would only have much later, if ever, been completed. Despite my many disagreements with Dewey's philosophy, this entire book constitutes an endorsement of Dewey's conviction that rationality and intelligence are central to education and to life. Because of this basic agreement, it seems most fitting that this work should have been carried out with the help of a Dewey Fellowship.

Finally, I would like to dedicate this work to the teachers and administrators of Everett High School, who—for the most part in spite of themselves—occasionally encouraged their students to think critically.

Acknowledgments

Several of the chapters which follow are based, either mainly or in part, on earlier articles of mine. Where no acknowledgment of earlier publications is made, the work appears for the first time here. I am grateful to the editors of the journals and collections involved for permission to use previously published material. (Reference information appears in the Bibliography.)

Chapter 1's last section is taken from "Educating Reason: Critical Thinking, Informal Logic, and The Philosophy of Education. Part One: A Critique of McPeck and a Sketch of an Alternative View." Much of the same material appeared later in "McPeck, Informal Logic, and the Nature of Critical Thinking." Chapter 1 also contains some bits from "Educational Ideas and Educational Practice: The Case of Minimum Competency Testing."

Chapter 2 draws upon "Critical Thinking As an Educational Ideal," and "Educating Reason: Critical Thinking, Informal Logic, and the Philosophy of Education. Part Two: Philosophical Questions Underlying Education for Critical Thinking."

Chapter 3 borrows from "Educating Reason," Parts One and Two, from "Critical Thinking as an Educational Ideal," and from "Rationality, Critical Thinking, and Moral Education."

Chapter 4 takes a bit from "Critical Thinking as an Educational Ideal." Although written first for this volume, the chapter has appeared in slightly altered form as "Rationality and Ideology."

Chapter 5 utilizes material from "The Response to Creationism," and "Rationality, Morality, and Rational Moral Education: Further Response to Freeman."

Chapter 6 is an amalgamation of several essays, including, "Kuhn and Critical Thought," "Kuhn and Schwab on Science Texts and the Goals of Science Education," "On the Distortion of the History of Science in Science Education," and "Relativism, Rationality, and Science Education."

Chapter 7 is taken mainly from "Educational Ideals and Educational Practice: The Case of Minimum Competency Testing."

I would also like to thank the following authors and/or publishers for permission to quote from the following works:

Richard Paul and *Informal Logic Newsletter* for "Teaching Critical Thinking in the Strong Sense";

G. V. Glass and the National Council on Measurement in Education, Washington DC for "Standards and Criteria";

Israel Scheffler for *Reason and Teaching*;

Thomas S. Kuhn and the University of Chicago Press for *The Structure of Scientific Revolutions*;

John McPeck and St. Martin's Press for *Critical Thinking and Education*.

Rationality, critical thinking and education

Critical thought is of the first importance in the conception and organization of educational activities.[1]

There is at present an unprecedented interest in critical thinking. National commissions on the state of education decry the lack of emphasis on the development of reasoning ability in schools and call for the inclusion of reasoning in the curriculum as the fourth "R"; educators of all stripes belittle rote memorization in favor of educational programs which teach students how to think; entire university systems require their students to take courses in critical thinking before graduation; and entire states test their public school students' critical thinking skills. It is a good time to be in the critical thinking business.

Alongside the rise in interest in critical thinking, recent years have witnessed the growth, in the philosophical community, of the Informal Logic Movement.[2] The Informal Logic Movement arose largely as a response to the domination of logic by formal methods, and with the conviction that formal logic did little to enhance the reasoning ability of students, especially with regard to the sort of reasoning required in ordinary, everyday situations. This focus on "everyday reasoning" is typically offered as a justification for including informal logic in the curriculum: it is desirable for students and citizens to be able to reason well in the situations in which they actually find themselves and about issues with which they are genuinely concerned, and facility in informal logic constitutes, or at least contributes to, this ability to reason well or think critically. Members of the Informal Logic Movement frequently hold that logic, construed informally, has much to contribute to the educational task of enhancing students' reasoning ability. Consequently many of those members consider the movement to be a leading force in the general educational effort to enhance reasoning ability, and construe it as a focus both for the intellectual clarification of the nature of reasoning and argument, and also for the practical, political and pedagogical tasks of establishing critical thinking as an effective and central curricular effort. As Richard Paul puts the point, the Informal Logic Movement "ought to move to become the professional group that superintends the teaching of logic-critical thinking skills in the public schools and so universalize its influence in education."[3] Here Paul—and I suspect many members of the Movement would agree—both identifies (informal) logic with critical thinking, thereby acknowledging the Movement's embracing of critical thinking as part of its "turf"; and also asserts the Movement's interest in and commitment to practical educational affairs.[4]

Because of the perceived connection between informal logic and critical thinking, most of the extant theorizing concerning the nature of critical thinking has been done by thinkers identified in one way or another with the Informal Logic Movement. Yet the notion of critical thinking remains obscure and ill-defined; the theoretical conflicts between the various analyses offered to date are significant. Consequently, the obvious starting point for the present effort is a review and analysis of the currently popular accounts of critical thinking. This I offer in chapter 1, focussing especially on the views of Robert Ennis, Richard Paul, and John McPeck. This leads naturally into my own positive account of critical thinking, which is presented in chapter 2. This conception, which holds that the critical thinker is one who is *appropriately moved by reasons* (henceforth "the reasons conception"), emphasizes the connection between critical thinking and rationality, and also emphasizes the importance of certain dispositions, habits of mind and character traits, in addition to reasoning skills, for a full conception of critical thinking. Perhaps most importantly, this conception stresses the point that, for critical thinking to be properly construed as central to educational affairs, as many within the Informal Logic Movement construe it, critical thinking must be conceived much more broadly than it usually is. It must be conceived not along the lines of informal logic, but as a fundamental educational ideal, infusing and informing the entire range of educational activities and affairs. Such a conception of critical thinking raises profound questions concerning the nature of education, questions traditionally treated in the philosophy of education. Because such questions must be faced if a viable conception of critical thinking is to be had, I argue that critical thinking theorists, and members of the Informal Logic Movement more generally, must confront the philosophy of education. One of the implicit aims of the present work is to help facilitate the integration of philosophy of education into the body of concerns of the Informal Logic Movement, by raising and grappling with some of the fundamental questions which a full theory of critical thinking must answer, and which the philosophy of education has long been concerned with.

One of these questions concerns the justification of educational ideals such as critical thinking. While it seems obvious to many that critical thinking is an important educational desideratum, the problem of justifying critical thinking as a central educational ideal is a crucial one, both philosophically and practically. In chapter 3 I explore the problem and attempt the justification.

A major stumbling block with respect to the justification of critical thinking as an educational ideal is the suggestion that this ideal is, necessarily, ideologically tainted. Many social theorists and philosophers of education have suggested that educational aims and ideals are inevitably bound up with prior ideological commitments, so that it is impossible to justify educational ideals except within the context of some ideological framework. "Neutral" justification is, on such a view, out of the question. In chapter 4 I examine several versions of this "ideology objection" to the justification of critical thinking as an educational ideal, and argue not only that it fails, but that a commitment to something very much like critical thinking is necessary even for the very posing of the objection.

In chapter 5 I consider the problem of indoctrination. Since there is at least a *prima facie* conflict between education for critical thinking and indoctrinative education, it is important to consider whether or not education for critical thinking can be conducted in a non-indoctrinative way. After exploring the repercussions for critical thinking of indoctrinative education, I argue here that it can, thus defeating a second possible objection to the ideal.

Chapter 5 completes the first section of the book, in which the focus is on the notion of critical thinking and its status as an educational ideal. In the two chapters which follow I explore some of the educational ramifications of the results of the first section.

Chapter 6 concerns science education. I argue that critical thinking conflicts with a Kuhnian-style education for "normal science," and that science education ought to be conducted so as to strive to produce (in Schwab's terminology) "fluid enquirers." The effort here is to evaluate alternative conceptions of science education from the point of view of the ideal of critical thinking, and to utilize that ideal in the formulation of the science curriculum. My hope is that the science curriculum can be seen as representative of other curriculum areas, so that the chapter can be seen as providing a general picture of the ramifications of critical thinking for the curriculum.

The ideal of critical thinking has ramifications for a wide variety of educational practices and policies. In chapter 7 I consider the widely utilized practice of minimum competency testing, and argue that it is incompatible with the conception of critical thinking articulated in chapter 2. Using minimum competency testing as an example, this chapter aims to demonstrate the power of the ideal to direct and assess educational policy and practice.

In the Postscript I suggest that the results of the present study lead naturally to epistemological questions concerning the nature of reasons, and of rationality more generally. The analysis of critical thinking offered needs ultimately to be deepened by being grounded in a general conception of rationality. This conception must be such that it can deal successfully with questions in a wide variety of philosophical contexts: for example, with questions concerning the rationality of theory choice in science; the relationship between rationality and morality; the nature of rational decision-making, including "paradoxes" like the prisoner's dilemma and Newcomb's problem; and so on. I suggest that pursuit of a general conception of rationality is a fundemental philosophical activity, and that it underpins philosophy of education as well as philosophy of science, ethics, decision theory, epistemology, etc. In this way the view of philosophy of education and critical thinking developed in the several chapters has the considerable merits of both:

1 relating philosophy of education to "pure" philosophy in a way that restores to the former some of its lost dignity; and
2 pointing the way to further philosophical insight—into education, and generally.

The book as a whole thus addresses fundamental questions within philosophy of education, developing and defending a basic educational ideal; questions within education itself, regarding curriculum, policy, and practice; and questions about philosophy of education, regarding its nature, purposes, power, proper pursuit, and connection with philosophy in general. It begins with a look, in chapter 1, at three influential contemporary discussions of critical thinking.

CHAPTER 1

Three conceptions of critical thinking

The whole concept of argument ... rests upon the ideal of rationality—of dicussion not in order to move or persuade, but rather to test assumptions critically by a review of *reasons* logically pertinent to them.[1]

The fundamental trait to be encouraged is that of reasonableness. ... In training our students to reason we train them to be critical.[2]

What is critical thinking? Despite widespread recent interest in critical thinking in education, there is no clear agreement concerning the referent of the term. But if that notion is to carry significant weight in our educational thinking and practice, it is essential that it be delineated with some precision, so that we will know what we are talking about when we talk of the desirability of critical thinking, or of educational efforts aimed at improving students' critical thinking ability. In this chapter I wish to discuss three accounts of critical thinking recently offered, those of Robert H. Ennis, Richard W. Paul, and John E. McPeck. These three thinkers are all identified with the Informal Logic Movement (though the last is generally seen as a critic of, rather than a friend of or participant in, the Movement), and reflect that Movement's commitment to the improvement of educational practice as well as the promulgation of informal over formal logic (again excepting McPeck, who is committed to educational improvement but is not as taken with informal logic, in education or elsewhere, as Ennis or Paul). In considering the merits of each account, as well as the conflicts among them, I hope to set the stage for my own positive account of critical thinking (in the next chapter), which has affinities with each. I begin with the work of Ennis.

1 Ennis's conception of critical thinking

Ennis has been concerned with critical thinking for many years; in fact contemporary interest in the notion and its relevance to education can be traced to his highly influential "A Concept of Critical Thinking."[3] In that paper Ennis explicates critical thinking as "the correct assessing of statements,"[4] and offers both a list of aspects of statement assessment and criteria for the correct assessment of various sorts of statements.[5] The discussion exhibits Ennis's usual care and clarity. But the details of the analysis are not germane for present purposes. Here I wish simply to draw attention to the fact that the conception of critical thinking offered in Ennis's paper focusses entirely on a person's ability correctly to assess or evaluate certain sorts of statements. A person is a critical thinker, on this view, if she has the skills, abilities, or proficiencies necessary for the proper evaluation of statements. Education for critical thinking, then, involves the imparting to students of the requisite skills, abilities, or proficiencies. (To illustrate with just one of Ennis's "aspects," a student would be a critical thinker with respect to inductive conclusions if and only if she had the skill requisite for mastery of and application of the complex set of criteria for correctly assessing the warrantedness of inductive conclusions.) No mention is made of the student's *actual utilization* of her skills and abilities—if she is able to assess statements correctly, she is rightly regarded as a critical thinker. Let us call this the "*pure skills*" conception of critical thinking: a person is a critical thinker if and only if she has the skills, abilities, or proficiencies necessary for the correct assessing of statements.[6]

This "pure skills" conception of critical thinking faces an obvious objection: it sanctions our regarding a person as a critical thinker even though that person never, or only infrequently, thinks critically. It would require us to regard our educational activities aimed at promulgating critical thinking as successful if, for example, students could pass tests designed to assess their critical thinking skills but did not utilize those skills in their ordinary statement-assessing activities (i.e. outside of the testing context). And of course examples abound of people who fit this description—who possess highly developed skills of statement assessment but who, for example, buy cars or vote for politicians for the most uncritical of reasons.[7] Thus something more than skills appears necessary for critical thinking.

Ennis has, since the paper being considered appeared, become aware of this difficulty, and in his more recent work he has attempted to shore up the "pure skills" conception by adding to skills (and good judgment) a set of *tendencies* requisite for critical thinking. After presenting his "perhaps overwhelming list of proficiency items," Ennis remarks that "Proficiency is not enough. There must be a tendency to exercise the proficiency."[8] On this "*skills plus tendencies*" conception, then, a critical thinker has both the skills or proficiencies necessary for the proper assessing of statements (and actions), and also the tendency to exercise those proficiencies in their ordinary statement- (and action-) assessing activities.

The "skills plus tendencies" conception of critical thinking does, I think, overcome the difficulty with the "pure skills" conception noted above, and is an important advance in Ennis's conceptualization of critical thinking. For, as I argue in chapter 2, critical thinking extends far beyond skills of statement assessment, and centrally includes certain dispositions, habits of mind, and (even) character traits; and the disposition to *be* a critical thinker—that is, the disposition to utilize appropriate criteria in the evaluation of statements and actions, and to value belief and action which is guided by reasons—is perhaps the most important "non-skill" component of critical thinking. So Ennis's addition of the tendency to utilize the proficiencies necessary for critical thinking to the list of ingredients of critical thinking is, in my view at least, a welcome one. However, this addition, however welcome, does not put to rest the task of conceptualizing critical thinking. For there remain some difficulties with the "skills plus tendencies" conception which demand attention.

First, there is a problem of emphasis. Ennis's list of proficiencies is extremely detailed and elaborate; he himself regards it as "perhaps overwhelming." The bulk of his work over the years has been with various dimensions of the items on the list, their philosophical foundations (concerning, for example, the nature of explanation and causation), and the vicissitudes of testing for them. By contrast, although according to the formal presentation of Ennis's conception proficiences and tendencies are on a par (along with good judgment), Ennis's discussion of the tendencies consists solely of a list of them (including, for example, the tendencies to be well-informed, to demand appropriate precision, etc.) with no elaboration. All of the tendencies on the list, moreover, are by his own word "in a way included in the list of proficiencies,"[9] except the tendency to exercise the proficiencies delineated by the list of proficiency items. So instead of two roughly equal components of critical thinking, proficiencies and tendencies, what Ennis's conception amounts to is actually a highly complex list of proficiencies coupled with the simple admonition to exercise the proficiencies. In this way, while Ennis's view is to be praised for its recognition of the importance of utilization of skills, the tendency to utilize critical thinking skills is under-analyzed and under-attended to in Ennis's work.

The under-attention to the tendency to utilize proficiencies can be seen in its absence from Ennis's work on testing for critical thinking. I think it is fair to say that Ennis is the leading theorist of critical thinking testing; his work in this area exhibits a rare mastery of both the philosophical and educational dimensions of critical thinking, and the psychology of testing. (In fact Ennis is the co-author of the highly influential and widely used Cornell Critical Thinking Tests, and is on the cutting edge of the development of a new generation of such tests.[10]) Yet his work on testing for critical thinking focusses, as far as I am aware, entirely on testing for proficiencies. Granting for the moment that testing for critical thinking is important, it is difficult to reconcile the claim that the tendency to utilize proficiencies is as important a component of critical thinking as the proficiencies themselves with the one-sided heroic effort to develop effective tests for the proficiencies in the total absence of effort to develop effective tests for the tendency.[11] In this way Ennis's work on testing for his revised conception of critical thinking, the "skills plus tendencies" conception, while acknowledging the importance of the tendency to utilize critical thinking proficiencies—to *be* a critical thinker, and not just to be *able* to be one—nevertheless under-emphasizes and under-values that crucially important tendency.[12]

Ennis also under-values the tendency to utilize proficiencies in his suggestion that we regard critical thinking, or rational thinking as the "fourth R" of education.[13] The original three Rs (reading, 'riting, and 'rithmetic) are typically regarded not as ideals of education, but as specific skill/competency areas which, because of their central importance in life and because they make possible all advanced study which presupposes them, are vitally important for students to master. On the view to be articulated in the next chapter, however, rational thinking is not simply another of these areas. Rather, it is the guiding ideal of educational endeavor, the "*first* R" which justifies and makes sense of our commitment to the other three. At present my point is simply that it under-values critical thinking to regard it simply as another (albeit important) skill area. It is, rather, best regarded as an educational ideal which involves dispositions, habits of mind, and character traits as well as skills.

(There is a difference between Ennis's view about the way dispositions or tendencies enter into an account of critical thinking and my own. (I mention it now; I hope it will become clearer in the next chapter.) Ennis's list of dispositions is composed of rather specific items—e.g. "Try to be well-informed"—whereas my discussion (in chapter 2) is concerned with the general, global disposition to pay attention to reasons and to regard them as important, i.e. to be "appropriately moved" by them. This latter disposition is best understood, I think, as a sort of character trait; a person who has it is not simply a person with a certain disposition, but a certain sort of person. I am concerned, then, with the global or "macro-disposition" to be moved by reasons and the implications of this for character; while Ennis's discussion is more concerned with specific "micro-dispositions" which might contribute to the satisfactory assessment of claims and actions. I do not believe there is any incompatibility between Ennis's discussion of dispositions and tendencies and my own. Our discussions reflect, rather, a difference in focus and target.[14])

Thus far I have been arguing that Ennis's conception of critical thinking under-values certain dimensions of that notion. I now wish to mention two ways in which Ennis's conception is under-developed; two issues which a full conception of critical thinking should address but which are not addressed in Ennis's analysis.

First, consider the tendency to think critically, i.e. to utilize the proficiencies Ennis discusses. Ennis and I are agreed that this tendency is an important component of critical thinking (although, as I have argued above, his analysis in several ways under-values it). Why should critical thinkers have this tendency? Ennis does not address this question. But it seems to me that the question ought to be addressed, for the answer tells us something important about critical thinking. The answer, I think, is that critical thinkers should be disposed to think critically, and tend to do so, because (i.e. for the reason that) they recognize the *value* of critical thinking. This recognition involves the recognition of related values, such as truth, intellectual honesty, and justice to evidence. Moreover, to recognize the value of critical thinking it is necessary that critical thinking *has* value; consequently, a fully worked out conception of critical thinking ought to demonstrate that value. Thus a full conception of critical thinking ought to offer a justification of critical thinking as an educational goal or ideal. This I attempt to do in chapter 3.[15]

Second, I wish to draw attention to the distinction between critical think*ing* and the critical think*er*, and to suggest that a full conception of critical thinking must provide not only criteria for assessing pieces of reasoning, but also a characterization of the attributes of the sort of person who is rightly regarded as a critical thinker. Ennis sees his project as delineating a conception of critical (or rational) thinking, and sees this as involving the development of a set of criteria for determining the goodness of pieces of thinking: "Criteria are needed for determining whether a given piece of thinking is rational. Providing such criteria (that is, providing a conception) is my goal."[16] Yet what Ennis goes on to provide is not just such a set of criteria, but rather such criteria mixed in with a characterization of critical think*ers*.[17] The tendency to utilize proficiencies, for example, may be a characteristic of a critical thinker, but it is surely not a criterion for determining the rationality of a given piece of thinking, since a piece of thinking, while it may be the result of that tendency, surely does not itself possess that tendency. Tendencies to think or act in certain ways are properties of persons, not pieces of thinking. Ennis's discussion slides over this distinction, but I think that distinguishing between the characteristics of pieces of good thinking and those of the critical thinker is important. For one thing, it underscores the importance of incorporating tendencies, dispositions, and habits of mind into the characterization of critical thinking. In doing so, moreover, it draws attention to the fact that critical thinking, conceived of as an educational ideal, concerns the characterization not simply of a set of cognitive skills or criteria of reasoning assessment, but more importantly of a certain sort of *person*. To recognize this is to recognize the depth of the concept of critical thinking, and the importance of character, values, and other moral dimensions of the concept. Ennis (and Paul and McPeck) is (are) agreed that the key task, so far as education is concerned, is that of articulating and defending a characterization of a certain sort of person—a critical/rational thinker. But his analysis dwells very lightly on these moral dimensions of the concept, and does not in my view distinguish sufficiently clearly between characteristics of pieces of good reasoning and characteristics of persons who are rightly regarded as critical thinkers. This is a lack that robs critical thinking of a considerable portion of its depth and significance. In chapter 2 I try to give these dimensions their due.

In ending this section I wish explicitly to acknowledge the obvious: Ennis's work on critical thinking is crucially important, pioneering, and basic to inquiry in the field. His list of proficiencies is by far the most detailed, complex, and useful to be developed; his work on testing for critical thinking is of fundamental importance. My critical suggestions are simply that, first, while Ennis's conception of critical thinking acknowledges the tendency to utilize proficiencies and be a critical thinker as a component of critical thinking, it nevertheless in certain respects under-values that component; and second, that certain questions which I think a full conception of critical thinking should address are not addressed by Ennis's conception. I address those questions in the next chapters. First, however, I turn to Richard Paul's conception of critical thinking.

2 Paul and critical thinking in the "strong sense"

Paul acknowledges, and indeed emphasizes, the importance of including the tendency or disposition to utilize proficiencies, to do critical thinking, in a full conception of critical thinking. This acknowledgment is part of Paul's more general distinction between two different senses of critical thinking: a "weak" sense and a "strong" sense. Our first task in this section is to explicate Paul's distinction.

The typical critical thinking students comes to us,[18] Paul suggests, already having:

a highly developed belief system buttressed by deep-seated uncritical, egocentric and sociocentric habits of thought by which he interprets and processes his or her experience....The practical result is that most students find it easy to question just, and *only*, those beliefs, assumptions and inferences that [they] have already "rejected" and very difficult, in some cases traumatic, to question those in which they have a personal, egocentric investment.[19]

Consequently, Paul claims, when learning techniques of argument assessment in "egocentrically neutral" cases, students do not (as we would like) simply transfer skills and techniques to more "loaded" contexts. Rather, they utilize their newly developed skills to fend off challenges to their deeply held beliefs; they become, in Paul's words, "more sophistic rather than less so, more skilled in 'rationalizing' and 'intellectualizing' the biases they already have."[20] Such is the result, Paul argues, of teaching critical thinking in the "weak" sense. The most problematic aspect of teaching critical thinking in the weak sense, Paul argues, is the assumption "that critical thinking can be taught as a battery of technical skills which can be mastered more or less one-by-one without any significant attention being given to the problems of self-deception, background logic, and multi-categorical ethical issues."[21] Weak sense critical thinking thus involves a commitment to an "atomistic" conception of critical thinking: uncritical thinking ultimately reduces to some combination of simple or atomic thinking errors, such as are picked out by standard lists of fallacies or by failures to utilize properly items on Ennis's list of proficiencies (e.g. mistaking a necessary for a sufficient condition, begging the question, generalizing from an undersized sample, etc.). To teach for weak sense critical thinking is to commit oneself to the view that critical thinking amounts simply to the mastery (and perhaps utilization) of those skills and techniques necessary for the avoidance of such "atomic" mistakes.[22]

Paul, as we have seen, rejects such a conception of critical thinking on the grounds that teaching based on it is likely to have the unhappy effect of producing sophists: students who are adept at manipulating argumentative exchanges in such a way that they can always "demonstrate," or at least protect from challenge, those deep-seated beliefs and commitments which they are not willing to explore or reject. Paul remarks that his effect is not the one

that we wish our teaching to have. I take it to be self-evident that virtually all teachers of critical thinking want their teaching to have a global "Socratic" effect, making some significant inroads into the everyday reasoning of the student, enhancing to some degree that healthy, practical and skilled skepticism one naturally and rightly associates with the *rational* person. This necessarily encompasses, it seems to me, some experience in seriously questioning previously held beliefs and assumptions and in identifying contradictions and inconsistencies in personal and social life.[23]

Atomistic, weak-sense approaches to critical thinking will not, Paul contends, have this happy effect.

What then is needed? Paul recommends that we replace weak-sense critical thinking with *strong*-sense critical thinking:

On this alternative view one abandons the idea that critical thinking can be taught as a battery of atomic technical skills independent of egocentric beliefs and commitments. In place of "atomic arguments" one focuses on argument networks (world views); in place of conceiving of arguments as susceptible of atomic evaluation one takes a more dialectical/dialogical approach (arguments need to be appraised in relation to counter-arguments, wherein one can make moves that are very difficult to defend or ones that strengthen one's position). One is led to see that atomic arguments (traditional conception) are in fact a limited set of moves within a more complex set of actual or possible moves reflecting a variety of logically significant engagements in the world. In this "real" world, whether that of "ordinary" or "philosophical" discourse, argument exchanges are means by which contesting points of view are brought into rational conflict, and in which fundamental lines of reasoning are rarely "refuted" by an individual charge of "fallacy," however well supported. The charge of fallacy is a move; it is rarely logically compelling; it virtually never "refutes" a point of view. This approach I believe, squares much more closely with our own and the student's experience of argument exchanges.[24]

There are several features of the "strong" sense of critical thinking Paul espouses which deserve specific attention. First, there is the rejection of "atomism" in favor of argument networks or "world views"; relatedly, there is the conception of argument exchange as being a clash of opposing perspectives in which the critical thinker seeks to transcend atomic bits of argument in order to achieve a sympathetic grasp of the underlying world view of her opponent. Second, there is a focus on self-deception, and a concomitant disposition for the critical thinker to "know herself" and understand the psychology of her "rational" commitments. Third, there is a sensitivity to egocentric and sociocentric components of one's own world view, and a commitment to overcome these components and "secularize" or depersonalize one's world view. Critical exchange thus appears more a matter of dialogue between opposing perspectives than a series of atomic criticisms and deflections. It is "global," rather than narrow and atomistic, in that it brings to bear a whole host of considerations absent from the atomistic approach. And it is Socratic in its dictate that the critical thinker should "know herself"; that is, should actively seek out and question her deepest beliefs and commitments, and challenge them with all the energy she devotes to the challenging of beliefs and commitments she does not hold.

There is, I think, much of merit in Paul's articulation of the "strong" sense of critical thinking. Perhaps most importantly, it emphasizes the very feature missing from the "pure skills" conception, namely that the critical thinker not simply master a set of atomic "moves" or skills, but that she utilize such skills. Indeed Paul takes this feature one step further than we have taken it so far, emphasizing as he does the necessity of utilizing one's critical thinking skills *on oneself*, of challenging one's own fundamental beliefs and attitudes and not simply those of one's opponents or the newspaper editorialist. Paul's calling our attention to the problem of "transfer" of critical thinking skills from "egocentrically neutral" to "egocentrically charged" contexts, and his insightful analysis of other practical pedagogical problems facing the critical thinking teacher, are also most instructive and most helpful to the carrying out of our practical task of actually getting our students to be, as much as possible, critical thinkers. Paul's analysis is, more than any of the others to be discussed (including my own), informed by his longstanding efforts to teach his students to be critical thinkers and by his genuine interest in taking seriously the practical, pedagogical implications of theorizing about critical thinking. His insistence on, and success at, bringing the ramifications of critical thinking theory to the practical world of education may well be his most important contribution to the critical thinking "movement."

I think, however, that, along with the benefits which accrue to an analysis of critical thinking informed heavily by classroom concerns, come some costs. Here I wish to mention two.

First, there are troubling aspects of Paul's conception of "strong sense" critical thinking as "dialectical/dialogical," according to which critical thinkers transcend atomistic analysis and endeavor to comprehend the issue at hand from the point of view, the "world view," of their "opponents." On some readings of "dialectical" there is no problem here: if one means by "dialectical" only that a critical thinker is sensitive to the give-and-take and development of extended arguments, and, for example, recognizes an objection to a line of reasoning as a matter demanding attention, then it seems uncontroversial that in this sense critical thinking is dialectical. But

Paul's couching the point in terms of "world-views" raises (in my view unnecessary[25]) difficulties. His idea, we have seen, is that whether or not a given bit of reasoning is fallacious, for example, depends on the world-view from which one addresses the issue at hand; what is question-begging (say) for the proponent of one world view is not for the proponent of another.[26] This suggests that the criteria of evaluation of informal arguments, and the criteria of critical thinking, are ultimately grounded in world views. Along with this suggestion, however, come a host of difficulties: What is a world view? How are world views individuated? Can criteria of evaluation of world views be "world view neutral," so that impartial assessment of world views is possible; or is the evaluation of world views necessarily question-begging, as each world view judges itself superior to rivals by virtue of its own "internal" criteria?[27] Worse yet, is critical thinking itself a world view, so that the value of critical thinking is itself contentious, and demonstrable only to those already committed to the critical thinking world view? In a clash of views that ultimately reduces to "You hold p because you are committed to the value of critical thinking, while I hold not-p because I am not," is the critical thinker left with nothing to do save see the issue from the perspective of the other's world view? Why should the world view which favours critical thinking be regarded any more highly than those which favor (say) dogmatism or close-mindedness? In short, are world views themselves rationally criticizable?

It seems to me that there are only two possibilities here: either world views admit of rational appraisal in terms of non-question-begging criteria (supplied by the theory of critical thinking), or they do not. If not, then, as the line of questioning above indicates, we are left with a vicious form of relativism in which all "rational" disputes boil down to unanalyzable differences in world view. In this case, critical thinking is a chimera, since no bit of thinking ever fails to be critical; all thinking is "critical" in that it is sanctioned by the criteria of some world view or other, and "critical thinking" fails to pick out any preferred set of pieces of "good" thinking. Besides the deep difficulties attending to such a form of relativism,[28] this alternative seems especially problematic in the present context because it makes a mockery of attempts to conceptualize critical thinking. Critical thinking collapses as a coherent notion distinct from "uncritical" thinking and as an educational desideratum.[29]

If, on the other hand, world views do admit of rational appraisal, then they must do so in accordance with "atomistic" criteria of appraisal. Criteria such as "considers all relevant evidence," "explains as well as alternative world views," "deals adequately with objections," and so on, are (on this view) to be thought of as criteria which can be brought to bear on the assessment of any particular world view.[30] Thus their proper application does not require commitment to any particular world view. Rather, they are to be conceived as "world view neutral," sanctioned by the theory of critical thinking (or, as I shall later argue, by the theory of rationality), in particular by that aspect of the theory concerned with the critical appraisal of world views. On this view relativism is avoided, but only by embracing "atomism," i.e. the possibility of identifying specific flaws in particular world views, which flaws, moreover, are recognizable—at least in principle—by the adherents of all world views, including the flawed one itself.

This second alternative is the one we must embrace. For the first relies on an unclear conception of world views; it is embroiled in a self-defeating relativism; and it undermines the very possibility of developing a conception or theory of critical thinking. The second, on the other hand, does justice to the unproblematic intuition that even very basic beliefs, such as those which make up the substance of world views, admit of rational criticism and appraisal. The resulting embrace of the sort of atomism described above seems perfectly appropriate here.[31] It suggests, however, that Paul's conception of "strong sense" critical thinking embraces a conception of dialectical analysis which problematically articulates dialectic in terms of world views; that conception concomitantly rejects too quickly all forms of "atomistic" analysis.[32]

The second difficulty with Paul's analysis of critical thinking in the strong sense has to do with its focus on the avoidance of ego- and sociocentrism and self-deception. Paul writes that:

> To teach critical thinking in the strong sense is to help the
> student to develop reasoning skills precisely in those areas where
> he is most likely to have egocentric and sociocentric biases. Such
> biases exist most profoundly in the area of his identity and
> vested interests. His identity and interests are linked in turn to
> his unarticulated and articulated world view(s). His unarticulated
> world view represents the person that he is (the view implicit in
> the principles he uses in guiding his action). His articulated view
> represents the person that he *thinks* he is (the view implicit in the
> principles he uses in *justifying* his action). The contradictions or
> inconsistencies that exist between the two represent, when they
> are not a matter of simple "mistake", the degree to which he
> reasons and acts in bad faith or self-deceptively.[33]

The point Paul makes here—that critical thinking is most difficult in just those situations in which it threatens to challenge one's self-interest—is, I think, an enormously important practical and pedagogical one. Nevertheless, it skews the theoretical account of critical thinking in an undesirable way, by focussing critical thinking theorizing on certain sorts of issues at the expense of other, more traditionally philosophical issues, and/or by placing too much weight on notions (e.g. egocentrism, sociocentrism, etc.) which are not sufficiently clarified in his discussion to bear the burden Paul places on them.

As Paul makes clear, it is in his view most difficult to think critically in those areas in which one has egocentric or sociocentric investment; in areas concerning one's "identity and vested interests." Which areas are these? Presumably, they are areas, or issues, in which one has a strong identification or commitment. Paul's examples of such areas are all of moral, personal, and political issues. (The extended example in the article under discussion concerns United States' involvement in El Salvador.) His idea is that many persons adopt world views which make their group and/or themselves "look good" and favor their interests; as a result, since critical thinking with respect to these areas challenges these interests, it is difficult to think critically with respect to these areas—the costs are too high. As Paul puts it:

> There are deep seated tendencies in the human mind to reason in order to maximize getting, and to justify getting, what we often unconsciously want. This typically involves using cognitive and affective processes to maintain self-serving or pleasant illusions, to rule out or unfairly undermine opposing ideas, to link our identity with ideas that are "ours" (such that disagreement is experienced as ego-threatening), and otherwise to disort or "misinterpret" our experience to serve our own advantage.[34]

Critical thinking is most difficult, Paul contends, in just those areas in which these "deep seated tendencies in the human mind" are most deep; and "strong sense" critical thinking must focus on just those areas in order to counteract those deep tendencies.

But are there separable areas of concern, e.g. areas involving personal identity, morality, or politics, in which these "deep seated tendencies" are deeper than in other areas? It is not clear that there are, for the simple reason that *any* area of concern or issue can be the locus of intense ego-involvement and commitment if the person in question ego-invests in that issue. One might be reluctant to change one's view, for example, of US involvement in El Salvador (to use Paul's example), because one might "sociocentrically" identify with (alleged) US interests there. Presumably, one would not similarly identify with a particular theory of black holes, since such matters are not typically central to one's world view. But it is easy to imagine cases in which one *is* deeply "invested" in such an issue—for example, if one is an astrophysicist whose professional reputation depends on such matters. In short, it would be a mistake to think that the deep-seated tendencies for self-deception which Paul points to are necessarily more germane to certain areas or issues than to others.

Now this point may be embraced by Paul. He need not hold that certain areas or issues manifest these tendencies more than others. He may hold that "strong sense" critical thinking involves concentration on those areas in which egocentrism, sociocentrism, and self-deception are most manifest, whatever areas those happen to be. Then, however, another question arises: how do we tell when these evils are manifesting themselves? How do we distinguish, for example, between the biologist who believes that lung cancer is caused by a virus because she is convinced by the experimental evidence, and the biologist who believes it because the originator of the theory is a personal idol or mentor? One may be tempted to reply that the first biologist would recant upon receipt of further confounding evidence, whereas the latter would not. But the demise of "naive falsificationism"[35] in the philosophy of science makes clear that the first biologist may be quite justified in clinging to her original opinion and rejecting the additional confounding evidence. The same problem arises for two Republicans, one who is convinced that US intervention in Central America is justified on the basis of carefully considered political principles and arguments, the other on the basis of a deep-seated need to maintain her self-image as an "ideologically pure" conservative. The line between "Smith believes *p* on the basis of argument and evidence" and "Smith believes *p* egocentrically (or sociocentrically or self-deceptively)" is a very difficult one to draw.

The point here is simply that Paul relies very heavily, in his characterization of "strong sense" critical thinking, on the ability to distinguish cases of egocentrism, sociocentrism, and self-deception from alternative sorts of cases. Short of detailed analyses of these philosophically contentious notions, however, which are not provided by Paul's analysis, it is not clear that they are sufficient to distinguish "strong" from "weak" critical thinking, or critical from uncritical thinking. If they are not, we would be better off to conceptualize strong sense critical thinking without recourse to them. Paul's insight into the psychological difficulty of overcoming the "deep seated tendencies of the human mind" he notes, while a point with profound practical, pedagogical consequences for the teaching of critical thinking, should not distort our best theoretical account of the nature of critical thinking itself.[36]

I conclude that Paul's account of critical thinking in the "strong sense" is problematic in the two ways noted. Nevertheless, his discussion is highly significant for two reasons. First, it emphasizes the importance of non-skill components of critical thinking, and the point that a person who masters certain "micro-skills" of argument analysis may nevertheless fail profoundly to exemplify our best conception of the critical thinker. Put more positively, Paul's insistence that critical thinking involves not just skills but is "ultimately intrinsic to the *character* of the person"[37] is a crucially important enlargement of our conception of critical thinking, which extends it beyond the domain, not only of the "pure skills" conception, but of the "skills plus tendencies" conception as well. (The idea that critical thinking involves character traits is developed further in the next chapter.) Second, it relates, better than any other discussion I am aware of, theoretical work on the nature of critical thinking to the practical world of education. There is much of merit, then, in Paul's account; the importance of his contribution to both the theory and the practice of critical thinking cannot be gainsaid. Nevertheless, for the reasons offered above, it is not a fully satisfactory account of critical thinking as it stands.[38]

Before turning to my own account of critical thinking, I wish to consider the widely-discussed analysis offered by John McPeck. McPeck's work is extremely controversial within the Informal Logic Movement, mainly because it challenges the idea that there are general and generalizable skills of reasoning that transcend relatively narrow disciplines or areas, and so challenges the idea that lists of skills and proficiencies (like Ennis's, and like the lists of "do's and don'ts" common to many informal logic texts) are useful for, or even relevant to, the development of critical thinking ability.

3 McPeck and the generalizability of critical thinking skills

Critical thinking is widely regarded as a generalized skill or ability (or set of such skills and abilities), which can be utilized or applied across a variety of situations and circumstances. (Ennis's conception, for example, surely fits this general description, as does Paul's.) In his recent book *Critical Thinking and Education*,[39] however, John McPeck challenges this view of critical thinking. McPeck argues provocatively that critical thinking cannot be regarded properly as a generalized skill, because there is not—and cannot be—any single critical thinking skill that can be applied generally across subject-area domains. This is because, according to McPeck, thinking (critical or otherwise) is never thinking *simpliciter*, but is always thinking about something or other: "thinking is always thinking *about* something. To think about nothing is a conceptual impossibility."[40] On the basis of this point, McPeck criticizes the sort of informal logic/critical thinking course associated with the Informal Logic Movement, namely a course which seeks to enhance students' thinking ability *in general*, i.e. without regard to any particular subject matter:

> In isolation from a particular subject, the phrase "critical thinking" neither refers to nor denotes any particular skill. It follows from this that it makes no sense to talk about critical thinking as a distinct subject and that it therefore cannot profitably be taught as such. To the extent that critical thinking is not about a specific subject X, it is both conceptually and practically empty. The statement "I teach critical thinking," *simpliciter*, is vacuous because there is no generalized skill properly called critical thinking.[41]

There are some obvious difficulties with this argument. Most fundamentally, it confuses thinking generally (i.e. as denoting a *type* of activity) with specific *acts* (i.e. tokens) or instances of thinking. McPeck's claim that "Thinking . . . is logically connected to an X"[42] reflects this confusion. A given act of thinking may, as McPeck suggests, always be about something or other; it may make no sense to say of a given episode of thinking that the thinker was thinking, but not about anything in particular. But it hardly follows from this that thinking, conceived as a general sort of activity which includes as instances all cases of particular acts of thinking—and such a conception must be possible, on pain of inability to identify all the specific acts as acts *of thinking*—must itself be construed as about something or other. Distinct acts or episodes of thinking, that is, may have all sorts of features in common; these common features may be said to be features of thinking, which manifest themselves in various distinct acts or episodes of thinking. It is not the case that the general activity of thinking "is logically connected to an X," any more than the general activity of cycling is logically connected to any particular bicycle. It is true that any given act of cycling must be done on some bicycle or other. But it surely does not follow that the general activity of cycling cannot be discussed independently of any particular bicycle. Indeed, we can state, and teach people, general skills of cycling (e.g. "lean to the left when making a left-hand turn;" "slow down before cornering, not during cornering," etc.), even though instantiating these maneuvers, and so exhibiting mastery of the general skills, requires some particular bicycle. As with cycling, so with thinking. Thus McPeck's suggestion that teaching critical thinking *simpliciter* is a conceptual impossibility is mistaken. As we can teach cycling, so critical thinking might be taught.

It makes perfect sense, for example, to claim that one teaches critical thinking, *simpliciter*, when one means that one helps students to develop reasoning skills which are general in that they can be applied to many diverse situations and subject matters. Contra McPeck, there is nothing vacuous or unintelligible about such a claim. This point is supported, moreover, by the fact that there are readily identifiable reasoning skills which do not refer to any specific subject matter, which do apply to diverse situations, and which are in fact the sort of skill which courses in critical thinking seek to develop. Skills such as identifying assumptions, tracing relationships between premises and conclusions, identifying standard fallacies, and so on do not require the identification of specific subject matters; such skills are germane to thinking in subject areas as diverse as physics, religion, and photography. So McPeck's argument that critical thinking is necessarily subject-specific and not generalizable, so that educational efforts (e.g. courses) aimed at developing general critical thinking skills are ill-advised, is not compelling. It fails to distinguish between specific acts of thinking, and thinking conceived as a general sort of activity which includes specific acts or episodes of thinking as instances; and it fails to take seriously obvious examples of general, i.e. not subject-specific, critical thinking skills and abilities.[43]

McPeck challenges this view of the matter. He argues that general skills, for example those of identifying assumptions or fallacies, are not really general in that one needs to have subject-specific information or knowledge in order to be able to exercise them. He writes that:

> phrases like ... "the ability to identify assumptions" ... etc. are phrases which semantically masquerade as descriptions of general abilities, but upon analysis, none of them actually denotes a generalized ability. Rather, each phrase subsumes a wide variety of *different* instances under its rubric, such that no singular ability could account for its diverse range of achievements. Take, for example, "the ability to recognize underlying assumptions." That this is not a singular ability can be appreciated by considering the fact that to recognize an underlying assumption in mathematics requires a different set of skills and abilities from those required for recognizing them in a political dispute, which are different again from those required in a scientific dispute.... Assumptions are not all cut from the same cloth. And even trained logicians cannot ... "readily identify them" within the various domains of human knowledge. You can, of course, logically characterize assumptions for students, that is, tell them what an assumption *is*, but this logical

knowledge will not enable them to discover the diverse
assumptions in the various knowledge domains and contexts.[44]

McPeck is, I think, half right. He is right that logical knowledge
regarding the nature of assumptions will not by itself enable students
to identify assumptions in all contexts. Specific knowledge of the
subject matter at hand is typically required as well.[45] But by the same
token, the specific knowledge by itself will equally fail to enable
students—let them know as much as you like about the specific
subject under consideration, they will not be able to identify
assumptions in arguments in that area if they do not know what an
assumption is. Thus logical knowledge concerning the nature of
assumptions, and subject-specific knowledge, are both necessary;
neither is by itself sufficient. So the logical knowledge is not vacuous,
or trivial, or eliminable from students' education, if we wish them to
have this ability or set of abilities.

The point can be illustrated by resorting again to the cycling
analogy. Suppose that, in teaching students the finer points of
cycling, we teach them that they should always inflate their tires
properly before setting out. McPeck criticizes "logical knowledge,"
essentially for being empty; the student may know what an
assumption is, but that will not enable the student to identify
assumptions without specific knowledge of the subject at hand. The
same is true of our cycling "logical knowledge"; "inflate tires properly
before setting out" is sage enough advice, but it won't enable the
student to avoid blowouts or achieve maximum performance
without specific knowledge of the tires in question. Proper tire
inflation requires knowledge of, for example, the sort of tire it is, the
manufacturer's recommended pressure, the sort of riding being done,
the length of the journey, the weight of the rider, the riding surface,
and so on. So specific knowledge is required for proper inflation to
be achieved. Nevertheless, the advice is good advice, and the student
who failed to inflate her tires properly before setting out would be
committing a "fallacy" of cycling. Similarly with general reasoning
skills such as identifying assumptions: knowing what an assumption
is is not sufficient for assumption identification, perhaps;
nevertheless, that logical knowledge is necessary for such
identification, and an ingredient of subject-specific good reasoning.

Perhaps a better way to put the point is as follows. McPeck writes
that "Knowing what an assumption *is*, and knowing what a valid
argument *is* is far from sufficient for enabling people to engage in
effective critical thinking,"[46] I agree. *But it helps.* How much it helps
is an empirical issue, and no doubt will vary from case to case, but
McPeck provides no reason for thinking that it won't help quite a lot
in some cases, and so might be (at least conceivably) quite an

important component of critical thinking.

Having criticized the conception of critical thinking as a (set of) generalized skill(s), McPeck offers a positive account of that notion. Noting that critical thinking "involves a certain skepticism, or suspension of assent,"[47] and that such skepticism must be reflective and judicious, McPeck suggests that critical thinking is "the appropriate use of *reflective skepticism* within the problem area under consideration.[48] Applying his earlier contention regarding the necessity of subject matter knowledge for critical thinking, McPeck argues that critical thinking is properly understood as subject-specific:

> Since critical thinking is always "critical thinking about X," it follows that critical thinking is intimately connected with other fields of knowledge. Thus the criteria for the judicious use of skepticism are supplied by the norms and standards of the field under consideration.[49]

After chiding informal logicians for neglecting or denying this "simple insight"[50] regarding the connection between critical thinking and specific subjects or fields, and so for conceiving critical thinking/informal logic as subject-neutral, McPeck suggests that "the core meaning of critical thinking is the propensity and skill to engage in an activity with reflective skepticism."[51] McPeck emphasizes that this propensity and skill requires thorough familiarity with the subject matter defining the activity; simply knowing some subject-neutral logic is not sufficient for critical thinking: "There is no set of supervening skills that can replace basic knowledge of the field in question."[52] And McPeck offers the following "more formal" conception of critical thinking:

> Let X stand for any problem or activity requiring some mental effort. Let E stand for the available evidence from the pertinent field or problem area. Let P stand for some proposition or action within X.
>
> Then we can say of a given student (S) that he is a critical thinker in area X if S has the disposition and skill to do X in such a way that E, or some subset of E, is suspended as being sufficient to establish the truth or viability of P.[53]

Notice first that the notion of "reflective skepticism" is unhelpful, and the definition of critical thinking in terms of it circular. A skeptic might be reflective, and yet her skepticism unjustified. And it will not do to justify skepticism in terms of its appropriateness, such appropriateness being determined by disciplinary or problem-area criteria, for often it is just those criteria about which one needs to be reflectively skeptical.[54] We would need to use critical thinking to determine whether any particular instance of reflective skepticism is or was in fact justified. Hence justified reflective skepticism *assumes* critical thinking; consequently it cannot in turn explicate or define critical thinking. McPeck's notion of reflective skepticism does not, therefore, afford any help in conceptualizing critical thinking.

The act of suspension McPeck highlights in his "formal" expression of his conception of critical thinking is worth a bit more scrutiny. Here I think McPeck is importantly right about something, although his concern with grinding his subject-specific axe has obscured this. Appreciating the point clearly, moreover, will open the way to what I hope is an incisive reformulation of our conception of critical thinking.

What is it for a critical thinker to have "the disposition and skill to do X in such a way that E (the available evidence from a field) is suspended (or temporarily rejected) as sufficient to establish the truth or viability of P (some proposition or action within X)?"[55] It is simply to say that the critical thinker has the disposition and skill to question the power of E to warrant P. That is, the critical thinker has the disposition and skill to query the extent to which E actually provides compelling reasons for P, or justifies P. This is, I think, the defining characteristic of critical thinking; the focus on reasons and the power of reasons to warrant or justify beliefs, claims, and actions. A critical thinker, then, is one who is *appropriately moved by reasons*: she has a propensity or disposition to believe and act in accordance with reasons; and she has the ability properly to assess the force of reasons in the many contexts in which reasons play a role.

McPeck rightly notes the two central components of this conception of critical thinking. There is, first, the ability to assess reasons properly. Call this the *reason assessment* component. There is, second, the willingness, desire, and disposition to base one's actions and beliefs on reasons; that is, to *do* reason assessment and be guided by the results of such assessment. This I call the *critical attitude* or *critical spirit* component of critical thinking. Both components are, I claim, essential to the proper conceptualization of critical thinking, the possession of which is necessary for the achievement of critical thinking by a person. They are jointly sufficient as well. The concept of critical thinking is captured by this "appropriately moved by reasons" (henceforth "reasons") conception.[56]

Although McPeck's conception of critical thinking hinges on the notion of "reflective skepticism," which I have argued is defective in certain ways, it is important to note that McPeck's analysis does recognize the components of, and is largely compatible with, the reasons conception. As has already been pointed out, McPeck's formal expression explicitly mentions the critical spirit component of that conception, and his subsequent discussion emphasizes this component: "It is sufficient for our purposes to recognize that training in particular critical thinking skills is not sufficient to produce a critical thinker. One must also develop the disposition to use those skills.[57] McPeck also emphasizes the central role of the reason assessment component of critical thinking. He labels his approach to critical thinking "epistemological" rather than "logical," because it focusses on the epistemology of various subject areas rather than on subject-neutral logic, and he notes that "the epistemological approach to critical thinking involves little more than providing ... [an] understanding [of] what constitutes good reasons for various beliefs."[58]

McPeck's detailed articulation of his conception of critical thinking thus approximates the reasons conception. However, his discussion frequently obscures this, for that discussion emphasizes issues which are tangential to the nature of critical thinking, and on which McPeck takes positions which are problematic—thus focussing attention on the tangential issues and his problematic positions on those issues, and thereby obscuring his correct identification of the two central components of the reasons conception of critical thinking. I wish now to:

1 Consider three such tangential issues;
2 show how McPeck's discussion of them is problematic; and
3 argue that the reasons conception is independent of these issues, and stands untouched by criticisms of McPeck's discussion of them.

(A) The relation of logic to critical thinking

McPeck is emphatic in his insistence that logic (formal or informal) is either largely or entirely irrelevant to critical thinking, and it is this view that most rankles with members of the Informal Logic Movement. He writes that:

the real problem with uncritical students is not a deficiency in a general skill, such as logical ability, but rather a more general lack of education in the traditional sense.... I shall attempt to show why courses in logic fail to accomplish the goal of developing critical thinkers and how the epistemology of various subjects would be the most reasonable route to that end ... there is both a conceptual and a pedagogic link between epistemology, critical thinking, and education, but the study of logic or critical thinking as such has no part in this linkage.[59]

> The standard approach for developing critical thinking ... has been to teach logic and various kinds of general reasoning skills. Presumably, the rationale for this approach is that since logic plays a role in every subject, and logic is intimately related to reasoning, the study of logic should improve one's ability to assess arguments and statements in any subject area. What I wish to argue is that the plausibility of this reasoning can be sustained only by seriously underestimating the complexity of the different kinds of information used in arguments and by overestimating the role of logic in these assessments. That is, even when the problem at issue is the rational assessment of some statement or argument, the major requirements for such assessment are epistemological, not logical, in character.[60]

(I note in passing McPeck's ambivalence as to whether logic is *entirely* irrelevant to critical thinking, or only *largely* irrelevant (so that logic is at least somewhat relevant). The former citation makes the first, stronger claim; the latter only the second, weaker claim.[61])

As noted earlier, McPeck agrees that reason assessment is a central component of critical thinking—indeed he emphasizes the point, since his "epistemological approach" places reason assessment at the heart of critical thinking. Thus logic can be irrelevant to critical thinking for McPeck only if logic has nothing to do with reason assessment. But this is false on its face: even if many, or even most, reasons are properly assessed only with reference to subjet-specific criteria, some (and perhaps many or most[62]) reasons are properly assessed at least partially in accordance with subject-neutral logical reasons. The fallacies furnish obvious examples here. Take just one. When Jehovah's Witnesses come to my door, and argue that I should believe in the divinity of the Bible because (for the reason that) the Bible proclaims itself to be the divine and so authoritative word of God, it does not take any theological or other subject-specific information or criteria to realize that the reason offered does not in fact support the claim it is offered in support of. Rather, it begs the question. (Similar remarks apply to the argument that "pro-life" persons make against abortion, namely that abortion is wrong because it involves a violation of the right to life of the "baby"—so that abortion is just "baby-killing." No biological or other subject-specific knowledge is needed to recognize that this argument (more exactly, the reason provided by the premise) begs the question against the "pro-choice" person who denies that the fetus is a person who has a right to life. (Of course the question whether or not the fetus is properly thought of as a person with a right to life can be addressed, but it is not addressed by this "pro-life" argument.)) Here logic *is* relevant to reason assessment, and so is relevant to critical thinking, even on McPeck's own terms. This example illustrates the relevance of *informal* logic to reason assessment, and so to critical thinking as McPeck construes it.

It is worth noting (although it is not clear to what extent McPeck would disagree, since, although his position seems to require him to reject both informal and formal logic as relevant to critical thinking, it is mainly the Informal Logic Movement-type informal logic course that McPeck criticizes in his book) that *formal* logic, as well as informal logic, is relevant to critical thinking. First, formal logic can be seen as providing a paradigm of good argumentation. A deductively valid formal argument is as strong an argument as it is possible to have; the connection between premises and conclusion of such an argument is as tight as any such connection can be. To put the point slightly differently, formal argumentation may profitably be seen (by the critical thinking student as well as the rest of us) as constituting an "ideal type" of argument, which (like ideal types in social science, or "ideal laws" like the gas laws in physical science) may not be typically, or ever, encountered in everyday discourse, but which nevertheless are central to our theoretical understanding of argumentation. Thus formal logic is a crucial sub-component of the reason assessment component of critical thinking.

A second reason for thinking formal logic to be relevant to critical thinking is that the latter is fundamentally concerned with the proper assessment of reasons, and formal logic provides an excellent source of clear reasons. For example, it is hard to imagine a more compelling reason for accepting some proposition "q" than the proposition "$pvq.-p$" ("p or q, and not p"). Given the latter proposition, we have conclusive reason for accepting the former. In fact, propositions which are themselves justified and which deductively entail some other proposition seem to me to be among the most compelling reasons for accepting the latter proposition there can be. Thus in this way, too, formal logic is relevant to reason assessment, and so to critical thinking (and exposure to formal logic is desirable for the critical thinking student, for it illustrates well the fundamental relation of "is a reason for").

Thus logic (both formal and informal) is relevant to reason assessment, and so to critical thinking, on McPeck's terms as well as my own. Logic is relevant to the determination of the goodness of reasons. Such determination is central to critical thinking. Thus his claim that logic is irrelevant (either largely or totally) to critical thinking is mistaken, and the Informal Logic Movement-type informal logic/critical thinking course which emphasizes general, subject-neutral material is, at least to some extent, vindicated.

(B) The relation of logic to information

McPeck draws a sharp distinction not only between logic and critical thinking. He also[63] distinguishes sharply between logic and (non-logical, subject-specific) information, and argues that the assessment of good reasons is determined (largely or wholly) by the latter. We have already seen that McPeck claims that "the major requirements for [the rational assessment of statements and arguments] are epistemological, not logical, in character."[64] His view is that the assessment of good reasons is dependent, not on logic, but on specialized, field-dependent knowledge:

> typically we are in a quandary less about the logical validity of an argument than about the truth of the putative evidence. We frequently cannot determine whether evidence is good or not, because such a judgment depends upon special knowledge. One has to be a fellow participant in the particular domain of meaning to appreciate the proper significance of the evidence.[65]

> critical thinking is linked conceptually with particular activities and special fields of knowledge.[66]

> specific content, knowledge and information cannot be coherently demarcated from critical thinking.[67]

McPeck is at least partly right here; the assessment of reasons often involves essential appeal to information which is subject-specific or field-dependent. But there are difficulties here as well. First, McPeck shifts, as earlier, between stronger and weaker claims: that logic is entirely irrelevant to reason assessment, or that it is only somewhat irrelevant (and so somewhat relevant); that information is sufficient for reason assessment, or only necessary; that information is always necessary for reason assessment, or only sometimes necessary. McPeck writes, for example, that "a minimal condition for understanding a good reason in any field is that one understands the full meaning of the specialized and often technical language in which such reasons are expressed."[68] True enough, in cases in which reasons are expressed in specialized and technical language. But frequently reasons are expressed in non-specialized, non-technical language. In such cases full understanding does not require mastery of specialized language or information. Reasoning occurs in specialized and technical, but also in non-specialized and non-technical, areas. Thus

McPeck's weaker claim that specialized information is sometimes required for reason assessment is sustained, but the stronger claim that it is always required is not. (How typical each sort of case is is an empirical matter.) Moreover, the weaker claim is an important point for critical thinkers to appreciate, but it is not itself a subject-specific point; it is, rather, a general, subject-neutral point that could well be made in a general critical thinking course.[69] Thus McPeck's weaker claim is well taken. But it must not be confused with the stronger claim. Nor does it cast any doubt on the utility of a general course in critical thinking. Indeed, points like the ones which McPeck is concerned to make, e.g. that specialized knowledge is frequently required for reason assessment, themselves belong to no specific technical field; to the extent that they are important points for a critical thinker to grasp, it seems highly appropriate to present them in a domain-neutral critical thinking course. Thus McPeck's argument does not only not undermine, it actually suggests the practical necessity and utility of general Informal Logic Movement-type critical thinking courses; such courses are important if there is general information—like McPeck's point, and like logic—that it is important for students to have. Once again the Informal Logic Movement-type critical thinking course is vindicated.

If there is a viable distinction to be drawn between logic and information, they are both relevant to reason assessment and so to critical thinking. McPeck does well to remind us of the importance of specialized information for critical thinking. But this in no way establishes the non-importance of non-specialized, non-technical, general information, or the inappropriateness of general critical thinking courses.

(C) The relation of critical thinking to rationality

We have already seen McPeck's emphasis on the role of good reasons in critical thinking. This naturally raises the question of the relation of critical thinking to rationality. McPeck suggests that critical thinking is a sub-species of rationality, but that the latter far outstrips the former:

> While critical thinking is perfectly compatible with rationality, and with reasoning generally, we should not regard the terms as equivalent. The concept of critical thinking denotes a particular type of thinking ... no injustice to rationality will result from simply construing it as the *intelligent use of all available evidence* for the solution of some problem. There are, of course, difficulties with the notion of evidence (what, for example, is to count as evidence?). Also, rationality may sometimes

countenance the disregarding of certain types of evidence. But it is precisely from these problematic junctures in reasoning that critical thinking derives its conceptual content and it is here the employment of critical thinking is perhaps most useful. Indeed, it requires critical thinking even to recognize that one has arrived at such a juncture. All this does not make critical thinking distinct from, much less incompatible with, rationality; rather rationality includes critical thinking as a particular aspect (or subset) of itself. The concept of critical thinking merely marks out the facet of rationality that comprises the disposition and skill to find such difficulties in the normal course of reasoning.[70]

McPeck suggests here that rationality is broader than critical thinking in that, while rationality includes within its domain all instances of the intelligent use of evidence in the solution of problems, critical thinking involves only some of those instances; namely, those instances in which the determination of relevant evidence is problematic. When one is engaged in intelligent problem solving, one is within the domain of rationality; when one is engaged in such a way that it is necessary to raise "meta-questions" concerning the constitution, relevance, or appropriateness of putative pieces of evidence to the solution of the problem at hand, one is in the sub-domain of critical thinking within the larger domain of rationality. Critical thinking, on this view, is a particular sort of rational thinking which takes place in a particular sort of problem-solving context.

The distinction McPeck draws here between critical thinking and rationality is, I think, untenable. McPeck limits the range of critical thinking to cases in which reasons or evidence are in some way problematic, and to reasoning about the problematic nature of the reasons or evidence in question. But this restriction is incompatible with McPeck's articulation, seen earlier, of his "epistemological approach" to critical thinking, according to which critical thinking involves the skill and disposition to seek out, understand, and base belief and action upon good reasons. If McPeck is to maintain his "epistemological" or "good reasons" approach to critical thinking, then he must reject the limitation he seems to want to place on the range of critical thinking in his distinction between critical thinking and rationality. The reason assessment component of critical thinking extends to the assessment of *all* reasons, not just "meta-reasons" concerning the constitution, relevance, or appropriateness of "ground floor" reasons. On McPeck's construal of critical thinking as a subset of rational thinking, a person who properly utilized available evidence in order to solve some problem or come to some belief, e.g. one who planned a trip route by carefully examining maps, noting terrain, balancing time demands against the goals of the trip, etc.—in short, one who planned the trip rationally—would *not* count as having engaged in critical thinking while planning it. This not only seems absurd on its face, it is incompatible with McPeck's "epistemological approach," according to which evaluating and utilizing reasons is central to critical thinking.

Once one rejects this limitation on the range of critical thinking, the distinction between critical thinking and rationality collapses. Critical thinking is coextensive with rationality, not merely a dimension of it,[71] for rationality and critical thinking are both "coextensive with the relevance of reasons."[72] The connection between rationality and reasons is as tight as can be. As Laudan puts it:

> At its core, rationality ... consists in doing (or believing) things because we have good reasons for doing so ... if we are going to determine whether a given action or belief is (or was) rational, we must ask whether there are (or were) sound reasons for it.[73]

In so far as rationality consists of believing and acting on the basis of good reasons, and in so far as we accept McPeck's epistemological approach—or any approach which makes reason assessment central—we must perforce regard critical thinking not as a dimension of rationality, but as its equivalent or educational cognate. Otherwise, we are forced to regard instances of believing and acting on the basis of good reasons as non-instances of critical thinking. Thus the distinction McPeck draws between critical thinking and rationality cannot be sustained.

It is time to regain the thread of the overall argument. I have been arguing that McPeck's discussions of the relations between logic and critical thinking, logic and information, and critical thinking and rationality are in their various ways problematic. This should not obscure the fact that we are fundamentally agreed that critical thinking centrally involves reason assessment and the disposition to engage in it; that is, that critical thinking involves both the reason assessment component and the critical spirit component of the reasons conception. That conception is unbesmirched by the difficulties with McPeck's analysis which I have been belaboring for the last few pages. In the end McPeck is importantly right about the nature of critical thinking, despite those difficulties.

As we saw earlier, the conceptions offered by Ennis and Paul also, despite their difficulties, have their affinities with the reasons conception. It seems, in fact, that that conception captures what all or most theorists would agree are the essential features of critical thinking. But so far I have done little more than name those features. In the next chapter I endeavor to lay out the conception in more detail; say more about each component, especially the "critical spirit" or "critical attitude" component; provide an underlying rationale for the reasons conception in terms of the conceptual connections between critical thinking, rationality, and reasons; and consider the relationship between critical thinking and education, and the sense in which critical thinking may be said to constitute a fundamental educational ideal. This last raises the problem of justifying the ideal, which is the topic of chapter 3. I should like to close the present chapter by noting once again that Ennis, Paul, and McPeck, despite their differences, have all contributed mightily to the conceptualization of critical thinking, to the establishment of critical thinking as a significant educational concern, and to the recognition of critical thinking as a concern alive with important philosophical dimensions. For these contributions we are all—educators, students, citizens, philosophers—in their debt.

CHAPTER 2

The reasons conception

At its core, rationality ... consists in doing (or believing) things because we have good reasons for doing so ... if we are going to determine whether a given action or belief is (or was) rational, we must ask whether there are (or were) sound reasons for it.[1]

Rationality ... is a matter of *reasons*, and to take it as a fundamental educational ideal is to make as pervasive as possible the free and critical quest for reasons, in all realms of study.[2]

Applying [the skills and understandings necessary for autonomous education] ... involves a *disposition* to do so, an attitude of "critical-mindedness", and a willingness to challenge prevailing norms. This disposition is almost never fostered in our public schools, which is one of our greatest *educational* failings.[3]

In chapter 1 I introduced the "reasons" conception of critical thinking, according to which a critical thinker is one who is *appropriately moved by reasons*. In this chapter I shall attempt to amplify and clarify this conception. I begin by exploring the connection between critical thinking and rationality, after which are examined the "reason assessment" component of critical thinking and the "critical attitude" component. The educational significance of the reasons conception, according to which critical thinking constitutes a fundamental educational ideal, is considered as well.

1 Critical thinking, rationality, and reasons

To be a critical thinker is to be appropriately moved by reasons. To be a rational person is to believe and act on the basis of reasons. There is then a deep conceptual connection, by way of the notion of reasons, between critical thinkers and rational persons. Critical thinking is best conceived, consequently, as the *educational cognate* of rationality: critical thinking involves bringing to bear all matters relevant to the rationality of belief and action; and education aimed at the promulgation of critical thinking is nothing less than education aimed at the fostering of rationality and the development of rational persons.

Rationality, in its turn, is to be understood as being "coextensive with the relevance of reasons."[4] A critical thinker is one who appreciates and accepts the importance, and convicting force, of reasons.[5] When assessing claims, making judgments, evaluating procedures, or contemplating alternative actions, the critical thinker seeks reasons on which to base her assessments, judgments, and actions. To seek reasons, moreover, is to recognize and commit oneself to *principles*, for, as R. S. Peters puts it, "principles are needed to determine the relevance [and strength] of reasons."[6] Israel Scheffler describes the relationship between reasons and principles in this way:

> reason is always a matter of abiding by general rules or
> principles ... reason is always a matter of treating equal reasons
> equally, and of judging the issues in the light of general
> principles to which one has bound oneself ... if I could judge
> reasons differently when they bear on my interests, or disregard
> my principles when they conflict with my own advantage, I
> should have no principles at all. The concepts of *principles*,
> *reasons* and *consistency* thus go together.... In fact, they define
> a general concept of rationality. A rational man is one who is
> consistent in thought and in action, abiding by impartial and
> generalizable principles freely chosen as binding upon himself.[7]

To illustrate the connection between reasons, principles, and consistency: suppose that Johnny's teacher keeps him after class one day as punishment for throwing spitballs. When asked by his parents why Johnny was kept after class, his teacher replies: "Johnny was kept after class because (i.e. for the reason that) he was disrupting the class." The teacher's *reason* for keeping him after class is that his behavior was disruptive. For this properly to count as a reason, the teacher must be committed to some *principle* which licenses or backs that reason, i.e. establishes it as a bona fide reason, e.g. "All disruptive behavior warrants keeping students after class" (or "This sort of behavior warrants keeping students after class"), which must be consistently applied to cases. If the teacher is not committed to some such principle, then her putative reason for keeping Johnny after class does not constitute a genuine reason; Johnny or his parents would be perfectly entitled to challenge the teacher, for example by noting that Mary, who also threw spitballs, was not kept after class. Johnny might well say: "Since you don't apply any relevant principle consistently, you have no reason to keep me after class. If throwing spitballs is not a reason for detaining Mary, it cannot be a reason for detaining me either." Of course there may be mitigating circumstances; Mary may be a first time offender and

Johnny a repeater, etc. Nevertheless, the point remains that the teacher's putative reason is rightly regarded as a reason, which warrants or justifies her behavior, only if it is backed by some principle which (can itself be justified and) is consistently applied in relevantly similar cases. To take a final example: if having a grade point average of 0.6 is a reason for having Mary repeat grade 10 (in light of the principle that a grade point average of 0.6 in grade 10 is insufficient for promotion to grade 11, or some similar principle), it is a reason for having Johnny repeat it as well. Here we see the connection between reasons, principles and consistency. In general, p is a reason for q only if some principle r renders p a reason for q, and would equally render p' a reason for q' if p and p', and q and q', are relevantly similar.

Because of this connection between reasons and principles, critical thinking is principled thinking; because principles involve consistency, critical thinking is impartial, consistent, and non-arbitrary, and the critical thinker both thinks and acts in accordance with, and values, consistency, fairness, and impartiality of judgment and action.[8] Principled, critical judgment, in its rejection of arbitrariness, inconsistency, and partiality, thus presupposes a recognition of the binding force of standards, taken to be universal and objective, in accordance with which judgments are to be made.[9] In the first instance, such standards involve criteria by which judgments can be made regarding the acceptability of various beliefs, claims, and actions—that is, they involve criteria which allow the evaluation of the strength and force of the reasons which may be offered in support of alternative beliefs, claims and actions. This leads us naturally into consideration of the reason assessment component of the reasons conception of critical thinking.

2 The reason assessment component

The basic idea here is simple enough: a critical thinker must be able to assess reasons and their ability to warrant beliefs, claims and actions properly. This means that the critical thinker must have a good understanding of, and the ability to utilize, principles governing the assessment of reasons.

There are at least two types of such principles: subject-specific principles which govern the assessment of particular sorts of reasons in particular contexts; and subject-neutral, general principles which apply across a wide variety of contexts and types of reason. Subject-neutral principles include all those principles typically regarded as "logical," both informal and formal. So, for example, principles regarding proper inductive inference, avoiding fallacies, proper deductive inference—in fact, virtually all that is usually included in informal logic texts, and virtually all of Ennis's list of proficiencies—count as subject-neutral logical principles. On the other hand, principles which apply only to specific subjects or areas of inquiry—e.g. principles governing the proper interpretation of bubble chamber photographs in particle physics, or those governing proper assessment of works of art, or novels, or historical documents, or the design of bathroom plumbing fixtures—are (as McPeck insists), though not general, nevertheless of central importance for critical thinking. There is no *a priori* reason for regarding either of these types of principles as more basic (or irrelevant) to critical thinking than the other; nor is there, at least to my knowledge, any significant empirical evidence to that effect. Similarly, there is no reason for regarding the skills associated with one sort of principle (e.g. the skill or ability to read a bubble chamber photo, a subject-specific skill) as more or less fundamental to critical thinking than the skills associated with the other sort (e.g. the skill or ability to reason well inductively, or assess the merits of observations, or recognize and avoid the fallacy of begging the question—all these being subject-neutral, logical skills).

This latter point is sufficient, I think, to establish that, from the educational point of view, the important question is not "Is there a generalized skill (or set of skills) of critical thinking?" but rather "How does critical thinking manifest itself?" The answer to this latter question is: "In both subject-specific and subject-neutral ways, for reasons, and the principles relevant to their assessment, are both subject-specific and subject-neutral." The McPeck-inspired debate over the first question, which has greatly preoccupied many members of the Informal Logic Movement of late, is thus in an important sense beside the point. There is no *a priori* reason for regarding either sort of principle or skill as more basic to critical thinking than the other; nor is there compelling empirical evidence to support such a judgment.[10]

Earlier I claimed that the reason assessment component of critical thinking requires that the student be able to assess reasons and their warranting force properly, and that this in turn requires that the student have a good grasp of the principles governing such assessment. A full account of the reason assessment component involves more than this, however. In addition to the ability to assess reasons and their warranting force (and a grasp of the related governing principles), critical thinkers need also to have a theoretical grasp of the nature of reasons, warrant, and justification, and so some understanding of why a given putative reason is to be assessed as it is. That is, the reason assessment component involves *epistemology*.

Perhaps the best way to get at this point is through a look at McPeck's discussion of the relation between critical thinking and epistemology. McPeck calls his approach to critical thinking the "epistemological approach," and he too argues that epistemology is central to critical thinking.[11] But McPeck's discussion of the relation between critical thinking and epistemology is problematic. For McPeck, the "epistemological approach" involves striving for an understanding of the constitution of good reasons for beliefs, so that:

> A student would learn not only what is thought to be the case in a given field (that is, the "facts") but also why it is so regarded. With this kind of understanding ... a person is then in a position to make the kinds of judgment required of a critical thinker.[12]

On this view, the student is a critical thinker in some content area, e.g. science, if the student understands the criteria of evaluation and justification of scientific beliefs. To have this understanding is to have an understanding of the epistemology of science. McPeck is quite explicit that good reasons, and so epistemology, are in his view subject-specific—not just reasons, but criteria for assessing the goodness of reasons are subject-specific; epistemology is to be replaced by a series of epistemologies, one for each "field of human endeavor":

> In chapter 2 it was argued that epistemology is, in effect, the analysis of good reasons for belief, including their specific character and foundation. Also, because collective human experience has discovered that different kinds of beliefs often have different kinds of good reason supporting them, it follows that there will be many different epistemologies corresponding to different fields of human endeavor. A corollary of this is that logic itself is parasitic upon epistemology, since logic is merely the formalization of good reasons once they have been discovered. Thus epistemology, and to some extent logic, have intrafield validity but not necessarily inter-field validity.... (Most programmes for critical thinking effectively deny this proposition, hence my disagreement with them.)[13]

There is a confusion here in McPeck's use of "epistemology." Epistemology is the *general* study of reasons, warrant, and justification, and a student striving to be a critical thinker in (e.g.) science does not study "the epistemology of science," understood to be distinct from "the epistemology" of other subject areas. Rather, the student strives to understand the specific principles and criteria by which scientific reasons are assessed, supplemented by a deeper understanding of the nature of reasons, warrant and justification generally. McPeck uses "epistemology" to refer both to subject-specific criteria of reason assessment, and to the general account of what it is to be a reason, to offer warrant for a belief, and to be justified. Once this conflation is noted, McPeck's claim that epistemology has "intra-field validity but not necessarily inter-field validity" collapses.[14] McPeck is surely right that students should come to learn why reasons for given claims in particular fields are rightly regarded as strong, powerful, compelling, weak, trivial, and so on according to the criteria for assessing reasons in those fields. But such an "epistemology of the subject" is only a part of epistemology as it is usually (and properly) understood. For the student who is to be a critical thinker must come to understand not only the criteria of reason assessment in specific fields, but also the nature of reasons generally and the fact that good reasons in different fields, singled out as good by different field-specific criteria, nevertheless stand in the same relation to the beliefs they support despite their being singled out by disparate criteria. If not, the student will have only the most shallow understanding of "the epistemology of the subject"—"*here* we regard *this* sort of thing as a good reason"—without understanding why this sort of thing should count as a reason here, but another sort of thing as a reason there. In short, McPeck's call for an epistemological approach to critical thinking stops short of a fully epistemological approach, for it fails to recognize that epistemology conceived as inquiry into the nature of reasons, warrant, and justification speaks to, and backs, the particular criteria of reason assessment McPeck refers to as "the epistemology of the subject."

It is perhaps worth noting that McPeck's own discussion belies his construal of epistemology as field- or subject-specific. For consider McPeck's claim that epistemology has intra-field but not necessarily inter-field validity, and the reasons he offers in support of that claim. Are those reasons, or the criteria which sanction them, field-specific? If so, to what field? To raise these questions is to realize that epistemology, understood as McPeck does as the analysis of good reasons, cannot be conceived of as subject- or field-specific. For:

1 many reasons and beliefs are not subject-specific, and so fall under no subject-specific set of reason- assessment criteria; and, more importantly,

2 critical thinking requires not simply a grasp of field-specific criteria of reason assessment, but also a general understanding of the nature of reasons, warrant and justification as these notions function across fields.[15]

To summarize: I have suggested thus far that a central component of critical thinking is the reason assessment component. The critical thinker must be able to assess reasons and their ability to warrant beliefs, claims and actions properly. Therefore, the critical thinker must have a good understanding of, and the ability to utilize, both subject-specific and subject-neutral (logical) principles governing the assessment of reasons. (This ability involves the "sub-ability" of determining which principle(s), and which sort of principle, are appropriate for the assessment of the putative reasons at hand.) A critical thinker is a person who can act, assess claims, and make judgments on the basis of reasons, and who understands and conforms to principles governing the evaluation of the force of those reasons. The account offered highlights the close conceptual connections between critical thinking and reasons, and between reasons and principles. The fact that there are (at least) two general types of principles of reason assessment—subject-specific and subject-neutral—suggests that much recent debate between various members of the Informal Logic Movement and McPeck concerning the generalizability of critical thinking skills is misconceived and irrelevant to the theory of critical thinking. McPeck and those members of the Movement are both right; both subject-specific, non-generalizable, and subject-neutral, generalizable skills, principles and information are highly relevant to reason assessment and so to critical thinking. Neither can be ruled out on *a priori* grounds; nor can either be ruled out—at least at present—on empirical grounds. (How central each is to the proper teaching of critical thinking is a matter to be resolved by further empirical study.) Finally, epistemology is also a crucially important component of a proper conception of critical thinking, for the critical thinker must have a good grasp of the nature of reasons, warrant and justification generally, as these notions function across fields, in order both to carry out and to understand the activity of reason assessment.[16]

Suppose that a student masters the reason assessment component of critical thinking, and is able to assess reasons, and to understand the nature of reasons and their assessment, in the ways articulated above. Has such a student earned the title "critical thinker"? So far, she has not, though she is undeniably well along the way to doing so. For, as we saw in the previous chapter, being able to assess reasons is not sufficient for being a critical thinker, though it is necessary. Equally necessary is that our student have an appropriate *attitude* toward the activity of critical thinking. This brings us naturally to the second component of critical thinking to be considered: the "critical attitude," or "critical spirit" component.

3 The critical spirit

In order to be a critical thinker, a person must have, in addition to what has been said thus far, certain attitudes, dispositions, habits of mind, and character traits, which together may be labelled the "critical attitude" or "critical spirit." Most generally, a critical thinker must not only be *able* to assess reasons properly, in accordance with the reason assessment component, she must be *disposed* to do so as well; that is, a critical thinker must have a well-developed disposition to engage in reason assessment. A critical thinker must have a *willingness* to conform judgment and action to principle, not simply an ability to so conform. One who has the critical attitude has a certain *character*[17] as well as certain skills: a character which is inclined to seek, and to base judgment and action upon, reasons; which rejects partiality and arbitrariness; which is committed to the objective evaluation of relevant evidence; and which values such aspects of critical thinking as intellectual honesty, justice to evidence, sympathetic and impartial consideration of interests, objectivity, and impartiality. A critical attitude demands not simply an ability to seek reasons, but a commitment to do so; not simply an ability to judge impartially, but a willingness and desire to do so, even when impartial judgment runs counter to self-interest.[18] A possessor of the critical attitude is inclined to seek reasons and evidence; to demand justification; to query and investigate unsubstantiated claims. Moreover, a person who possesses the critical attitude has habits of mind consonant with the just-mentioned considerations. Such a person habitually seeks evidence and reasons, and is predisposed to so seek—and to base belief and action on the results of such seeking. She applies the skills and abilities of reason assessment in all appropriate contexts, including those contexts in which her own beliefs and actions are challenged. For the possessor of the critical attitude, nothing is immune from criticism, not even one's most deeply-held convictions. Most fundamentally, the critical attitude involves a deep commitment to and respect for reasons—indeed, as Binkley puts it, a *love of reason*:

> the attitudes we seek to foster in the critical reasoning course might be summed up under the label "love of reason." We not only want our students to be *able* to reason well; we want them actually to do it, and so we want them to be eager to do it and to enjoy it—to think it important. We want it to assume an important place in their lives.[19]

This is, we want our students to *value* good reasoning, and to be disposed to believe and act on its basis. This is the heart of the critical attitude.[20]

Such a view as this, which includes attitudes, dispositions, habits of mind, and traits of character in a conception of critical thinking, seems to violate the time-honored distinction between cognition and affect (or thinking and feeling, or thought and value, or reason and emotion).[21] This violation, however, is as it should be. For the idea that reasons and emotions are unconnected, and the related idea that the exercise of reason requires complete independence from the emotions,[22] must both be rejected. As many recent writers have suggested, the "life of reason"—that is, the life of the critical thinker, who bases belief, attitude and action upon appropriate reasons and evidence—must have appropriate attitudes, passions, and interests as well as sufficient skills of reason assessment.[23] The conceptions of the reasonable person as one without emotion, and as one who "turns off" her emotions while engaging in reason, are untenable. Rather, the reasonable person has integrated with her reason assessment skills a host of *rational passions*, which together constitute and instantiate the critical attitude. Such a person actively seeks reasons and evidence on which to base judgments; such an attitude involves:

a love of truth and a contempt of lying, a concern for accuracy in observation and inference, and a corresponding repugnance of error in logic or fact. It demands revulsion at distortion, disgust at evasion, admiration of theoretical achievement, respect for the considered arguments of others.[24]

As Paul puts it, the rational passions include:

A passionate drive for *clarity*, accuracy, and fair-mindedness, a fervor for getting to the bottom of things ... for listening sympathetically to opposition points of view, a compelling drive to seek out evidence, an intense aversion to contradiction, sloppy thinking, inconsistent application of standards, a devotion to truth as against self-interest—[which are] essential components of the rational person.[25]

The critical thinker, finally, must *care* about reason and its use and point. She "must care about finding out how things are, about getting things right, about tracking down what is the case,"[26] and must have "the feeling of humility which is necessary to the whole-hearted acceptance of the possibility that one may be in error."[27] In sum, the image of the critical thinker/rational person as a "bloodless reasoning machine" will not do.[28] The critical thinker has a rich emotional make-up of dispositions, habits of mind, values, character traits, and emotions which may be collectively referred to as the critical attitude. This attitude is a fundamental feature of the critical thinker, and a crucially important component of the reasons conception of critical thinking.

As Peters puts it, "the use of reason is a passionate business."[29] The reasons conception reflects this fact, and rejects the commonly-drawn distinction between cognition and affect. Besides the emotional and attitudinal dimensions of critical thinking already considered, a person who is to be a critical thinker must be, to the greatest extent possible, emotionally secure, self-confident, and capable of distinguishing between having faulty beliefs and having a faulty character. A positive self-image, and traditionally-conceived psychological health, are important features of the psychology of the critical thinker, for their absence may well present practical obstacles to the execution of critical thinking.[30]

All of this suggests that education aimed at the development of critical thinking is a complex business, which must seek to foster a host of attitudes, emotions, dispositions, habits and character traits as well as a wide variety of reasoning skills. Since this cluster of traits to be fostered are traits of persons, not acts of thinking, the present discussion raises again the distinction between an account of critical think*ing* and an account of the critical think*er*. I would like to close out the present section by briefly returning to that distinction.

On the reasons conception, critical thinking involves actions which are not just acts of thinking.[31] For the critical thinker is appropriately *moved* by reasons; she acts in accordance with the force of relevant reasons. Thus the critical thinker is, importantly, a rational actor.[32] As important to critical thinking as rational action is, however, it is crucial to see that critical thinking far outstrips rational action. For a critical thinker is not simply a person who acts rationally (and who has well-developed skills of reason assessment). A critical thinker not only *acts* in certain ways. A critical thinker *is*, in addition, a certain sort of person.[33] Dispositions, inclinations, habits of mind, character traits—these features of the critical thinker are present, and definitive of the critical thinker, even when they are not being utilized or acted upon. Just as sugar has the disposition to dissolve in water while still in the sugar bowl, so does the critical thinker have the dispositions, habits of mind and character traits we have considered while not engaged in reason assessment or (other) rational action. The conception of critical thinking being offered here is as much a conception of a certain sort of person as it is a conception of a certain set of activities and skills. When we take it upon ourselves to educate students so as to foster critical thinking, we are committing ourselves to nothing less than the development of a certain sort of person. The reasons conception is a conception, not only of critical thinking, but of the critical thinker as well.[34]

These last remarks call attention to a matter that has been neglected for the last several pages. So far in this chapter I have endeavoured to articulate the reasons conception: to motivate it in terms of the relations between critical thinking, reasons, and rationality; to consider the detailed aspects of its two components, the reason assessment component and the critical spirit component; and to draw attention to the fact that the reasons conception—as any fully-developed conception of critical thinking must be—is a conception not only of a certain sort of activity, but of a certain sort of person. It remains to consider the way in which critical thinking, and in particular the reasons conception, functions as an educational notion and impacts on our educational ideas. We must, that is, consider the relation between critical thinking and education.

4 The relevance of critical thinking to education

(A) Critical thinking and the ethics of education

A striking feature of critical thinking (understood, from now on, as the reasons conception) is its impressive generality and wide-ranging relevance to education. Critical thinking is relevant to, and has implications for, the ethics of education as well as the epistemology of education. It touches the manner as well as the content of education. It will be worthwhile to spell out in some detail this wide-ranging relevance and generality.

Critical thinking is relevant to the *ethics* of education in at least two ways. First, ethical considerations arise in educational contexts in that how we teach—our *manner* of teaching—has an ethical as well as an instrumental side. We want to teach effectively, so that learners stand a good chance of learning; however, our methods of instruction must meet certain moral standards if they are to be acceptable. For instance, instructional methods which call for physical or psychological abuse of the learner are morally objectionable, no matter how effective. The way in which critical thinking is tied up with the manner of teaching will be dealt with below; this is the first way in which critical thinking is linked with the ethics of education.

The second way concerns the learner's moral education. Educators are bound, both morally and practically, to contribute to the moral education of the learner. Exactly how moral education is to proceed is a matter of some dispute, but it is clear that the learner's moral education should include, at least, instruction aimed at the inculcation in the student of certain intellectual habits, dispositions, and reasoning skills necessary for the learner to reach moral maturity. For example, moral education must seek to develop in the student a willingness and an ability to face moral situations impartially rather than on the basis of self-interest, for adequate moral behavior demands such impartiality. Hand in hand with impartiality is empathy, for the mature moral agent must be able to put herself in the position of others, and grasp their perspective and feelings, if they are to take seriously into consideration the interests of others; the development of empathy as a moral sentiment is thus equally a part of adequate moral education. Likewise, a morally mature person must recognize the centrality and force of moral reasons in moral deliberation, and moral education must strive to foster that recognition. Such "rational virtues" as impartiality of judgment, ability to view matters from a variety of non-self-interested perspectives, and recognition of the force of reasons, to name just three such virtues, are indispensable to moral education. They are also, we have seen, central aspects of critical thinking. Here, then, is the second way in which critical thinking is relevant to the ethics of education.[35]

(B) Critical thinking and the epistemology of education

Equally informed by critical thinking is the *epistemology* of education. A learner is, if she is successfully educated, expected to come to know many things. The "items of knowledge" a learner is expected to come to know are tremendously diverse, from simple "facts" to complex theories. Such facts and theories, moreover, are to be understood as well as known. It is not enough simply to know (in the sense of being able to repeat) the axioms of Euclidean geometry, for example; the learner is expected to understand them as well (as evidenced by, for example, the ability to utilize them correctly in formulating proofs of theorems). Such knowledge and under-standing demands, among other things, a proper understanding of the relevance of reasons and rules of inference and evidence. Without understanding the way in which (for example) the parallel line axiom offers a reason for taking the angle-side-angle theorem to be true, the learner cannot be said to understand fully either the axiom or the theorem. Moreover, the principles governing the correct assessment of inference and evidence are themselves important features of the curriculum. That is to say, a learner may profitably study canons of argument and evidence appraisal in their own right as objects of study, as well as master them in order to understand other items of knowledge which understanding depends on such mastery. Such items of the curriculum, then, are central to the education of the learner; to grasp the connection between premise and conclusion or evidence and conclusion is to understand the way in which premises and evidence constitute or provide reasons for conclusions. To understand the role of reasons in judgment is to open the door to the possibility of understanding conclusions and knowledge-claims generally. And, as we have seen, the ability to recognize the importance of and properly assess reasons is a central feature of critical thinking. Here, then, is the way that critical thinking is relevant to the epistemology of education.

(C) Critical thinking and the content of education

Intertwined with aspects of the ethics and epistemology of education are the content and manner of education. We can usefully divide the realm of education into two distinct parts: the *content* of education, which includes all that educators seek to impart to their students; and the *manner* of education, which includes the ways in which educators try to impart that content. Critical thinking has ramifications for both of these domains. We can see in another way the generality of critical thinking by spelling out the ramifications of critical thinking for both domains.

Critical thinking is highly relevant to the *content* of education. Accepting Ryle's distinction between knowledge how and knowledge that,[36] educational content includes both the development of skills and specific abilities (knowledge how), and propositional information (knowledge that). Critical thinking is relevant to both these types of educational content.

Critical thinking includes an important set of skills and abilities which education seeks to foster. As such, it is part of the "knowledge how" of educational content. We want students to be critical thinkers, and we seek to develop in them skills to that end, much as we seek to develop their reading, spelling, and computational skills. (These skills have of course been considered under the "reason assessment" component of critical thinking.) Similarly, we try to inculcate in students attitudes, dispositions, and habits likely to improve both their ability to think critically, and their inclination to do so. That is to say, we seek to instill in students the critical spirit, in that we try to impart to them the dispositions, habits of mind, and character traits which constitute that spirit. Since these skills and habits fall under the general heading of "knowledge how," we may say that critical thinking is part of the "how" of our educational content.

Critical thinking also falls under the "knowledge that" portion of educational content. We want to get students to be able to think critically, and that means, in part, getting them to understand what the rules of assessment and criteria of evaluation of claims are. We want our students to learn, for example, the evidential criteria underlying our judgments that some piece of evidence supports claim X, but that another piece does not support claim Y. We want students to learn *how* to apply such criteria. This, we have seen, is part of the way in which critical thinking concerns the "knowledge how" portion of educational content. But we also want students to be able to *reflect* on these criteria, and to endeavor to improve them.[37] In addition, we want students not simply to apply criteria blindly, but to understand their point, the justification of claims that they offer, and the higher-order justifications of them as legitimate criteria of assessment and evaluation that we can offer in their behalf. All this is part of our educational content of the "knowledge that" sort. So, critical thinking is an important part of the content of education, touching both the "knowledge how" and "knowledge that" portions of that content.

(D) Critical thinking and the manner of education

Perhaps most significant of all the connections between critical thinking and education are those between critical thinking and the manner of teaching—the *critical manner*. The critical manner is that manner of teaching that models and reinforces the critical spirit. A teacher who utilizes the critical manner seeks to encourage in his or her students the skills, habits and dispositions necessary for the development of the critical spirit. This means, first, that the teacher always recognizes the right of the student to question and demand reasons; and consequently recognizes an obligation to provide reasons whenever demanded. The critical manner thus demands of a teacher a willingness to subject all beliefs and practices to scrutiny, and so to allow students the genuine opportunity to understand the role reasons play in the justification of thought and action. The critical manner also demands honesty of a teacher; reasons presented by a teacher must be genuine reasons, and the teacher must honestly appraise the power of those reasons. In addition, the teacher must submit her reasons to the independent evaluation of the student:

> To teach ... is at some points at least to submit oneself to the understanding and independent judgment of the pupil, to his demand for reasons, to his sense of what constitutes an adequate explanation. To teach someone that such and such is the case is not merely to try to get him to believe it: deception, for example, is not a method or a mode of teaching. Teaching involves further that, if we try to get the student to believe that such and such is the case, we try also to get him to believe it for reasons that, within the limits of his capacity to grasp, are *our* reasons. Teaching, in this way, requires us to reveal our reasons to the

> student and, by so doing, to submit them to his evaluation and
> criticism.... To teach is thus ... to acknowledge the "reason" of
> the pupil, i.e. his demand for and judgment of reasons.[38]

Teaching in the critical manner is thus teaching so as to develop in
students the skills and attitudes consonant with critical thinking. It
is, as Scheffler puts it, an attempt to initiate students "into the
rational life, a life in which the critical quest for reasons is a
dominant and integrating motive."[39] Here reasons, rationality, and
teaching come together in the critical manner. Teaching in the critical
manner is thus perhaps the clearest way in which critical thinking
appropriately guides educational practice.[40]

5 Critical thinking as an educational ideal

We have seen thus far that critical thinking has ramifications for
both the ethics and the epistemology, and both the content and the
manner, of education. These ramifications are numerous, varied, and
wideranging. They demonstrate the impressive generality of critical
thinking as an educational notion. But what sort of notion is it? How
should we conceive of the *educational* notion of critical thinking?

We should, I think, conceive of it as an educational *ideal*. Critical
thinking, at least in the way it has been conceptualized in the present
chapter, speaks to virtually all of our educational endeavors. It
provides both important goals for our educational efforts, and
direction for the achievement of those goals. It is highly relevant to
the determination of what we should teach, how we should teach,
how we should organize educational activities, what the points of
many of those activities are, how we should treat students and others
in the educational setting, and so on. Perhaps most importantly, it
provides a conception of the sort of person we are trying, through
our educational efforts, to create, and the sort of character to be
fostered in such a person. Critical thinking provides an underlying
rationale for educational activities, a criterion for evaluating those
activities, and a guiding principle for the organization and conduct of
those activities. Surely such a broad-gauged notion is properly
thought of as an ideal.

In fact, I should like to suggest, critical thinking is best thought of
as a *regulative* ideal. It defines regulative standards of excellence
which can be used to adjudicate between rival educational methods,
policies, and practices. We have spelled out some of the features of
critical thinking: certain skills, attitudes, habits, dispositions and
character traits of the learner; certain sorts of practices, qualities and
attitudes of the teacher; certain sorts of content of the curriculum;

and certain sorts of properties, both contentual and organizational, of educational activities. To say that critical thinking is a regulative educational ideal is to say that the notion of critical thinking, or its constituent components, can and should be used as a basis by which to judge the desirability and justifiability of various features of or proposals for the educational enterprise. For example, according to the regulative ideal of critical thinking, whichever of two rival teaching methods conforms more closely to the manner of teaching described above as the critical manner is *prima facie* more desirable and ought to be utilized. Similarly, of two educational practices, whichever tends to develop in students those skills, habits, dispositions and character traits central to critical thinking is *prima facie* more desirable and ought to be chosen. In general, our guiding question in assessing educational activities should be: does this manifest, and foster, critical thinking? To the extent that we take this as our guiding evaluative question, we take critical thinking to be a fundamental educational ideal. In this way, critical thinking regulates our judgments and provides standards of excellence on which to base evaluations of educational practices, and so is usefully called a *regulative* ideal. It aids us in evaluating, and choosing between, alternative curricula, teaching methods, theories, policies, and practices.[41]

It should be clear that taking critical thinking to be an educational ideal is a highly significant move, with potentially far-reaching, even revolutionary, consequences. Hence it is far from clear that we should take it as such. The aim of this chapter has been simply to set out a conception of the ideal. The task of justifying the ideal, that is of providing reasons for granting the notion of critical thinking the prestige, force and power to guide education that I have just suggested it ought to be granted, is the topic of the next chapter.

CHAPTER 3

The justification of critical thinking as an educational ideal

Whatever we do, I believe we ought to keep uppermost the ideal of rationality and its emphasis on the critical, questioning, responsible free mind.[1]

Mankind in the main has always regarded reason as a bit of a joke.[2]

1 Why does the ideal need to be justified?

All of us right-thinking people regard the skills and dispositions constitutive of critical thinking as desirable things to have, and a critical thinker as a desirable thing to be. We think it important that our children, and young people generally, be educated in such a way as to foster in them the development of the traits of the critical thinker. Our efforts to write textbooks, design curriculum materials and courses, and encourage educators at all levels to incorporate critical thinking into the curriculum attest to our belief in the importance of, and commitment to, the fostering of critical thinking through education. What is the basis of our conviction? How do we justify educational interventions aimed at the development of critical thinking in students?

The question is not an idle one. For it is not the case that critical thinking is in fact universally accepted as an educational ideal.[3] For example, various defenders of "scientific" creationism deny that science education should strive either to expose students to scientifically legitimate alternative theories, or to help students to become capable of objectively evaluating evidence for, and of fairly assessing the merits of, those alternatives. While some only implicitly deny this, and pay lip service to critical evaluation, others explicitly suggest that science education ought to conform, not to the ideal of critical thinking, but rather to basic religious tenets.[4] More generally, fundamentalists of various stripes, and "TV preachers" such as Jerry Falwell, argue that parents *own* their children and have an unbridled right to indoctrinate their children into beliefs of all sorts.[5] More generally still, members of the general public—not to mention members of school boards and school administrations—often argue against the exposure of students to "dangerous" ideas, e.g. to "revisionist" ideas in US and world history and politics courses, to (non-distorted) communist/socialist/Marxist ideas in economics courses, to "liberal" (or "conservative") ideas regarding sex and related matters in health and hygiene courses, to ideas of all sorts in literature courses, etc. As a strictly political, practical matter, those who have opinions about, and determine the direction of, the education of children and young adults are not universally agreed that critical thinking ought to be regarded as a fundamental educational ideal.

But the challenge to critical thinking is mounted not only at the level of the "common," practical person who may or may not be active in the guidance of the education of young persons. The ideal is also challenged by several factions of the academic/intellectual community; that is, there are *theoretical* objections to taking critical thinking to be a fundamental educational ideal. For example, many feminist scholars distinguish between "male" and "female" thinking, label rational thinking (which I argued earlier is coextensive with critical thinking) as "male," and decry it as incomplete, biassed, sexist, or worse. The educational vision promulgated by such theorists is not one which is compatible with the ideal of critical thinking as delineated here.[6] Similarly, in literary theory deconstructionists such as Derrida deride rationality as "logocentric."[7] Further, as I consider in the next chapter, some Marxists and other ideologues reject critical thinking as biassed and bound up with unacceptable hegemonic interests. In addition, a suprising number of contemporary epistemologists and philosophers of science endorse views which favor one or another form of epistemological relativism,[8] which undercut the ideal of critical thinking, or more directly disparage rationality. Feyerabend is perhaps the most extreme, but he is not alone, when he castigates reason and rationality as oppressors of the human spirit, and eagerly anticipates their demise:

> Reason, at last, joins all those other abstract monsters such as Obligation, Duty, Morality, Truth and their more concrete predecessors, the Gods, which were once used to intimidate man and restrict his free and happy development: it withers away.[9]

More generally, writers from a variety of domains echo this sentiment, expressed by Dostoevsky, concerning a widely shared skepticism regarding rationality: "in some cases it is really more creditable to be carried away by an emotion, however unreasonable ... than to be unmoved ... a ... man who is always sensible is to be suspected and is of little worth."[10] So within the scholarly and literary community, no less than in the wider community, there are those who reject the idea that our educational institutions and activities ought to be organized and carried out with a view to fostering critical thinking.

Finally, I wish simply to point out that the simple *assumption* that critical thinking is a worthy educational goal is contentious, and masks enormous allied assumptions concerning the nature of education and the educated person. Many educational theorists have denied and would deny not only that critical thinking is a fundamental educational ideal, but that it is a worthwhile ideal at all. For many such theorists have favored educational ideals which are not only alternatives to, but are incompatible with, the ideal of critical thinking. Such alternatives include the production of docile citizens or good workers; the maximization of individual happiness; the fostering of ideological purity and commitment; and so on. In short, the aims of education are controversial and contentious. It is not *obvious* that the fostering of critical thinking is a good thing or a worthy aim of our educational endeavors.

The immediate lesson to be drawn from this point is that critical thinking, like any other putative educational ideal, must be justified if educational activities carried out in its name are to be justified; reasons must be given for its adoption, objections and criticisms answered, etc. A second, equally important lesson to be drawn is this: defenders of any educational ideal, and educators whose activities presuppose one or another ideal (as all such activities do), must squarely face central questions concerning the nature of education and the educated person. Such questions are traditional in the philosophy of education. Defenders of critical thinking, then, no less than proponents of alternative educational goals and activities, must confront the philosophy of education.

We could, of course, simply ignore the several foes of critical thinking just noted, and ignore the obligation to confront the philosophy of education and attempt to justify critical thinking as an educational ideal, secure in the knowledge that we right-minded thinkers recognize a fundamental educational ideal when we see one. But this will not do, so long as we regard ourselves as critical thinkers who honor the demand for reasons and justifications of our convictions. To justify critical thinking as an educational ideal is to offer a positive account of the desirability and worthiness of educational efforts which have as their aim the fostering of critical thinking in students; it is also to show that the sorts of challenges to the ideal just reviewed can be met, that the ideal can survive criticisms made against it. This is a large task. I do not claim to have completed it in what follows. But I do hope that it is a start, that it provides at least provisional justification for regarding critical thinking as a fundamental educational ideal, and that it encourages members of the Informal Logic Movement, educators and educational theorists, and philosophers of education to engage in serious reflection concerning critical thinking, the nature and existence of educational ideals, and the justification of those ideals.

2 What sort of "justification" is wanted?

A word concerning the sort of justification wanted, and the audience to whom the justification is addressed, is here in order.[11] It would be one thing—and an important thing—to offer a justification of critical thinking that spoke to its practical utility, and was addressed to school administrators, legislators, school board members, etc. Convincing the "movers and shakers" of education, the people who can actually get critical thinking to be taken as a focus of educational activities, that it would be a good idea to do so is a task of the utmost practical importance. Nevertheless, this task—offering a "pragmatic" justification for critical thinking, addressed to the people who hold the strings governing educational policy—is not, however important practically, what I shall seek to offer below. What I am after, rather, is a "philosophical" justification of critical thinking: production of reasons for regarding critical thinking as a fundamental educational ideal which are rationally persuasive to a rational, objective (perhaps ideal) inquirer into the question of the proper aims of education. The justification is not aimed at any particular audience, save perhaps an ideal one. In particular, it is not aimed at the local high school principal, the school board member, or the curriculum designer, though of course to the extent that such persons are themselves critical thinkers and so appropriately moved by reasons they should recognize and acknowledge the force of the reasons produced. My aim is to show that critical thinking *is* a justified ideal, that there *are* reasons which establish its worthiness as a focus for educational affairs. These reasons are not aimed at anyone in particular—but of course they are offered to all who wish to be, and claim to be, rational in that they are moved by reasons.[12]

Because I am after a philosophical rather than a pragmatic justification, certain powerful pragmatic considerations which speak in favor of critical thinking will not serve my purposes. For example, Michael Scriven, Ralph Johnson and J. Anthony Blair, and many others have urged critical thinking on the grounds that students need protection, self-defense, from unscrupulous advertizers, ideologues, and other potential manipulators of students' beliefs. This seems to me an enormously important practical point. But it will not serve as a philosophical justification of critical thinking, for it presupposes that it is a good thing for students to be free of such manipulation—a seemingly obvious point, perhaps, but one which nevertheless must be (and below will be) argued for. Other pragmatic considerations could be listed, to the same effect. In seeking a philosophical rather than a pragmatic justification, I am in no way intending to belittle the latter. On the contrary, I believe that, if we truly seek to get our students to be critical thinkers, attention to pragmatic considerations is essential, and should be a focus of concern for us all. Nevertheless, if we are truly justified in so seeking, then philosophical considerations are more basic, for they ground the commitment to the educational vision which the pragmatic activity strives to realize. So pragmatic considerations, e.g. that critical thinking will help students to avoid being snookered and sucked in by bad arguments, however important in other contexts, are not what I am after here. It is a philosophical justification that I am attempting to provide in what follows. Such is required if our efforts to make critical thinking central to our educational endeavors are ultimately to be justified.[13] (Henceforth all mention of "justification" should be taken to refer to philosophical justification, as just delineated.)

3 An unsuccessful attempt

It may be instructive to consider an effort to justify critical thinking which, while right-spirited, fails to establish it as an educational ideal. The effort is McPeck's, and, although he does not couch his discussion in terms of justification, its relevance to the justification of critical thinking is immediate and obvious.

McPeck argues that the relation between education and critical thinking is one of logical entailment; that critical thinking is a necessary condition for education:

> what I shall argue is not only that it would be a good thing if our educational institutions could get students to be critical thinkers, but also that, insofar as the purpose of schools is to educate, this task logically cannot be accomplished without critical thinking. In short, critical thinking is a necessary condition for education.[14]

If McPeck is right, then the justification of educational efforts aimed at fostering critical thinking is automatic; if one is engaged in education, one is, as a matter of logic, *eo ipso* engaged in the fostering of critical thinking. Unfortunately, the justification of educational practices and ideals is not so easy.

McPeck's argument for the logical necessity of critical thinking in education comes to this:

1 Education entails the acquisition of knowledge.
2 Knowledge presupposes justification.
3 Justification requires the temporary suspension of belief in order to assess the coherence of the evidence for the belief.
4 Such suspension and assessment simply is critical thinking.
5 Therefore, justification requires critical thinking.
6 Therefore, knowledge presupposes critical thinking.
7 Therefore, education entails critical thinking.

McPeck summarizes his argument's conclusion as follows: "Critical thinking must, therefore, command a place in any institution committed to the pursuit of education because critical thinking is a necessary condition of it."[15]

McPeck's argument founders on its very first step. McPeck puts it this way:

> Whatever else an analysis of education might reveal, it surely entails the acquisition of knowledge. Conceptual analysts and curriculum theorists might argue over the various types of knowledge that form constituents of education, but I can think of no one who would seriously doubt that knowledge of some sort is entailed by education.[16]

Unfortunately, this sort of reliance on conceptual analysis will not secure McPeck's point. No analysis of the concept of education will secure such a point, for what a concept entails depends crucially on whose concept it is.[17] In fact it is easy to think of persons who *would* seriously doubt that knowledge is entailed by education, if knowledge is taken (as McPeck here takes it) as essentially involving rational justification. The ideologue who views education as a means of attaining or insuring ideological purity; the political, cultural, or religious conservative who views education as a means of maintaining the *status quo*; the "social systems manager" who views education as a means of maintaining a docile and compliant citizenry—all these and many others as well would indeed seriously doubt that education entails knowledge (taken to involve rational justification).[18] One cannot settle the deep disputes that exist between those (like McPeck) who believe that education entails knowledge, and those who believe that education entails the passing on of basic religious (political, moral, etc.) commitments *sans* justification, by appealing to ordinary-language or conceptual analysis.

I am not suggesting that such disputes are not rationally adjudicable. On the contrary, I believe not only that they are; I believe that they must be addressed if the vision of education McPeck and other friends of critical thinking propound is to be justified, or even taken seriously. It is of fundamental importance to justify critical thinking as an educational ideal, and so to establish the fostering of critical thinking as a justifiable educational aim and efforts at such fostering as justifiable activities. My point here is simply that McPeck's view of the relation between education and critical thinking—that the one entails the other, and that this entailment relation is established by conceptual analysis—will not do. If education for critical thinking is rationally preferable to education for ideological purity, maintenance of the political and social *status quo*, maintenance of a docile and unquestioning citizenry, the transmission of fundamental religious commitments, or any other "uncritical" educational aim, that rational preferability must be established by means of substantive philosophical argument concerning educational ideals and the aims of education. If critical thinking is to be a central focus of our educational efforts, this cannot be justified on the basis of the meaning of "education," but only on the basis of our best-justified educational ideals. In short, and to repeat, those who take seriously the educational agenda of the Informal Logic Movement, and defenders of critical thinking more generally, must squarely face basic issues in the philosophy of education. I have criticized McPeck's account of the relationship between critical thinking and education, but I applaud his recognition that that relationship must be addressed, and not simply assumed, by proponents of critical thinking who themselves endeavor to justify their commitment to that ideal. It is crucial that we who value critical thinking attend to the task of justifying our allegiance to that value. Onward, then, to the justificatory task at hand.

4 Some final preliminaries

If we accept critical thinking as a fundamental educational ideal, we explicitly acknowledge the desirability of the attainment by students of self-sufficiency and autonomy. If we think it good that a student become a critical thinker, we must approve as well of the student's ability and disposition to consult her own independent judgment concerning matters of concern to her. The critical thinker must be *autonomous*—that is, free to act and judge independently of external constraint, on the basis of her own reasoned appraisal of the matter at hand.[19] Relatedly, if we take the ideal of critical thinking seriously, we must endeavor to render the student self-sufficient and capable of determining (insofar as is possible) her own future. In this way we aim to bring the student quickly to the point at which she can join the adult community and be recognized as a fellow member of a community of equals. Critical thinking, in its open striving for the student's early achievement of a significant degree of autonomy and self-sufficiency, is incompatible with any educational plan which aims at the preparation of the student for some preconceived adult role or pre-established slot in some social arrangement. Rather, critical thinking aims at getting the student to be an active participant in the establishment and creation of her adult life, and of the social arrangements in which she is engaged.

As these preliminary remarks make clear, critical thinking is no rubber-stamp friend of the *status quo*; indeed, it is an enemy of the unjustifiable *status quo*.[20] This is not only an important fact about critical thinking; it also makes clear how threatening a full embrace of the ideal can be to the maintenance of the established social order, and so explains a certain sort of resistance to that embrace. Making critical thinking a basic aim of our collective educational endeavors in effect grants those endeavors a special status: it establishes education, and its concern for critical thinking, as an independent critic and guide of democratic society. This conception of education, and its role in and relationship to the larger society, is a profound one, and indicates the immense depth of the philosophical issues raised by a consideration of critical thinking. I regret that I cannot pursue the matter here.[21] It is long past time that the task of justification be faced.

5 The justification of the ideal

How can the educational ideal of critical thinking—which promulgates the development in students of autonomy, self-sufficiency, the skills of reason assessment, and the attitudes, dispositions, habits of mind, and character traits of the critical spirit, and erects those features of persons as the fundamental guidelines for the evaluation and transformation of society—be justified? I would like to offer four considerations which I hope constitute at least the beginning of a justification.

(A) Respect for students as persons

The first consideration involves our moral obligations to students, and is most directly relevant to that portion of critical thinking which has to do with the manner of teaching. That is, it purports to justify the claim that our manner of teaching ought to accord with the critical manner.

This first consideration is simply that we are morally obliged to treat students (and everyone else) with respect. If we are to conduct our interpersonal affairs morally, we must recognize and honor the fact that we are dealing with other persons who as such deserve respect—that is, we must show *respect for persons*. This includes the recognition that other persons are of equal moral worth, which entails that we treat other persons in such a way that their moral worth is respected. This in turn requires that we recognize the needs, desires, and legitimate interests of other persons to be as worthy of consideration as our own. In our dealings with other persons, we must not grant our interests any more weight, simply because they are *our* interests, than the interests of others. The concept of respect for persons is a Kantian one, for it was Kant who urged that we treat others as *ends* and not means.[22] This involves recognizing the equal worth of all persons. Such worth is the basis of the respect which all persons are due.

It is important to note that respect for persons has ramifications far beyond the realm of education. All persons, in all situations, deserve to be treated with respect; to be regarded as morally significant and worthy entities. This general point includes educational situations, since educational situations involve persons. Here is the relevance of the Kantian conception of respect for persons to education. It is also worth pointing out that the obligation to treat students with respect is independent of more specific educational aims. It is an obligation binding on us generally, and so is not part of any particular educational setting or system. Whatever else we are trying to do in our educational institutions, we are obliged to treat students with respect.

The Kantian principle of respect for persons requires that we treat students in a certain manner—one which honors students' demand for reasons and explanations, deals with students honestly, and recognizes the need to confront students' independent judgment. For what does it mean for a teacher to recognize the equal moral worth of students and to treat them with respect? Among other things, it means recognizing and honoring the student's right to question, to challenge, and to demand reasons and justifications for what is being taught. The teacher who fails to recognize these rights of the student fails to treat the student with respect, for treating the student with respect involves recognizing the student's right to exercise her independent judgment and powers of evaluation. To deny the student this right is to deny her the status of "person of equal moral worth." To treat students with respect is, moreover, to be honest with them. To deceive, indoctrinate, or otherwise fool students into believing anything, even if true, is to fail to treat them with respect.

The general moral requirement to treat persons with respect thus applies to the teacher's dealing with her students simply because those students are persons and so are deserving of respect. It is independent of any specific educational aim. Nevertheless, it offers justification for the ideal of critical thinking in that the way one teaches, according to the critical manner, is in crucial respects isomorphic to the way one teaches so as to respect students. In both, the student's right to question, challenge, and seek reasons, explanations, and justifications must be respected. In both, the teacher must deal honestly with the student. In both, the teacher must submit reasons for taking some claim to be true or some action to be justified to the student's independent judgment and critical scrutiny. In most respects, then, teaching in the critical manner simply *is* teaching in such a way as to treat students with respect; the obligation to treat students with the respect they are due as persons thus constitutes a reason for adopting the critical manner. In short, this manner of teaching is morally required; it is also part and parcel of the ideal of critical thinking. So morality provides one powerful reason for operating our educational institutions, and conducting our educational affairs more generally, in ways which accord with that ideal.[23]

(B) Self-sufficiency and preparation for adulthood

The second reason for taking critical thinking to be a worthy eductional ideal has to do with education's generally recognized task of preparing students to become competent with respect to those abilities necessary for the successful management of adult life. We educate, at least in part, in order to prepare children for adulthood. But we cannot say in advance that Johnny will be a pilot, for example, and arrange his education accordingly, for Johnny might well decide to be something else. In general, when we say that education prepares children for adulthood, we do not mean for some specific adult role. Rather, we mean that education strives to enable children to face adulthood successfully. In particular, we hope that education fosters in children the power and ability to control, insofar as they are able, their own lives. We guide a child's education primarily because the child cannot responsibly guide it herself, but we seek to bring her, as quickly as possible, to the point at which she can "take over the reins" and guide her own education and life generally. That is, we seek to render the child *self-sufficient*; to *empower* the student to control her destiny and to *create* her future, not submit to it.[24] To get the student to the point at which she can competently control her own life and responsibly contribute to social life is to bring the student into the adult community, to recognize the student as a fellow member of a community of equals. To thus empower the student is to raise her, in the most appropriate sense of the term, to her "fullest potential," for any such potential surely includes the power to shape and choose, and to attain, possible potentials.[25] Indeed, this is a fundamental obligation to children. Without proper education, children would not get to the point at which they could competently control their own destinies; many options would be forever closed to them because of their poor education. To meet our obligation to children to prepare them well for adulthood, we must strive to educate them in such a way that they are maximally self-sufficient.[26]

How can we organize educational activities so as to empower the student? My suggestion, predictably enough, is that we organize those activities according to the dictates of critical thinking. To help students to become critical thinkers is to "encourage them to ask questions, to look for evidence, to seek and scrutinize alternatives, to be critical of their own ideas as well as those of others."[27] Such encouragement conforms well to the effort to encourage self-sufficiency, since, as Scheffler puts it:

> This educational course precludes taking schooling as an
> instrument for shaping [students'] minds to a preconceived idea.
> For if they seek reasons, it is their evaluation of such reasons
> that will determine what ideas they eventually accept.[28]

By encouraging critical thinking, then, we teach the student what we think is right, but we encourage the student to scrutinize our reasons and judge independently the rightness of our claims. In this way the student becomes a competent judge; more importantly for the present point, the student becomes an independent judge. That is, the student makes her own judgments regarding the appropriateness of alternative beliefs, courses of action, and attitudes. Such independence of judgment[29] is the *sine qua non* of self-sufficiency. The self-sufficient person is, moreover, a *liberated* person; such a person is free from the unwarranted and undesirable control of unjustified beliefs, unsupportable attitudes, and paucity of abilities, which can prevent that person from competently taking charge of her own life. Critical thinking thus liberates[30] as it renders students self-sufficient. Insofar as we recognize our obligation to help children become competent, self-sufficient adults, that obligation provides a justification for the ideal of critical thinking, for education conceived along the lines suggested by that ideal recognizes that obligation explicitly. Here, then, is a second reason for taking critical thinking to be a legitimate educational ideal.

(C) Initiation into the rational traditions

As argued earlier, critical thinking is best seen as coextensive with rationality, and rationality is concerned with reasons. For a person to be rational, that person must (at least) grasp the relevance of various reasons for judgments and evaluate the weight of such reasons properly. How does a person learn how to evaluate reasons properly?

One plausible account suggests that a person learns the proper assessment of reasons by being initiated into the traditions in which reasons play a role. Education, on this view, amounts to the initiation of the student into the central human traditions.[31] These traditions—science, literature, history, the arts, mathematics, and so on—have evolved, over the long history of their development, guidelines concerning the role and nature of reasons in their respective domains. Thus, for example, a science student must learn, among other things, what counts as a good reason for or against some hypothesis, theory, or procedure; how much weight the reason has; and how it compares with other relevant reasons. Science education amounts to initiating the student into the scientific tradition, which in part consists in appreciating that tradition's standards governing the appraisal of reasons.[32]

Such appraisal is, moreover, not static. Standards of rationality evolve and must be seen as part of a constantly evolving tradition:

> Rationality in natural inquiry is embodied in the relatively young tradition of science, which defines and redefines those principles by means of which evidence is to be interpreted and meshed with theory. Rational judgment in the realm of science is, consequently, judgment that accords with such principles, as crystallized at the time in question. To teach rationality in science is to interiorize these principles in the student, and furthermore, to introduce him to the live and evolving *tradition* of natural science. . . .
> Similar remarks might be made also with respect to other areas, e.g. law, philosophy and the politics of democratic society. The fundamental point is that rationality cannot be taken simply as an abstract and general idea. It is embodied in *multiple evolving traditions*, in which the basic condition holds that issues are resolved by reference to reasons, themselves defined by *principles* purporting to be impartial and universal.[33]

If we can take education to involve significantly the initiation of students into the rational traditions, and such initiation consists in part in helping the student to appreciate the standards of rationality which govern the assessment of reasons (and so proper judgment) in each tradition, then we have a third reason for regarding critical thinking as an educational ideal. Critical thinking, we have seen, recognizes the importance of getting students to understand and appreciate the role of reasons in rational endeavor, and of fostering in students those traits, attitudes, and dispositions which encourage the seeking of reasons for grounding judgment, belief, and action. Understanding the role and criteria of evaluation of reasons in the several rational traditions is crucial to being successfully initiated into those traditions. If education involves initiation into the rational traditions, then we should take critical thinking to be an educational ideal because so taking it involves fostering in students those traits, dispositions, attitudes and skills which are conducive to the successful initiation of students into the rational traditions. Seeing education as initiation thus offers justification for the ideal of critical thinking.[34]

(D) Critical thinking and democratic living

Finally, consider the relation between critical thinking and democracy. It is a truism that the properly functioning democracy requires an educated citizenry. What sort of education does such a citizenry require?

The answer is not one-dimensional. The democratic citizen requires a wide variety of the many things which education can provide. She needs to be well-informed with respect to all sorts of matters of fact; to grasp fully the nature of democratic institutions and to embrace fully their responsibilities; to treat her fellow democrats as equal partners in political life, etc. She also needs to be able to examine public policy concerns: to judge intelligently the many issues facing her society; to challenge and seek reasons for proposed changes (and continuations) of policy; to assess such reasons fairly and impartially, and to put aside self-interest when it is appropriate to do so; and so on. If the democratic citizen is not a critical thinker, she is significantly hampered in her ability to contribute helpfully to public life. Democracies rely for their health and well being on the intelligence of their citizens. My point is simply that such intelligence, if it is truly to be of benefit, must consist in part of the skills, attitudes, abilities and traits of the critical thinker. It is not simply an intelligent citizenry, but a critical one, which democracy wants.

Indeed, the relationship between critical thinking and democracy is a very close one. For democracy, at least ideally:

aims so to structure the arrangements of society as to rest them ultimately upon the freely given consent of its members. Such an aim requires the institutionalization of reasoned procedures for the critical and public review of policy; it demands that judgments of policy be viewed not as the fixed privilege of any class or elite but as the common task of all, and it requires the supplanting of arbitrary and violent alteration of policy with institutionally channeled change ordered by reasoned persuasion and informed consent.[35]

The fundamentality of reasoned procedures and critical talents and attitudes to democratic living is undeniable. Insofar as we are committed to democracy, then, that commitment affords yet another reason for regarding critical thinking as a fundamental educational ideal, for an education which takes as its central task the fostering of critical thinking is the education most suited for democratic life.[36]

These four putative reasons for regarding critical thinking as a fundamental educational ideal—morality and respect for persons, self-sufficiency and preparation for adulthood, initiation into the rational traditions, and the requirements of democratic living—are clearly not the last word. Much more needs to be said concerning all of them. Perhaps there are other justifications to be brought forth. I hope that the discussion offered thus far helps to stimulate members of the Informal Logic Movement, philosophers of education, and all who are interested in and/or committed to critical thinking to join in the investigation of the justificatory question. For, as I argued earlier, the ideal needs to be justified if our commitment to it is to be so. It is an important philosophical matter which underlies our practical endeavors and commitments.

As noted earlier, a full justification of the ideal would include not only positive reasons for embracing the ideal (four of which have just been given), but also rebuttals of independent objections and challenges to it. The next two chapters attempt to respond to two such challenges.

CHAPTER 4

The ideology objection

Abstract and remote, pretending to an objective standpoint beyond politics, bloodlessly rational and calculating, philosophy (they say) diverts energy from the imperative task of altering an utterly evil *status quo*. Blind to the human misery around it, it callously plays words instead of helping to mobilize militant revolutionary sentiments and radical action. By such intellectual diversion, it helps in fact to rationalize and bolster existent evils and enters into complicity with them. Its vaunted rationality, like that of science, is in fact merely its capacity to shape men to the specifications of a repressive industrial society.[1]

Critical thinking cannot be viewed simply as a form of progressive reasoning; it must be seen as a fundamental, political act.[2]

1 The objection and its significance

The task of justifying critical thinking as an educational ideal amounts to that of establishing that critical thinking is an ideal worthy of guiding educational endeavors. This presupposes that critical thinking, and alternative educational ideals and values, are amenable to rational evaluation. The objection to be considered in this chapter—the "ideology objection"—denies that educational ideals such as critical thinking do in fact admit of rational evaluation. Such ideals and values, rather, are determined by prior ideological commitment; a "justified" educational ideal is simply an ideal which is sanctioned by one's ideology. On this view, "rationality justified" is simply a misleading honorific. When we say that an educational ideal is justified, or that there is good reason for regarding some putative ideal as an ideal, we are simply noting the compatibility of the ideal and some ideology to which we are already committed. Behind every rational appraisal, in short, lies a prior ideological commitment which renders other educational commitments "rational."

Notice that the objection is not an objection only to the ideal of critical thinking. It is perfectly generalizable, and so casts aspersions on the rational justification of any educational ideal, and indeed on the very possibility of rational justification itself. Nevertheless, the objection poses a serious problem for the present endeavor, for if critical thinking can be "rationally justified" only insofar as it is sanctioned by our prior commitment to an ideology which honors it, then our rational justification appears to be no more than a question-begging rationalization, and our ideal not rationally justified at all. Our commitment to and pursuit of an educational plan which seeks to foster critical thinking must be seen, in this light, as arbitrary; and critical thinking seen as no more worthy an educational ideal than any other. Thus, if the objection holds, our project of justifying critical thinking fails. Hence the need for this chapter.

In what follows I will attempt to spell out the objection more fully and carefully, so as to assess its force. I hope to isolate and assess those considerations which might seem to show that rational justification presupposes prior ideological commitment. This inquiry will force consideration of a self-reflexive question: namely, does the effort to assess the ideology objection itself beg the question against the proponent of that objection, by presupposing prior standards of argument appraisal? This in turn will raise the question of the general relationship between rationality and ideology. I will agree with the skeptic regarding the non-ideological justification of educational ideals that, in order for critical thinking to be rationally justified as a fundamental educational ideal, it must be shown that that justification rests on no prior ideological commitment. Unlike that skeptic, however, I will suggest that non-ideological justification is possible. I will argue further that, in the relevant sense, rationality *transcends* ideology, and is capable of assessing the worth both of alternative ideologies and of alternative educational ideals. In this way, I will argue that the present effort—of articulating and defending critical thinking as a fundamental educational ideal—can meet the challenge of the ideology objection.

I hasten to point out the limited scope of the chapter. The philosophical literature on ideology is vast, and the philosophical difficulties (and insights) afforded by that notion are legion. Full consideration of the notion of ideology and the philosophical questions it raises is beyond my talent, and my patience. I intend only to treat the ideology objection—a large enough task—and, hopefully, to establish that the ideal of critical thinking can be justified, and the objection met. I will try to show, that is, that considerations of ideology do not undermine the legitimacy or justifiability of the educational ideal of critical thinking.

2 What is ideology?

This is not an easy question to answer, for, as Roger Simon puts it, "Readers familiar with current literature in political and social theory as well as sociology of education know too well that 'ideology' is a term currently in *semantic disarray*."[3] "Semantic disarray" captures neatly the difficulty we face: "ideology" has no definite meaning; it refers to no specific entity or phenomenon. Rather, writers of very different orientations use the term in a variety of loosely connected ways.

Perhaps the most central notion which "ideology" seeks to capture is that of a general framework, set of basic beliefs, or set of practices, which in some way helps to constitute or shape individual consciousness and which orients humans in the world and guides belief and action. According to this meaning of "ideology," a person's ideology enables that person to make sense of her experience and of the world she lives in, and guides the formation of her beliefs, intentions, attitudes, and actions. Ideology is thus a framework for the interpretation of experience. C.A. Bowers, for example, writes that:

> The term "ideology" designates an interlocking set of beliefs and assumptions that make up the background or horizon against which the members of society make sense of their daily experience.... ["Ideology"] denotes a socially constructed and maintained belief system or cosmology that provides the overarching rules and assumptions for symbolizing reality.[4]

Snook offers a characterization of (the liberal conception of) ideology as "any set of directive ideas."[5] Rohatyn defines it as "the central tenets of a culture."[6] Burbules offers a similar account of ideology as "a framework of explanation and justification," although he (like other writers) limits the bounds of the framework to the social world.[7] Apple suggests that it is relatively uncontroversial to "talk about ideology as referring to some sort of 'system' of ideas, beliefs, fundamental commitments, or values about social reality," although he notes the existence of controversy concerning the scope of ideological phenomena and the function of ideology.[8] Geertz regards ideologies as symbol systems which afford ways of making "otherwise incomprehensible social situations meaningful."[9]

The sense of "ideology" these varied accounts attempt to capture—that of a general framework that shapes individual consciousness, guides and legitimates belief and action, and renders experience meaningful—is the most widely shared sense of the term I am aware of. But "ideology" has been used in many different ways by different theorists, some of which bear noting.

Perhaps most famous is the notion usually attributed to Marx, which regards ideologies as fictions or distortions of objective reality.

On this view, ideologies betoken false consciousness; the person in the grip of an ideology suffers from a conception of reality which is necessarily misrepresentative of the world and the person's relation to it. On this "pejorative" sense of "ideology,"[10] an ideology is something undesirable and to be overcome.[11] Closely related to this sense of "ideology" is the claim that ideologies are typically politically oppressive, foster class conflict, and serve to legitimate unjustifiably[12] the *status quo*. Thus Louis Wirth characterizes ideologies as "complexes of ideas which direct activity toward the maintenance of the existing order."[13]

Contrary to this conception of ideologies as undesirable and as something to be overcome, ideologies are sometimes conceived as necessary, unavoidable mediators of thought. On this view, an ideology is a "constitutive medium,"[14] something required for comprehension. Consequently, on this conception of "ideology," ideologies are not something to overcome; they are, rather, necessary for thought. The critical task is then not to forswear ideology, which is impossible, but to adopt the best ideology one can.[15] This sense of "ideology", unlike the Marxist sense just noted, takes ideologies to be necessary and unavoidable, and uses "ideology" in a non-pejorative way.

It is worth noting as well that while some writers regard ideologies fundamentally as systems of ideas, others make much of the fact that ideologies have "non-discursive" as well as "discursive" elements,[16] arise from lived experience,[17] and are embedded in practices.[18]

As the reader is no doubt aware, these several alternative conceptions of ideology raise a host of difficult issues which theorists of ideology must face. Fortunately, in order to pursue the task of this chapter we needn't come to grips with the plethora of meanings of the term, or with the host of issues which divide rival theories of ideology,[19] for in order to express and consider the ideology objection, all that is required is a very general characterization of ideology, one which makes possible the forceful articulation of the objection. Let us, then, with full recognition of the vast and complex literature on ideology we are ignoring, regard an ideology as a general framework that shapes individual consciousness, guides and legitimates belief and action, and renders experience meaningful. With this notion of ideology we are able to articulate and assess the ideology objection.

3 The ideology objection

The proponent of the objection[20] rejects the idea that fundamental educational ideals, like critical thinking or rationality, can be justified without reference to some prior ideological commitment.

On this view, ideological commitment is logically prior to a commitment to educational ideals. I have been suggesting thus far that critical thinking can be justified as an educational ideal independently of ideological commitment. According to the objection, however, such a view puts the cart before the horse, for the justification of any ideal will be persuasive only to the extent that reasons offered in support of an ideal will be recognized as having force; and such recognition depends on a prior ideological commitment. To take the example of the last chapter, the reasons put forward in support of the ideal of critical thinking—Kantian respect for persons, self-sufficiency, initiation into the rational traditions, and the requirements of democratic living—will demonstrate the worthiness of the ideal only if those putative reasons are recognized as legitimate reasons by one's ideology. If one's ideology denies that these putative reasons are in fact warrant-conferring, then one would reject the ideal. Thus the justification of critical thinking as an educational ideal—and by parity of reasoning, the justification of *any* educational ideal—depends on the ideological stance from which judgment is to be made. So ideological commitment is basic; not only is it prior to justificatory tasks, it determines the epistemic force of putative reasons. What counts as a reason depends on what one's ideology recognizes as a reason. Rationally itself, and so epistemology,[21] is ideology-dependent. Ideology is basic and pervasive; educational ideals (and all other "reasoned" commitments) inevitably reflect and are a function of the ideological viewpoint of their proponents.

As noted above, the ideology objection raises dramatically the question of the relationship between rationality and ideology. We shall return to this fundamental question in due course. First, however, let us consider the question with specific attention to the justification of educational ideals. What reasons can be given in favor of the view that educational ideals are reflections of, and dependent upon, prior ideological commitment?

(A) There can be no neutrality in education; everything educational is fundamentally political

The first reason for thinking that educational ideals are dependent upon prior ideological commitment rests upon the recognition of the political nature of education. Many educational theorists emphasize that educational institutions are necessarily political in nature. This is a central theme, for example, of Paulo Freire's work. Perhaps the central tenet of Freire's writing is that "there is no truly neutral education."[22] Henry Giroux, in his fine discussion of Freire's perspective, characterizes it as follows:

> In essence all pedagogy, according to him [i.e. Freire], is
> essentially a political issue and all educational theories are
> political theories. Inherent in any educational design are value
> assumptions and choices about the nature of humankind, the use
> of authority, the value of specific forms of knowledge and,
> finally, a vision of what constitutes the good life. Freire's work
> represents a critical attempt to illustrate how ideologies of
> various means and persuasions reflect, distort, and prevent men
> and women from becoming socio-political actors in the struggle
> against an oppressive society. Thus, to understand his pedagogy
> one must begin with a recognition that it is both a call for
> liberation and an ongoing process of radical reconstruction. All
> of his major themes follow from this premise....
> Freire never tires of insisting that schooling is not neutral.[23]

Freire is, of course, not the only theorist to insist that education is
fundamentally political. Jonathan Kozol, for example, in his
fascinating account of Cuba's recent literacy campaign, suggests that
"All learning is ideological in one way or another.... All education,
unless it is hopelessly boring and irrelevant, is political.... Education
is either for domestication or for liberation."[24] In addition to Freire,
Kozol cites as fellow travelers in the "all education is political and
ideological" tradition Bowles and Gintis, Ivan Illich, Michael B.
Katz, and Joel Spring.[25] Bowers, too, suggests that in education it is
impossible to avoid ideology.[26] And Kevin Harris asserts that
"Education ... is a distinctly non-neutral political mechanism or
institutionalized process that largely provides and legitimises the
ways and perspectives by which and from which we shall come to
know the world."[27] Harris suggests as well that ideology is both
inescapable and "necessarily political."[28]

Given that education is inescapably political, and that the political
is entwined with the ideological, it is easy to see how the "everything
is political" thesis can be seen to afford a reason for thinking that
educational ideals—critical thinking or any other—presuppose prior
ideological commitment. For any educational ideal, according to this
thesis, presupposes or reflects a view of the sociopolitical character of
educational institutions, and any view of the political character of
education will inevitably be bound up with ideological considerations. Consequently, the thesis under discussion seems to imply
that educational ideals are dependent upon prior ideological
commitment. Hence this route to the ideology objection.

I say "*seems* to imply" because, as the reader might have guessed, I
believe that things are not so straightforward as the "all education is

necessarily political" theorists suggest. Before examining the matter, however, let me briefly mention another reason for thinking that educational ideals are dependent upon prior ideological commitment—that is, another reason for thinking that the ideology objection undermines the effort to justify critical thinking (or anything else) as a fundamental educational ideal.

(B) Ideology shapes consciousness

This reason is easy to state; one need go no further than the classic analysis of ideology offered by Mannheim. The fundamental idea—reflected in our earlier characterization of ideology—is that ideology in some sense shapes consciousness, and so materially affects the contents of thought. Thought, on this view, is determined by the social context in which we happen to find ourselves. What we think, and what we think about what we think—that is, how we evaluate and criticize our own and others' thinking—is according to this conception bound by the context of our culture. People from different social contexts, and so of different ideological persuasions, will judge matters differently; and since there is no escaping from ideological restrictions on thought, the comparative evaluation of alternative beliefs and viewpoints depends fundamentally on the viewpoint from which one stands when judging. As Mannheim articulates the point with reference to political thought:

> The significant element in the conception of ideology, in our opinion, is the discovery that political thought is integrally bound up with social life. This is the essential meaning of the oft-quoted sentence, "It is not the consciousness of men that determines their existence but, on the contrary, their social existence which determines their consciousness."[29]

Harris similarly suggests that:

> we might never be able to escape the prevailing ideology of our time and place. If this were so, then we could be regarded as victims of our social-historical circumstances, who in certain situations might have little alternative but to see the world in the disguised and distorted form in which it was misrepresented to us, or in which we misrepresent it to ourselves.
> This, to large extent, is so. We all live in historical-social settings, and we see the world as determined by those settings . . . in general there is no escape from ideology.[30]

The upshot of all this is clear. If thoughts are ideologically bound social products, our educational ideals, like all other thoughts,[31] are likewise products of our ideological environment. Not only is the educational ideal in question ideologically determined; what counts as a reason for favoring that ideal is similarly determined. Thus the epistemic force of putative reasons depends on the ideological stance from which one evaluates such reasons; determination precludes there being any sort of ideologically-neutral evaluation of the force of reasons. For the ideological determinist, then, rationality itself is a function of ideology; and what counts as good reason will depend on the ideological stance from which one evaluates reasons. The project of justifying an educational ideal—critical thinking or any other—is then doomed, for "rational justification" is reduced to an empty honorific which is attached to any idea which is sanctioned by one's ideology. Hence this second route to the ideology objection.[32]

We have, then, two main arguments for thinking that ideology precludes the rational justification of educational ideals. The first challenge to the enterprise of justifying critical thinking (or anything else) as an educational ideal hinges on the idea that everything educational is fundamentally political. The second is based on a strong thesis of the ideological determination of thought. It is time to evaluate these two challenges.

4 The objection considered

(A) Is everything educational political?

It depends. The claim that education is inevitably political is ambiguous.[33] Let us separate out two possible senses of the phrase "everything is political," as applied to educational ideals:

1 all educational ideals have political ramifications; and
2 all educational ideals are politically or ideologically biassed; the acceptance of any ideal is a function of prior political or ideological commitment. No independent (i.e. non-political or - ideological) support for any educational ideal is possible.

Sense 1 is unexceptionable. Every educational ideal does have political ramifications, for the simple reason that such ideals help to shape people's collective attitudes and commitments; moreover, educational institutions and practices which are informed by ideals, being social, inevitably impact the body politic in multifarious ways and are in that sense inevitably political. Critical thinking, for example, has ramifications undesirable for the fascist, since the attitudes, traits, dispositions, habits of mind, and skills to be fostered according to that ideal would tend to undermine the authority of any fascist leader, and similarly would tend to undermine the subservience of the citizenry on which a fascist (and many another) regime depends. By the same token, a fascist educational ideal (if it could be called such) would have ramifications undesirable for the democrat, for the attitudes and dispositions to be fostered under that ideal would work to undermine the free flow of information, and the equal participation and diversity of opinion of the populace, required of genuinely democratic social organization. In short, educational ideals inform educational institutions and practices; these institutions and practices impact upon social and political beings and organizations; consequently education—ideals as well as institutions and practices—is inevitably political. Education takes place in a political context, and thinking about education is thinking about an activity which inevitably takes place in a political context. In this sense, Freire and company are correct: everything educational is indeed political.

The correctness of sense 2, however, is more dubious. It is not so clear that the acceptance of any educational ideal is a function of prior political or ideological commitment, or that it is not possible to provide independent support for an educational ideal. It does not follow from the fact that all educational ideals have political ramifications that no independent support for some ideals can be found, for to say that educational institutions and practices are not *politically* neutral, that they affect the body politic, is not to say that educational ideals are not *intellectually* neutral. The practice of education may well be non-neutral, in that it always impacts upon persons and social arrangements, but that is very different from educational ideals being incapable of neutral, i.e. non-question-begging, reasoned defense.

Consider, for example, the first reason given in chapter 3 for regarding critical thinking as a fundamental educational ideal—the Kantian principle of respect for persons. If we are morally bound to treat others with respect, and to recognize their equal moral worth, we are bound to do so across the board of possible political and social arrangements. That is to say, the principle of respect for persons, if correct, does not apply to some arrangements and not others; rather, it is applicable to all personal and interpersonal interactions. Its support derives from general considerations concerning the nature of persons, the world, and morality.

Of course the principle of respect for persons might be incompatible with some forms of social organization—for example, certain forms of fascism and totalitarianism which fail to afford respect for persons. As such the principle eliminates those forms as *moral* forms of social organization. The principle, then, and educational ideals which derive support from it, have political ramifications; this is sense 1 above. Nevertheless, the principle is itself politically neutral in that its putative justification is independent of strictly political considerations. One need not adopt some prior political or ideological stance in order to defend the principle of respect for persons or to recognize it as binding on all personal and interpersonal, including educational, relationships. This is of course compatible with the principle constituting support for the ideal of critical thinking but not all other, rival ideas; that is, the ideal can enjoy non-political or -ideological support, yet still have political ramifications. This is exactly to note the distinction between sense 1 and sense 2 of "everything is political."[34]

Of course it is possible to reject the above line of argument, and to reject the idea that educational ideals such as critical thinking can enjoy support of a non-ideological sort. I suggested above that the ideal of critical thinking gains support from the Kantian principle, which is itself justified in terms of general (i.e. non-political or -ideological) considerations concerning the nature of persons, the world, and morality. One may deny, however, that considerations concerning the nature of persons, the world, and morality are truly non-ideological. On the contrary, one may hold that views about persons, the world and morality are fundamentally shaped by one's ideology; that there are no genuinely non-ideological considerations to be brought to bear on such matters as the nature of persons, the world, or morality—or education. On this view there is no escape from ideology. We find the Kantian principle plausible not because we recognize the force of non-ideological considerations which support it, but because it is congenial to the (Western, liberal, enlightenment) ideology to which we are already committed. Our ideology conditions that which we find compelling, and the reasons we find justificatory.

This, of course, is a statement of the second reason mentioned above in support of the ideology objection; our ideology shapes our consciousness, and so determines that which we find plausible and compelling. Not only are our basic views about persons, the world, morality, and education dependent on our prior ideological commitment; so too are the "reasons" we offer in support of those views. We must, then, turn our attention to this second reason.

(B) Does ideology shape consciousness?

According to the ideological determinist, not only what we believe, but also what we regard as reasons for our beliefs, are determined by our ideologies. There are many questions to ask here, in particular concerning the nature of the alleged "determination," but I wish to focus on only one problem the ideological determinist faces, which has to do with the status of the determinist thesis itself. What reasons are there for accepting the thesis?

It appears that there can be none. For consider some putative reason for the thesis p. Does p actually afford warrant for the thesis? Does it count in favor of the thesis? Does it offer us some reason for thinking the thesis true?

The determinist has two options here; either p is a reason which genuinely supports the thesis, or not. If not, then we have no reason to believe the thesis. Ideological determinism is no more plausible than its alternative. If so—that is, if p is held genuinely to support the thesis—then the determinist faces a different difficulty, for according to the thesis, what counts as a reason is itself ideologically determined. Consequently, the determinist, in order to be consistent with the thesis, must hold that p is a reason for the thesis only if one's ideology recognizes it as such. If one's ideology does not so recognize it, p is not rightly regarded as a reason for the thesis. But then p cannot be counted unequivocally as a reason for the thesis; p can be so counted *only if one is already committed* to an ideology which recognizes it as such. Moreover, if a person's ideology does not recognize p as a reason for the thesis, then the determinist is committed to the view that for that person p has no cognitive or intellectual force. For such a person there is no reason which supports the determinist thesis.

The ideological determinist is thus in a bind. Either there exists some good reason for embracing the determinist thesis or not. If there is not, then there is no good reason for embracing that view; the determinist's acceptance of the thesis is arbitrary and without merit. On the other hand, if there can be good reason for embracing the thesis, then the thesis is undercut, for asserting that there can be good reason to embrace it is tantamount to asserting that such good reason can be independent of prior ideological commitment—which is just what the thesis denies. In this case, whatever good reason there might be for embracing the thesis in fact forces the rejection of the thesis as self-defeating. Either way the determinist goes, the determinist thesis must be given up.[35]

5 The relationship between rationality and ideology

All of this raises the question of the relationship between rationality and ideology. On the determinist thesis, ideology is basic and rationality is relative to prior ideological commitment, in the sense that what counts as good reason for any claim is determined by prior ideological commitment. But one needs only to ask what reason there might be for thinking that ideology is basic to realize that the determinist has put the ideological cart before the rational horse (or, to alter the figure, has the ideological tail wagging the rational dog), for whether we ought to embrace the thesis of ideological determinism—or any other thesis—depends precisely on what reasons can be mustered in support of the thesis or claim in question, and on the cogent assessment of the rational force those reasons offer for that claim. Thus it is rationality which is basic, not ideology. One must take rationality, and reasons, seriously in order even to raise the question of the possible influence of ideology on the evaluation of reasons. The ideology objection thus *presupposes* a commitment to rationality. One could non-arbitrarily embrace the thesis of ideological determination only if one had good reasons for doing so—in which case one could not embrace the thesis, for having such (non-arbitrary, non-question-begging, non-ideologically-bound) good reasons, and recognizing them as such, forces the rejection of the thesis, which denies that very possibility. Rationality must therefore be conceived of as autonomous from ideological constraints, and indeed as providing the ground from which alternative ideologies can themselves be evaluated.[36]

In fact, many writers on ideology—both those who embrace determinism, and those who don't—honor (sometimes unwittingly) this point, and attempt to criticize offensive ideologies. Harris, for example, despite his embrace of determinism, devotes a large portion of his book to the detection of ideological misrepresentation and to the criticism of the ideology of "capitalist liberal democracy" and the more positive evaluation of Marxist ideology.[37] Giroux, whose stand on determinism is less clear, unequivocally and enthusiastically (and in my view correctly) criticizes ideological stances incompatible with his favored ideology of democracy, emancipation and liberation.[38] Bowles and Gintis happily criticize "technocratic-meritocratic ideology" and defend their socialist alternative.[39] Burbules also commits himself, as do the critical theorists generally, to the possibility of the rational critique of ideology and to the fostering of dispositions and skills conducive to rational evaluation.[40] In general, most writers on ideology regard the reasoned assessment of ideology as not only possible but of the utmost importance. To that extent they are committed not to the fundamentality of ideology, but rather to the fundamentality of rationality.

In short, the possibility of the (non-ideological) rational critique of ideology is basic to the very possibility of inquiry into the nature of ideology. Rationality, not ideology, is fundamental; rationality transcends ideology in the sense that any worthwhile analysis of ideology presupposes standards of rationality and the recognition of the cognitive force of reasons. Here is the proper understanding of the relationship between rationality and ideology.

6 Is rationality a reflection of ideology?

The reader might suspect that I have not been quite fair in the preceding discussion, for in arguing that the analysis of ideology presupposes a commitment to rationality and reasoned assessment I have neglected the fact that some theorists of ideology suggest that that commitment is itself an ideological one, and reflects particular ideological, cultural and class interests. The citation which opens this chapter gives the general flavor of this view, but it is articulated most clearly and most seriously (to my knowledge) by Bowers.

Bowers calls into question the "neutrality" of the ideals of rationality and critical thinking as they are fostered or imposed cross-culturally. According to Bowers, Freire's radical pedagogy, which takes as central the development of the critical consciousness of the oppressed, reflects the "Western mind set" which "takes for granted Western assumptions about progressive change, the power and legitimacy of critical reflection, the moral authority of individualism, and a secular-humanist view of the universe."[41] As Bowers makes clear, he regards Western liberal ideals of reason, criticism and reflection as tied to specific enlightenment ideologies; these ideals run the risk of hegemony when foisted upon cultures informed by radically divergent ideologies.[42] Bowers suggests that this ideological bias in favor of individualistic critical reflection, extolled throughout "neo-Marxist educational thought," is in fact intrinsically related to Western individualistic romanticism and is only problematically related to orthodox Marxist philosophical anthropology.[43] And he denies that one can criticize any ideology from some ideologically-neutral perspective:

> In suggesting that it is wrong for education to reduce the dialectic between human consciousness and belief system by representing the belief system as objectified reality one is not escaping into a form of enlightened rationalism that is free of ideology. The proposal, which I wish to make, that education should not restrict the student's consciousness by passing on the dominant belief system as taken-for-granted reality is thus not free from ideology. The idea of critical consciousness is tied to the traditional view of individual dignity and a reconstituted view of the rational process. In effect, an alternative to socializing students to the technocratic ideology is also grounded in an ideology, but one that does not subordinate the individual to the technique or to the status of an "output".[44]

Here Bowers makes clear his view that ideology is inescapable, that one cannot criticize an ideology from a position of "enlightened rationalism that is free of ideology." But one *can* nevertheless criticize an ideology; in this passage Bowers criticizes "technocratic ideology" for "subordinat[ing] the individual to the technique or to the status of an 'output.'" In subsequent discussion Bowers makes clear that he regards alternative ideologies as criticizable, and as more or less "defensible."[45]

How are we to understand the claim that ideology is both inescapable and criticizable? Presumably Bowers regards his criticism of "technocratic ideology" as telling, as providing at least some reason for rejecting that ideology. But if the ideology of "enlightened rationalism" is really an ideology, why should we regard criticism flowing from it as in any way compelling? For that matter, how are we to regard Bowers' claim that ideology is inescapable? Is it too the product of some particular ideology, which has no legitimacy for persons of alternative ideological persuasion? Or has Bowers offered us reasons for accepting the claim that ideology is inescapable, even if our presently-held ideology does not honor the claim?

The bind I have here outlined should be familiar from our earlier discussion. To claim that ideologies are more or less defensible is to commit oneself to the view that ideologies are escapable, at least in the sense that one can gain critical leverage on them and offer reasons for regarding them as more or less worthy which have epistemic force for all inquirers—whatever their ideology—who raise the question of their legitimacy. Thus, while it may be that in some sense "enlightened rationalism" is "just another ideology," this way of speaking renders the notion of ideology so thin and all-encompassing that it loses its critical usefulness. For "enlightened rationalism" is presupposed by the very study of ideology. To say anything about ideologies—how they function, how they legitimate (in either sense), in what ways some are preferable to others, or whether or not they are escapable—one presupposes the possibility of a critical stance from which defensible claims about ideology can be made. To reject this possibility is to give up the possibility of intelligent evaluation of ideology.

Thus "enlightened rationalism," i.e. the general view which takes rationality and critical thinking to be fundamental intellectual ideals, cannot be regarded as just another ideology. If one insists on regarding it as an ideology, one must recognize it not only as a necessary one, but as the *best* or most defensible one, for it alone sanctions the critical evaluation of all ideologies—including, if one insists on so regarding it, itself.[46]

(One might reject the criterion here relied upon as the fundamental criterion of ideology evaluation—namely, making possible rational inquiry concerning ideology—as a question-begging criterion of ideology evaluation which is of importance only to rationalist ideology. But to do so is to give up the project which licenses that rejection, for in criticizing that criterion, or any other, as ideologically biassed, one has already embraced the possibility of rational criticism of ideology (e.g. as biassed). Rejection of the criterion presupposes its acceptance; in this sense the criterion is necessary to the very project of the study of ideology, and its rejection is self-refuting.[47])

In short, one can engage in the rational evaluation of ideology only by adopting an "ideological" stance which renders such study possible. To fail to adopt that stance is to prevent oneself from even raising questions concerning the nature of ideology and the possibility of its rational study. But this cannot be the position of the person who attempts to answer such questions, e.g. who claims that ideology is inescapable. One can non-self-contradictorily make such a claim only if one embraces the "ideology" of rationality. Thus it is a mistake to regard rationality as "just another ideology," for it is the "ideology" forced upon as by the very study of ideology. We are all—necessarily—rationalists here.[48]

7 Critical thinking and liberationist ideology

Many of the educational theorists we have considered thus far call for an increased emphasis on education's task of *empowering* and *liberating* students. This is a central theme of Freire's work, which emphasizes the development of critical consciousness and the self-reflective overcoming of oppressive and dis-empowering social arrangements. Giroux, too, shares this basic concern for liberation by way of critical reflection, as does Kozol. So do Bowles and Gintis,[49] and Burbules.[50] Even Bowers, who, as we have seen, worries that education for the enhancement of critical reflection and empowerment reflects not educational or pedagogical radicalism but rather an elitist cultural imperialism of Western enlightenment ideology, appears to advocate similar educational desiderata; he simply wants less culturally question-begging justification.[51] So all hands, or at least most, whatever their views concerning ideology, are committed to seeing education as centrally concerned with the enhancement of liberation and empowerment. How does the ideal of critical thinking fit with this sentiment?

As should be clear, it fits very well indeed, for, as argued in chapters 2 and 3, the ideal of critical thinking is likewise reflective of a commitment to liberation and empowerment. Moreover, the ideal of critical thinking, like the several radical theorists discussed, portrays education for liberation and empowerment as potentially revolutionary; as no friend of the *status quo* as such, but as a friend only of the *justified status quo*, and enemy of the unjustified. The potentially revolutionary nature of critical thinking has been long recognized and embraced by educational theorists:

> if we once start thinking no one can guarantee where we shall come out, except that many objects, ends and institutions are surely doomed. Every thinker puts some portion of an apparently stable world in peril and no one can wholly predict what will emerge in its place.[52]

The advantage of the present analysis is that the honoring of liberation and empowerment as desirable educational outcomes does not rest on a dubious or question-begging appeal to ideology. As we have seen, such an appeal will not work. Rather, the honoring in question is grounded in *reasons*—reasons for regarding critical thinking as a fundamental educational ideal, offered in chapter 3— *not* ideology. This is as it should be, for to pursue the educational goals of liberation and empowerment *justifiably*, there must be good reasons for doing so. And it is rationality, not ideology, which sanctions and allows for the possibility of good reasons.

I conclude that the ideal of critical thinking survives the ideology objection. We need not regard educational ideals as fundamentally ideological; nor must we regard critical thinking as itself ideologically bound or as tied to specific cultural or class interests. Rather, as we have seen, critical thinking and rationality are basic in the sense that they alone allow for the possibility of the intelligent evaluation and criticism of ideology. To take the study of ideology seriously is to rely on the critical leverage afforded by critical thinking and (non-ideological) rational analysis.

CHAPTER 5

The indoctrination objection

In all education propaganda has a part. The question for the educator is not whether there shall be propaganda but how much, how organized and of what sort.[1]

If you bring children up to think for themselves, it is now intelligible to say, in general, that you have indoctrinated them: because "indoctrination" is opposed to "thinking for oneself."[2]

1 The objection and its significance

Can education aimed at the cultivation of critical thinking avoid indoctrination? Or must a student be indoctrinated in order to become a critical thinker?

The question is troublesome, for if it becomes clear that education for critical thinking is necessarily indoctrinative, then the ideal becomes significantly tarnished. Indeed, if indoctrination is unavoidable, it is not clear that critical thinking can rightly be regarded as a fundamental educational ideal. This is the force of the "indoctrination objection"—if it cannot be rebuffed, it threatens to undermine the ideal.

How, exactly, does the objection purport to undermine the ideal? Consider the several constituent components of critical thinking. For example, earlier I suggested that the critical thinker values critical thinking and reasons, and values more highly beliefs and actions which are supported by reasons than beliefs and actions which are not (or are less) supported. If this value must be indoctrinated, then students must be unable to embrace it on its merits; that is, students who are critical thinkers would have the value, but they would not critically hold it, i.e. hold it for good reasons. Either the value of critical thinking would not, in this circumstance, be rationally supportable; or, alternatively, the student would not accept the value for the reasons which in fact support it. Either way, the student is not valuing critical thinking critically, and so is not being a critical thinker with respect to this value.

Similarly, the critical thinker has beliefs of various sorts which are tied to her commitment to critical thinking. For example, she believes that holding beliefs on the basis of reasons which support them is preferable to holding beliefs which are not rationally supportable. If she must be indoctrinated into this belief, then it is itself not held critically, and so she is not, at least with respect to this belief, being a critical thinker.[3]

Similar remarks apply to the dispositions and habits of mind associated with the critical thinker—if these too must be indoctrinated, can we credit the possessor with having critical, or critically sanctioned, dispositions and habits of mind? Worse yet, can we speak of the critical thinker as having a certain sort of character, if the character traits require indoctrination? Can a person be autonomous if her autonomy is the result of indoctrination? All of these features of the critical thinker seem to be undermined if indoctrination into critical thinking is unavoidable. Here is the significance of the indoctrination objection: it threatens to expose the critical thinker in all her uncriticality, and to expose the ideal as an empty or unattainable sham.

Before we are convinced by this objection, however, some careful consideration is in order. For one thing, it is not clear that at least some features of critical thinking can properly be said to be indoctrinated, e.g. habits of mind, dispositions, and character traits, because indoctrination is often taken to pertain solely to beliefs. The claim that education for critical thinking necessarily involves indoctrination must be sharpened. For another, the case for the inevitability of indoctrination has yet to be made. These two topics are taken up in the next two sections.

2 What is indoctrination?

The notion of indoctrination has exercised analytic philosophers of education greatly, and over the last two or three decades a sizable literature on the topic has grown. A systematic study of the question would be out of place here, but something must be said if the indoctrination objection is to be clearly set out.

If X's getting Y to believe that Z is rightly thought of as X's indoctrinating Y into the belief that Z, what must be going on with respect to X, Y, and Z? One view of indoctrination has it that the case is one of indoctrination if X's *aim* or *intention* is of a certain sort, namely that X intends to or aims at getting Y to believe that Z, independently of the epistemic status of or evidence for Z.[4] A second view holds that indoctrination is a matter of *method*, so that our putative case of indoctrination is a genuine one if X's method of getting Y to believe that Z is of a certain sort, namely one which tends to impart to Y a belief that Z, independently of the evidence for Z, and without Y's questioning Z; a method, that is, which suppresses or discourages Y's critical consideration of the case for Z.[5] A third view regards indoctrination as a matter of *content*, so that our case is a case of indoctrination if Z is false or unjustified, independently of X's intentions and methods.[6]

I will not here try to analyze the dispute between these three views of indoctrination. For the three have in common a feature that serves well to distinguish indoctrination from other modes of belief inculcation. That feature concerns the *way* in which Y holds the belief that Z. Our case is a case of indoctrination if Y believes that Z in such a way that Z's being held is not a function of evidence for Z, and if evidence contrary to Z is, for Y, irrelevant to the belief that Z. Thomas F. Green, in an excellent discussion, puts the point in terms of Y's *style of belief*—our case is one of indoctrination if Y believes Z *non-evidentially*, and X is best regarded as an indoctrinator if her aims, intentions or methods are such that they encourage a non-evidential style of belief:

> when, in teaching, we are concerned simply to lead another
> person to a correct answer, but are not correspondingly
> concerned that they arrive at that answer on the basis of good
> reasons, then we are indoctrinating; we are engaged in creating a
> non-evidential style of belief.[7]

If a belief is held non-evidentially—that is, held in such a way that it is held without regard to evidence relevant to its rational assessment, and is impervious to negative or contrary evidence—then the belief is an indoctrinated one, and the believer a victim of indoctrination, for the believer, in such a case, is incapable of critically inquiring into the worthiness of the belief. If a "teacher" intends to foster such a non-evidential style of belief, or utilizes methods which tend to so foster, or seeks routinely to impart to students beliefs without regard to their truth or justifiability, and in so doing suppresses students' rational evaluation of said beliefs, then the "teacher" is rightly regarded as an indoctrinator, and the student is a victim of indoctrination.[8]

Students, in short, are indoctrinated if they are led to hold beliefs in such a way that they are prevented from critically inquiring into their legitimacy and the power of the evidence offered in their support; if they hold beliefs in such a way that the beliefs are not open to rational evaluation or assessment.[9] Indoctrination may be regarded as the collection of those modes of belief inculcation which foster a non-evidential, or *non-critical*, style of belief. And here we see the full force of the indoctrination objection. For indoctrination, whatever else it may be, is *anti-critical*; consequently, if indoctrination is inevitable, then critical thinking—at least a thorough-going critical thinking—is impossible. Whether or not the indoctrination objection undermines the ideal of critical thinking, then, depends on the inevitability of indoctrination.

3 Is indoctrination inevitable?

Is it the case, as this chapter's opening motto suggests, that education necessarily involves "propaganda"? Is indoctrination inevitable? Many have argued for affirmative answers to these questions. Such arguments are often tangled up with a distinct question, namely: Is indoctrination always wrong or unjustified? If we think that indoctrination is never justified, then we might strive to show that it is avoidable; if, on the other hand, we think that indoctrination is sometimes justified, then we will not be concerned to deny its inevitability, so long as *unjustified* indoctrination can be avoided.

Wilson, espousing a view largely compatible with the ideal of critical thinking, suggests that the crucial question does not involve indoctrination, but the enhancement of rationality: "The important point ... is not so much whether we call something 'indoctrination' or not, but whether a particular process increases or diminishes rationality."[10] If an educational process enhances rationality, on this view, that process is justified, if we choose to call it an indoctrinative; process, then we have a case of an educational process which is indoctrinative but nevertheless justified—a case of justified indoctrination.[11]

What would such a case look like? Consider imparting to a young child the belief that reasons are important, and that acting on the basis of reasons is to be preferred to acting impulsively or without due consideration of the consequences of one's actions. Imparting this belief cannot be a matter of rationally convincing the child of its worthiness, for the child, in lacking the belief, has no reason (so to speak) for taking reasons offered on the belief's behalf seriously—*ex hypothesi*, she does not yet honor reasons or accept their force; consequently, giving reasons for the belief would be pointless. More importantly, the young child needs to learn what a reason is, and this, it seems, can surely not be learned by offering reasons for regarding certain things as reasons. The child must come to understand what a reason is before she can reasonably adopt a belief concerning the value of reasons, and such coming to understand cannot result from reasoning with the child. Yet adopting the belief in question will undeniably enhance the child's rationality. Here, then, we have a case which might be rightly regarded as a case of justified indoctrination—indoctrination because we get the child to adopt the belief in the absence of good reasons which she appreciates for adopting it; justified because the belief, adopted on whatever basis, enhances her rationality.

It would be so regarded, at any rate, if we are correct in calling this case of belief-inculcation a case of indoctrination. Should it be so called? On some views of indoctrination, it should be. Paul Wagner, for example, defines indoctrination as "causing a person to hold a belief which they [sic] are unable to justify on rational grounds."[12] For a variety of reasons, among them youth, inexperience, naivete, and lack of knowledge, children—like the rest of us—may come to hold beliefs which they are unable to justify rationally. If this is the mark of indoctrination, as Wagner suggests, then indoctrination is indeed inevitable, and sometimes justified.[13]

It is undeniable, I think, that we seek to cause young children to hold beliefs in advance of their being able to justify them rationally. Parents and others spend quite a bit of time imparting to children a wide variety of beliefs—that they ought not to hit little sister, that they ought to share their toys with their friends, that they ought to avoid interacting with strangers, that Mommy and Daddy will protect them, etc.—well before the children could give reasons for the beliefs, or even know what reasons are. We are agreed that such belief-inculcation is desirable and justifiable, and that some of it might have the effect of enhancing the child's rationality. Should we call it indoctrination? This seems partly, at least, a verbal quibble. If we call it so, we are forced to give up the idea that indoctrination is always unjustified or evil, since we agree that some cases are justified. If we do not call such belief-inculcation indoctrination, we preserve that term's pejorative flavor, but must give up Wagner's definition.

Clarity and educational theory are served, I believe, by taking the latter route. For if the considerations of the last section are well-taken, indoctrination involves primarily the style in which beliefs are held. Granting that many of the child's early beliefs are held in the absence of rational justification, we must distinguish between two crucially distinct cases: that in which the lack of justifying reasons is permanent; and that in which it is temporary. There is a world of difference between causing Johnny to believe things in such a way that they are now held *sans* rational justification, and in such a way that he comes never to see the importance or relevance of inquiring into the rational status of his beliefs; and causing Janie to believe things in such a way that they are now held *sans* rational justification, but with the view that this lack is temporary, and with an eye to imparting to Janie at the earliest possible time a belief in the importance of grounding beliefs with reasons and to developing in her the dispositions to challenge, question, and demand reasons and justification for potential beliefs. In Janie's case, her independence of mind and the development of an evidential style of belief are taken to be central educational desiderata; her inculcation into unjustified beliefs temporary, and, while practically necessary given her youth and cognitive situation, to be replaced by justified beliefs as soon as possible. Calling Janie's case one of indoctrination, because it includes the inculcation of beliefs which she is at the moment unable to justify, obscures the fundamental difference between her case and Johnny's. For that reason it is best to reject the idea that all cases of belief-inculcation in which the believer is unable to provide rational justification for the belief are cases of indoctrination. It is better to reserve the label for cases like Johnny's, in which the beliefs are inculcated without justification; in which that state of affairs is taken as unproblematic, and acceptable as permanent; and in which an evidential style of belief is discouraged, and a non-evidential style encouraged. In this way we distinguish *indoctrination* from non-indoctrinative belief-*inculcation*.

Of course we could still see the question as largely a verbal one, and could still use "indoctrination" to pick out cases like Janie's as well as Johnny's. We could do this as long as we distinguished in other ways between the two cases: in particular, if we considered cases of indoctrination to be justified if, like Janie's, they involved instances of belief-inculcation *sans* justification only to the extent necessary for the further enhancement of rationality, and if they involved the development and encouragement of an evidential style of belief.

Granting, then, the necessity—both practical and conceptual—of belief-inculcation in the absense of justification, we have good reason for not taking this to be the mark of indoctrination. Or, alternatively, if we do take this as the mark, then we must acknowledge that indoctrination is sometimes justified, and may enhance rationality—and so can be engaged in in the service of critical thinking. Either way, the indoctrination objection fails as an objection to the ideal of critical thinking.

Green takes it the latter way when he writes that:

> Indoctrination has a perfectly good and important role to play in education ... [and] may be useful as the prelude to teaching ... we need not offer reasons for every belief we think important for children and adults to hold. On the other hand, we have no warrant to inculcate beliefs for which there is no good reason or for which we can offer no good reason, and we must be prepared to offer reasons or evidence when they are requested.... Indoctrination ... may be sanctioned only in order that beliefs adopted may later be redeemed by reasons.[14]

Here Green echoes Wilson in suggesting that the crucial question is the enhancement of rationality, and that indoctrination is justified insofar as it is necessary and causally efficacious for such enhancement. Taking "indoctrination" as "inculcating belief *sans* rational justification," I agree. But Green curiously ignores here his earlier emphasis on the desirability of the development of an evidential style of belief, and of a non-evidential style as the mark of indoctrination. Taking "indoctrination" in this latter way, we should regard the cases being considered—namely, cases in which beliefs are inculcated without rational justification, but in which those beliefs may later be "redeemed by reasons," i.e. given rational justification—not as cases of justifiable indoctrination, but as cases of non-indoctrinative belief-inculcation, for in such cases beliefs are inculcated without rational justification only if:

1   they help to develop in the believer an evidential style of belief; and
2   they are themselves to be "redeemed by reasons," i.e. the believer's belief in them without rational justification is regarded as temporary, and is to be replaced by belief which is rationally grounded.

To consider such cases indoctrinative is to give up the idea that a necessary condition for holding a belief indoctrinatedly is not just holding it in the absence of rational justification, but holding it non-evidentially, so that reasons, evidence, and so rational justification are irrelevant to its being held. This seems an idea worth keeping. For one thing, it allows us easily to distinguish between the cases of Johnny and Janie. For another, perhaps more important, it is only with this notion of indoctrination that we can make sense of a belief's being "redeemed by reasons." If I believe p non-evidentially, my belief cannot be redeemed by reasons, for in holding it non-evidentially I will not be moved by reasons for or against p. As Green himself puts it, "beliefs held non-evidentially cannot be modified by introducing evidence or reasons or by rational criticism."[15] But if I believe p without rational justification, but nevertheless have an evidential style of belief (or at least do not have a non-evidential style), I will be moved by reasons for p, and will happily redeem my previously adopted-but-ungrounded belief. In short, beliefs which are indoctrinated in that they are held without rational justification can be redeemed; beliefs which are indoctrinated in that they are held non-evidentially cannot. Given the central importance of such redemption, the importance of the enhancement of rationality, which requires such redemption, and the common sentiment, expressed by Wilson, that indoctrination and "thinking for oneself" are contraries, we do better to regard indoctrination as involving, not simply beliefs held without rational justification, but beliefs held irrespective of such justification—that is, non-evidentially.[16]

If the preceding paragraphs are correct, then Green has it nearly right, but not quite, for he should regard the inculcation of beliefs which are redeemable by reasons not as cases of sanctioned or justified indoctrination, but rather—since their redeemability implies the absence of a non-evidential style of belief—as cases of non-indoctrinative belief-inculcation, in which reasons which justify the beliefs have not been passed on to the believer, but could have been, and in any case are in the possession of the inculcator. He should regard things in this way, that is, if he wishes his discussion of redemption to be consistent with his discussion of style of belief, for beliefs held without rational justification can be redeemed by reasons only if the believer is open to reasons and rational considerations which favor such beliefs. To be open in this way is to have an evidential style of belief (or at least not to have a non-evidential style). Such a case cannot consistently be regarded by Green as one of indoctrination, if he wishes to maintain his analysis of indoctrination in terms of style of belief (which, as I argued above, there are good reasons for maintaining). This is why the passage cited above cannot be quite right. On the "style of belief" analysis of indoctrination, there can be no such thing as a belief which is indoctrinated but yet redeemable—for if it is redeemable, then the believer must not have a non-evidential style of belief, in which case the belief cannot be an indoctrinated one. (To put the point in terms of an economic metaphor, the currency of redemption—reasons—has no purchasing power in a non-evidential economy.) In short, if indoctrinated, the belief cannot be redeemable; if redeemable, it cannot have been indoctrinated.[17]

But the important point lies elsewhere. It is, to repeat, that, however one parses "indoctrinate," it nevertheless remains that indoctrination is not unavoidable in any sense in which it prevents the development of rationality. We may justifiably strive to impart to students the skills, attitudes, dispositions and character traits of the critical thinker, whether we take cases of belief-inculcation *sans* rational justification (but which enhance the development of rationality) to be indoctrinative or not. Consequently, the indoctrination objection fails as a challenge to the idea of critical thinking.

4 A further difficulty?

One might think that a problem still remains. For how, specifically, can a child be brought to embrace unindoctrinated beliefs, in the absence of the capacity to judge the extent of reasoned support those beliefs enjoy? It seems undeniable that, however the child is brought to embrace early beliefs, insofar as the child lacks the concept of reasons and lacks an understanding of reasons and their force in justifying potential beliefs, her embrace will be non-rational. It is crucial for the enhancement of the child's rationality that we get the child to embrace non-rationally a belief in the power and value of reasons. To that extent, a critic might seem within her rights to insist that, despite what has been said thus far, it nevertheless remains that the child must be indoctrinated into the beliefs constitutive of the commitment to rationality (and so critical thinking). And if the child must in this way be indoctrinated into critical thinking, the indoctrination objection remains. How, in short, can we get the child to appreciate reasons, and adopt the belief that it is a good thing to believe and act in accordance with reasons, except by indoctrination? As Suttle poses the problem, "if educators desire students to believe that they ought to want to develop and utilize their rational capacities, then educators may very well have to indoctrinate the students in this belief."[18]

R.S. Peters puts the problem, which he refers to as the "paradox of moral education," in this way:

> given that it is desirable to develop people who conduct
> themselves rationally, intelligently and with a fair degree of
> spontaneity, the brute facts of child development reveal that at
> the most formative years of a child's development he is incapable
> of this form of life and impervious to the proper manner of
> passing it on.[19]

Since the child is at this stage "incapable of the [rational] form of life," she cannot be brought to it by rational means. How, then, can she be brought to it? According to some, only by way of indoctrination.[20]

A classic answer to the paradox of moral education appeals to *habit*. As Peters puts it, echoing thinkers as diverse as Aristotle and Dewey, "in spite of the fact that a rational code of behaviour and the 'language' of a variety of activities is beyond the grasp of young children, they can and must enter the palace of Reason through the courtyard of Habit and Tradition."[21] Does the development of proper habits allow us to escape the paradox, and inculcate a commitment to rationality without indoctrinating children into that commitment? It does, if it be granted that habits can themselves become criticizable. If we develop in a child the habit of searching for reasons which justify a potential belief before adopting the belief, that habit not only enhances her rationality; it also admits of rational evaluation itself, for the child can (and we hope will) question the reasons which recommend that habit as a worthy one, and assess the force of those reasons herself. The development of rational habits, then, does not require either indoctrination or the forsaking of rationality. Rather, such development simply helps us to impart to children traits we believe desirable, in the face of "the brute facts of child development."

Grant that we inculcate, at first, *sans* reasons. In doing so, it is hoped, we transform the child from one who cannot appreciate and be moved by reasons to one who can; from a pre-rational person to a rational one. To focus on *how* the transformation is accomplished, however, is to focus on the wrong concern.[22] The important question is not "How is the transformation accomplished?"—admittedly, it is accomplished by non-rational means in that the child is not rationally persuaded to become rational—but rather "Does the transformation, however accomplished, enhance the child's rationality and foster an evidential style of belief?" If the answer to this latter question is affirmative, then we need not fear the charge of indoctrination. To label the development of early beliefs and habits "indoctrinative" is to take indoctrination to be the inculcation of beliefs which the believer cannot rationally justify. Earlier we saw the problems attending this conception of indoctrination. On a preferable conception—which takes indoctrination to be largely a matter of the style in which one holds beliefs—early belief- and habit-inculcation is not indoctrinative, so long as the beliefs and habits inculcated enhance the child's rationality, foster an evidential style of belief, and admit of rational justification which the child is encouraged to seek, grasp, and use to "redeem" the previously inculcated beliefs and habits as soon as she is able. Thus we may grant the unavoidability of early inculcation of beliefs and habits in the absence of rational justification, without running foul of the indoctrination objection. The fostering of rationality, and so of critical thinking, may proceed in the absence of a damning or damaging indoctrination.

5 The right to avoid indoctrination

What is so awful about indoctrination, anyway? Supposing that the argument advanced thus far succeeds, and indoctrination is avoidable, why should we avoid it?

These questions are insightfully considered, I think, in the context of the ideal of critical thinking. As argued earlier, indoctrination, insofar as it is a matter of fostering a non-evidential style of belief, is anti-critical. There is a deep, although obvious, connection between style of belief and critical thinking. A person who has an evidential style of belief has a disposition to seek reasons and evidence, and to believe on that basis; and this, we have seen, is a central component of critical thinking. A person with a non-evidential style of belief, on the other hand, lacks this key feature of critical thinking. In chapter 3 I offered a general defense of the ideal of critical thinking; here I would like to say something about the harm the ideal suffers at the hands of indoctrination.

If I have been indoctrinated, and so have developed or had fostered in me a non-evidential style of belief, I have been significantly harmed. My autonomy has been dramatically compromised, for I do not have the ability to settle impartially questions of concern to me on the basis of a reasoned consideration of the matter at hand. I am in an important sense the prisoner of my convictions, for I cannot decide whether my convictions ought to be what they are, and I am unable to alter them for good reasons, even if there are good reasons for altering them. Indeed, lacking the disposition to seek reasons, I am doomed to an unawareness of the desirability of aligning my beliefs and actions with the weight of relevant evidence. Consequently, my life is limited; options with respect to belief and action—and indeed of basic aspects of my life-style and beliefs about the worthwhile life (if I have any)—are forever closed to me, due to my predisposition against the contemplation both of challenges to my unreasoned but presently held convictions and of alternatives to them. I have been trapped in a set of beliefs I can neither escape nor even question; this is how my options, and my autonomy, have been limited. I have been shackled, and denied the right to determine, insofar as I am able, my own future. In being indoctrinated, I have been placed in a kind of cognitive straightjacket, in that my cognitive movements have been severely restricted. Worse, like the typical straightjacketed person, I have also been sedated—drugged—so that I don't even realize my restricted plight.[23] Such a limited life cannot be what we desire for our children, any more than we desire it for ourselves.[24]

The child has an overwhelming interest in avoiding indoctrination. To be so shackled, and to have her options and future limited, is to narrow her life in a way which is as unacceptable as it is out of her control. In being indoctrinated, the child is cut off from all but a narrow band of possibilities. Her freedom and her dignity are short-circuited, her autonomy denied, her control over her own life and her ability to contribute to community life truncated, her mental life impoverished.[25] This is more apt a description of child abuse than of acceptable education. As we have a moral obligation to stand against child abuse, so we have a similar obligation with respect to indoctrination.[26] Here, against the background of a comparison with critical thinking, we see what is so awful about indoctrination.

6 Concluding considerations

As has been argued, it is best not to regard all cases of belief-inculcation *sans* rational justification as cases of indoctrination. It must be granted that we sometimes have no alternative but to teach children, or at least to inculcate beliefs, without providing them with reasons which serve to justify those beliefs, for, before we can pass along reasons which the child can recognize as reasons, she must come to understand what a reason is. Nevertheless, we can inculcate beliefs which enhance rationality, and help to develop an evidential style of belief. Such belief inculcation, even though it does not, out of necessity, include the passing on of reasons which are seen by the believer as warrant for the inculcated beliefs, ought to be considered non-indoctrinative belief-inculcation rather than indoctrination.

If I get a young child to believe that the sun is 93,000,000 miles from the earth (on average), that it is better to share her toys with her friends than not to share, that $2+2=4$, or that it is desirable to believe on the basis of reasons, I am not necessarily indoctrinating. I am idoctrinating only if I pass on these beliefs in such a way that the child is not encouraged to, or is prevented from, actively inquiring into their rational status—that is, if her rationality is stunted, and if she is brought to develop a non-evidential style of belief.[27] If we inculcate beliefs *sans* reasons, but encourage the development of rationality and an evidential style of belief—that is, if we encourage the development of critical thinking—we are not indoctrinating. We cannot start out giving reasons, for the child has to learn what a reason is, and what counts as a good reason—that is, the child has to learn how to evaluate reasons—before giving reasons even makes sense.[28] Consequently, we have no choice but to begin by inculcating beliefs in the absence of justifying reasons. But this should not blind us to the central distinction between doing so as a necessary prelude to the development of rationality and an evidential style of belief, and doing so without regard to such further development. Only the latter is appropriately considered indoctrinative. We avoid indoctrination by taking the former path: by encouraging the student to become our "critical equal" and assess for herself the strength of the support which reasons offer for inculcated beliefs; to subject reasons which we take as justificatory to her independent judgment; and to transcend her intellectual dependence on us and drive, ever more competently, her own doxastic engine. We avoid indoctrination, in short, by taking seriously—even as we inculcate beliefs, as we sometimes must, in the absence of reasons which justify those beliefs—the ideal of critical thinking.

Recalling the close conceptual connection between critical thinking and rationality, and that critical thinking is best thought of as the educational cognate of rationality, we see that the (conclusion of the) argument of this chapter—that we can enhance rationality and encourage the development of an evidential style of belief without engaging in indoctrination—shows that we can non-indoctrinatively educate for critical thinking. The indoctrination objection fails to challenge successfully the educational ideal of critical thinking.

7 Taking stock

We have now completed our general philsophical treatment of critical thinking. In the preceding chapters I have tried to review and assess the most important extant accounts of critical thinking (chapter 1), offered as an alternative the reasons conception (chapter 2), attempted to justify that conception and the ideal of critical thinking (chapter 3), and argued against two important objections to the ideal—the ideology objection (chapter 4) and the indoctrination objection (chapter 5). These five chapters, taken together, are meant to provide the beginnings of a systematic account of the nature of critical thinking: what it is; why it is important; and how it functions as an educational ideal. In what follows I seek to demonstrate the relevance of the ideal to two central aspects of education—curriculum (chapter 6), and policy and practice (chapter 7).

CHAPTER 6

Science education

It is not *what* the man of science believes that distinguishes, him, but *how* and *why* he believes it. His beliefs are tentative, not dogmatic; they are based on evidence, not on authority or intuition.[1]

1. Science, scientists, and critical thinking

Science has traditionally been seen as the home of critical thinking, and the apex of rationality. The scientist, as the traditional image has it, is the dispassionate seeker of the truth—the person in the lab coat, untroubled by passion or emotion, unbiassed by prior conviction, guided only by reason, patiently observing, experimenting, following the evidence wherever it leads. On this image, the scientist believes and acts entirely on the basis of evidence and reasons. What better personification of the critical thinker could there be?

This image has, alas, been thoroughly exploded. Contemporary research in the history, philosophy, sociology and politics of science has revealed a more accurate picture of the scientist as one who is driven by prior convictions and commitments; who is guided by group loyalties and sometimes petty personal squabbles; who is frequently quite unable to recognize evidence for what it is; and whose personal career motivations give the lie to the idea that the scientist yearns only, or even mainly, for the truth. Under the weight of this new image, many philosophers and others have questioned the notion that science is the apex of rationality, and that the scientist is the critical thinker *par excellence*. And if science and scientists are as uncritical, and as unguided by reasons and evidence, as the new image suggests, then how, and to what end, shall science education be shaped by the ideal of critical thinking?

Given the nature of the present effort, a direct treatment of the massive philosophical and other literature on the nature of science and its rationality would be out of place here.[2] Nevertheless, recent work in philosophy of science, especially the groundbreaking work of Thomas S. Kuhn and the Kuhnian-inspired "new philosophy of science",[3] offers our best entry into the questions to occupy us in this chapter. Kuhn's characterization of science presents not only a profound challenge to more traditional conceptions; it also suggests the need for a radical reconceptualization of science education—one that is not friendly to a view of science education which takes seriously the ideal of critical thinking.[4]

2. Kuhn on science and science education

Kuhn's characterization of science is by now well known; consequently, I offer here only a brief sketch of it, focussing more on his related discussion of science education.[5]

Kuhn's fundamental notion is that of a "paradigm", a "universally recognized scientific achievement that for a time provides model problems and solutions to a community of practitioners."[6] Paradigms guide ordinary scientific practice, which Kuhn labels "normal science," which is "research firmly based upon one or more past scientific achievements, achievements that some particular scientific community acknowledges for a time as supplying the foundation for its further practice."[7] Paradigms guide normal science, in that they provide rules, procedures, and standards by which to conduct normal scientific research. Likewise, normal science is simply research carried out in accordance with the rules, procedures and standards of some particular paradigm. Not all science is normal science, however; occasionally the "puzzles" which normal scientific research is concerned to solve resist the efforts of the research community. When this happens, an unsolved puzzle/unexplained phenomenon is said to constitute an "anomaly." When anomalies get either frequent or serious, the paradigm under whose normal scientific research they appear is said to be in "crisis." Once a paradigm is judged to be in crisis, scientists begin to hunt around for new paradigms, paradigms which promise to resolve the anomalies that brought the old paradigm into crisis. When such new paradigms are under consideration, and the old paradigm is dispensable (for the old one cannot be discarded, according to Kuhn, until a new one is available), scientists engage in "revolutionary science," in which the rival paradigms fight for the allegiance of the scientific community. In a revolution the old paradigm is superseded by a new alternative.

A key process in revolutionary periods is "paradigm debate," in which proponents of competing paradigms attempt to convince the members of the relevant scientific community to accept their candidates. Kuhn argues that such debate boils down to persuasion; that the proponents of competing paradigms inevitably "talk through each other"; and that there is never better than "partial communication" between proponents of competing paradigms, who speak "across the revolutionary divide."[8] Furthermore, Kuhn views the scientist's decision to accept a new paradigm as a "gestalt switch," a "conversion experience that cannot be forced," and "a transition that must occur all at once ... or not at all."[9] Paradigm debate is so uncommunicative, according to Kuhn, because paradigms are "incommensurable" — that is, they cannot be judged according to paradigm-neutral criteria of evaluation. Paradigm debate and paradigm choice are, then, not at all like the critical discussion and reasoned argument (to say nothing of the straightforward comparison of predictions with experimental outcomes) that standard philosophy of science makes them out to be. For Kuhn, despite disclaimers to the contrary, paradigm debate and choice is by and large an irrational affair.[10]

Kuhn's conception of science is incompatible with the ideal of critical thinking in several respects. On his portrayal, both normal science and revolutionary science are anti-critical. So too is his relativistic conception of scientific knowledge. Perhaps most importantly for our purposes, his discussion of science education is anti-critical: both in its suggestion that we routinely do, and ought to, indoctrinate students into the "dogma" of the current paradigm; and that we routinely do, and ought to, distort the history of science in science education in order to facilitate the just-mentioned dogmatic indoctrination. Let us briefly look at these aspects of Kuhn's discussion in turn.

(A) Normal science and critical thinking

The transition to a scientific from a pre-paradigmatic, pre-scientific stage of development is, according to Kuhn, "precisely the abandonment of critical discourse."[11] By this Kuhn means that the transition to a science is marked by an initial period of normal science, and such a period, like all normal scientific periods, is marked by a lack of debate about fundamentals. The picture of the normal scientist Kuhn draws is not that of a curious, open-minded investigator, who is committed to following the evidence wherever it leads her, wilfully letting the truth fall where it may. Rather, the Kuhnian normal scientist is an ingenious puzzle-solver, who accepts certain goals, presuppositions, and rules of procedure without question, and employs them in attempting to solve various puzzles which the paradigm suggests. The goals, rules, and presuppositions which the normal scientist unquestioningly accepts are of course those of the paradigm which guides the normal scientific research in question.

It is not surprising that some philosophers have taken issue with this picture of the practising scientist. John Watkins, for example, takes Kuhn's view of normal science to be an abhorrent one, for he rightly views Kuhn's conception of normal science as not only uncritical, but anti-critical. Watkins describes the Kuhnian normal scientific community as "a closed society of closed minds,"[12] and as one "whose chief characteristic is 'the abandonment of critical discourse'."[13] Karl Popper takes up Watkins' cause in his own reply to Kuhn, and, like Watkins, finds Kuhn's view of the normal scientist abhorrent because of its anti-critical nature. Popper writes that:

> The "normal" scientist, in my view, has been taught badly. I believe ... that all teaching on the University level (and if possible below) should be training and encouragement in critical thinking. The "normal" scientist, as described by Kuhn, has been badly taught. He has been taught in a dogmatic spirit; he is a victim of indoctrination.[14]

Here Popper indirectly links the notion of critical thinking with education; critical thinking is, for Popper, fundamental to both scientific and educational affairs. The important point for present purposes, however, is simply that on Kuhn's conception of science normal science is decidedly anti-critical.[15]

(B) Revolutionary science and critical thinking

If normal science stands in contrast to the ideal of critical thinking, so too does revolutionary science, for revolutionary science is as anti-critical as normal science, albeit for different reasons. In periods of revolutionary science, it will be recalled, scientists of competing paradigms engage in paradigm debate. Such debate is viewed by Kuhn as being "partial" at best, at "cross-purposes," and as being much less than fully communicative, since all parties bring to the debate the meanings and presuppositions of their respective paradigms. Scientists of competing paradigms cannot rationally assess competing paradigms, for each paradigm brings with it its own criteria of evaluation. Consequently, proponents of competing paradigms, since they are "locked in" to their own paradigm's criteria of evaluation, cannot agree on neutral criteria by which to judge the merits of their respective paradigms. Furthermore, their paradigm-bound criteria of evaluation will always be incompatible, and so yield incompatible judgments of the adequacy of their respective paradigms, since the paradigms those criteria stem from are incommensurable. There is no hope, then, of critical appraisal—paradigm debate is "necessarily circular" and so irrational; a scientist's decision to adopt a given paradigm is likened by Kuhn to a "conversion experience" and a "gestalt switch" — neither of which are paragons of rational deliberation.

Kuhn's conception of paradigm debate is open to overwhelming criticism, and is problematic in several respects. I will not review the critical literature here, however,[16] for the crucial point at present is simply that Kuhn's conception of revolutionary science, like his conception of normal science, is anti-critical. On the Kuhnian view, the revolutionary scientist, like the normal scientist, cannot participate in critical discourse—since paradigms are incommensurable, there can be no critical discussion concerning the merits of competing paradigms; and theory choice (or paradigm adoption) is closer to a religious than an intellectual endeavor.

(C) Relativism

On the Kuhnian view, scientific knowledge is relative. What one "knows" depends on one's paradigm. Since paradigms are incommensurable, one cannot evaluate conflicting claims in an objective, paradigm-neutral way. So, while a Ptolemaian may "know" that the earth is at the center of the solar system, the Copernican "knows" it is rather the sun that occupies that place; likewise, while the Newtonian "knows" that space is absolute and Euclidean, the Einsteinian "knows" that space is rather "curved" and non-Euclidean.[17] This sort of relativism must be deemed anti-critical for the obvious reason: because competing paradigms are incommensurable, argument concerning the relative merits of incompatible, rival claims which stem from such paradigms cannot be rationally had, for what counts as a good reason for a claim depends on the paradigm one judges from, and what is rational from one point of view will be seen as wildly irrational from another. Reasons, and critical thinking itself, are on this view relative, and the rationality of the proponents of competing paradigms is restricted— not to say nullified—by the fact that it is impossible for those proponents to be rational or critical concerning their paradigm itself. They are trapped by their paradigmatic presuppositions and commitments, and are incapable of critical thinking concerning those. Thus paradigms and incommensurability render scientific belief and "knowledge" anti-critical, and critical thinking concerning pardigm-bound belief impossible.[18]

(D) Science education as dogmatic indoctrination

According to Kuhn, science education generally has been and should be geared to the inculcation in the student of the dominant scientific paradigm of the day. Much of science education aims at the production of competent researchers, and successful research can occur only in accordance with the methods and meanings of the paradigm which defines the problems being researched. Science textbooks, accordingly, are typically designed so as to enable the student to master the techniques and conceptions of the relevant paradigm. Kuhn himself points to the dogmatism inherent in this approach to science education: "science education remains a relatively dogmatic initiation into a pre-established problem-solving tradition that the student is neither invited nor equipped to evaluate."[19] Elsewhere he describes this approach at length:

> In these fields [the natural sciences] the student relies mainly on textbooks until, in his third or fourth year of graduate work, he begins his own research. Many science curricula do not ask even graduate students to read in works not written specially for students. The few that do assign supplementary reading in research papers and monographs restrict such assignments to the most advanced courses and to materials that take up more or less where the available texts leave off. Until the very last stages in the education of a scientist, textbooks are systematically substituted for the creative scientific literature that made them possible. Given the confidence in their paradigms, which makes this educational technique possible, few scientists would wish to change it. Why, after all, should the student of physics, for example, read the works of Newton, Faraday, Einstein, or Schrodinger, when everything he needs to know about these works is recapitulated in a far briefer, more precise, and more systematic form in a number of up-to-date textbooks?
>
> Without wishing to defend the excessive lengths to which this type of education has occasionally been carried, one cannot help but notice that in general it has been immensely effective. Of course, it is a narrow and rigid education, probably more so than any other except perhaps in orthodox theology. But for normal-scientific work, for puzzle-solving within the tradition that the textbooks define, the scientist is almost perfectly equipped.[20]

Kuhn argues here that a major aim of science education is the production of competent normal scientists; that a highly effective way of doing this is by educating in a "narrow," "rigid," "dogmatic" way in which textbooks are designed to indoctrinate science students into the paradigm in question; and that such an education, given its effectiveness in achieving its aim, is highly desirable for education in science. He is, that is, both describing and advocating science education which rejects critical thinking in favor of indoctrination into the dogma of the currently favored paradigm.[21] Once again we see the anti-critical thrust of the Kuhnian view, this time with specific reference to science education.

(E) The distortion of the history of science in science education

Effectiveness in educating competent normal scientists is a reason, according to Kuhn, not only for dogmatic paradigm indoctrination. It is also a reason for distorting the history of science.

On Kuhn's view, science texts typically have offered, and typically offer, a distorted account of the history of science. They do so since, being written from the point of view of some paradigm, they "inevitably disguise not only the role but the very existence of the revolution that produced them."[22] Textbooks, according to Kuhn, are designed to perpetuate normal science, which means that they are written in the language, and in accordance with the principles, of the dominant paradigm of the day. Consequently, texts view the history of their field "through the eyes of" the dominant paradigm, making the history of the field look like a steady progression to that paradigm, with earlier scientists conceiving of the discipline and its problems in terms of the presuppositions of the currently dominant paradigm—rather than a history full of revolutions, in which earlier scientists conceived of the discipline and its outstanding problems in terms uncongenial to the current view. In this way, the revolutionary nature of science is underplayed, and a faulty picture of science as cumulative is propagated.

Kuhn argues not only that science textbooks do in fact distort the history of science. He argues as well that they *should* so distort. The distortion of the history of science in science education is desirable because it helps to inculcate science students into the dominant paradigm of the day, and so is effective in the training of competent normal scientists:

> To fulfill their [textbooks] function they need not provide authentic information about the way in which those bases [of the new paradigm] were first recognized and then embraced by the profession. In the case of textbooks ... there are even good reasons why, in these matters, they should be systematically misleading.[23]

The "good reasons" Kuhn here refers to are of course pedagogical—textbooks should be systematically misleading, and biased in favor of the perspective of the current paradigm, because such bias will facilitate the inculcation in the student of the currently dominant paradigm. The non-distorted history of the discipline might actually be detrimental to the student, since in such study the student "might discover other ways of regarding the problems discussed in the textbooks, but ... he would also meet problems, concepts, and standards of solution that his future profession has long since discarded and replaced."[24] Kuhn concludes that if we, as science educators, are to produce competent scientists, we had better keep students away from the undistorted history of science, and present to the student an "unequivocal," paradigm-bound view of the history of the discipline:

> I ... hope that [this] paper has indicated why an educational system best described as an initiation into an unequivocal tradition should be thoroughly compatible with successful scientific work. And I hope, in addition, to have made plausible the historical thesis that no part of science has progressed very far or very rapidly before this convergent education and correspondingly convergent normal practice became possible.[25]

So: normal science—"convergent normal practice"—is a necessary condition of scientific progress;[26] convergent practice goes hand in hand with "convergent education," i.e. education which distorts the history of science to make that history appear to converge; consequently, the distortion of the history of science is a good thing, even a necessary thing, for successful science education. Kuhn thus recommends that we present the history of science as an "unequivocal tradition," notwithstanding the fact that we are well aware that the tradition has not, in fact, been so unequivocal:

> Textbooks thus begin by truncating the scientist's sense of his discipline's history and then proceed to supply a substitute for what they have eliminated. Characteristically, textbooks of science contain just a bit of history, either in an introductory chapter or, more often, in scattered references to the great heroes of an earlier age. From such references both students and professionals come to feel like participants in a long-standing historical tradition. *Yet the textbook-derived tradition in which scientists come to sense their participation is one that, in fact, never existed.* For reasons that are both obvious and highly functional, science textbooks ... refer only to that part of the work of past scientists that can easily be viewed as contributions to the statement and solution of the texts' paradigm problems. Partly by selection and partly by *distortion*, the scientists of earlier ages are implicitly represented as having worked on the same set of fixed problems and in accordance with the same set of fixed canons that the most recent revolution in scientific theory and method has made seem scientific.[27]

A clearer statement of Kuhn's view could hardly be wanted: because it is functional or effective for the training of the competent normal scientist to be inculcated into a distorted view of the history of her discipline, it is a desideratum of science education to so inculcate—notwithstanding the fact that, as the educator is well aware, the view is distorted, i.e. false; that the tradition in which the scientist is led to sense her own participation is one which, as Kuhn candidly acknowledges, never existed.

I needn't belabor the anti-criticalness of this view of the role of the history of science in science education. Not only is its justification the effectiveness in training for normal science, which is itself of dubious merit from the point of view of critical thinking. In addition, this view systematically distorts, and actively seeks to keep students from knowing about, the actual history of their field. It discourages students questioning their current paradigm and its standards, concepts, and methodology; it seeks to prevent students from conceiving of their discipline and its problems from alternative paradigmatic points of view. It encourages a narrowness, a blindness to alternatives, in students. Perhaps most dramatically, its sanctions lying to students. Surely this conflicts with the respect for students as persons which the ideal of critical thinking takes as fundamental.

In all these ways, then, Kuhn's conception of science and science education conflicts with the ideal of critical thinking. Our question is: Is Kuhn right? Is an anti-critical science education the sort of science education we should be providing our students? Predictably, I shall argue against this Kuhnian conception of science education.

3 Arguments against anti-critical science education

(A) The nature of science and the education of scientists

Is the goal of science education simply the production of competent normal scientists? For Kuhn's description of the typical science textbook and science education program to be prescriptively adequate, this question must be answered in the affirmative. Yet there is overwhelming reason to believe that such a conception of the goal of science education is far too narrow and constricting to be adequate. Science education, it must be granted, does recognize the goal of producing competent scientific researchers. However, it recognizes other goals as well, among them the education of persons who do not intend to become and will not become future scientists but who wish or need to have a basic understanding of science, and also the production of certain attitudes and habits of thought which are antithetical to the uncriticalness required by science education as Kuhn describes it. These other goals suggest a science education quite different from the sort Kuhn describes. Such a science education would emphasize critical skills rather than the uncritical research of normal science; it would accentuate the fallibility and potential for improvement of the paradigm of the day. The science student and future scientist would be encouraged to question and challenge the paradigm accepted by the community of specialists, and actively to seek its improvement.[28]

Such a view of science education is proposed, for example, by Joseph J. Schwab. In his *The Teaching of Science As Enquiry*, Schwab argues for a view of science education much like the one just sketched—that is to say, one which stresses the importance of potentially revolutionary thinking to the science student. He emphasizes the role of critical thinking in science education and the recognition that science "is a mode of investigation which rests on conceptual innovation, proceeds through uncertainty and failure, and eventuates in knowledge which is contingent, dubitable, and hard to come by."[29] Schwab's view of science education is, in its emphasis on the critical side of science, thus at odds with the Kuhnian view.

Precisely because opposite conclusions for science education are obtainable from their characterizations of the scientific enterprise, it is important to note that Kuhn and Schwab conceive of that enterprise in remarkably similar ways. Kuhn conceives of scientific activity of two distinct sorts: normal and revolutionary. Schwab likewise conceives of two distinct sorts of scientific enquiry: *stable* and *fluid*. Stable enquiry is much like Kuhn's normal science; and the role of the stable enquirer is, according to Schwab, much like the role of the normal scientist:

> It is the business of the stable enquirer ... to construct an edifice, not to question its plan. Each stable enquiry is concerned to fill a particular blank in a growing body of knowledge. The shape of the blank space and the way to go about filling it are conferred by principles of enquiry, but the stable enquirer has no traffic with these principles as such. He receives them from others and treats them as matters of fact. He uses them as means of enquiry and not as objects to be enquired into. The principles define his problem for him and guide the pattern of experiment which will solve it, but the principles are not treated as problems in themselves.[30]

Kuhn conceives of normal science as uncovering anomalies which eventually lead to the paradigm which guides normal research into crisis. Schwab, similarly, views stable enquiry as eventually leading to problems which undermine the principles guiding stable research: "There comes a time, however, when a given set of principles no longer defines effective problems. Stable enquiries falter. Contradictory data are obtained ... Such events mark the senescence of a set of principles."[31] The "senescence" here described by Schwab is strikingly like Kuhn's account of anomaly-induced crisis. Moreover, Schwab's analogue of normal science, stable enquiry, leads to his analogue of crisis, senescence, much like Kuhn's model.

Finally, as crisis leads to revolutionary science for Kuhn, senescence leads to fluid enquiry for Schwab:

> Its [fluid enquiry's] task is to study the failure of the stable enquiries in order to discover what is lacking in the principles which guided them. Fluid enquiry then proceeds to the invention of new conceptions and tests of them for adequacy and feasibility. Its immediate goal is not added knowledge of the subject matter, per se, but development of new principles which will redefine that subject matter and guide a new course of effective, stable enquiries.[32]

The parallel between revolutionary science and fluid enquiry as sketched by Kuhn and Schwab is unmistakable. While there are some differences between the two—most notably, Schwab's allowance for the rational development of fluid enquiry, as contrasted with the lack of that allowance, by Kuhn, for revolutionary science—Schwab's and Kuhn's portraits of the scientific enterprise are highly similar. Not only do they compartmentalize different aspects of scientific practice analogously, they envision the role and function of each aspect similarly.

Given the remarkable similarity of these two conceptions of the dynamcs of science, it becomes a problem to explain the dissimilarity of their respective recommendations for science education. An educational program based on Kuhn's conception of science might be said to advocate education for normal science, while a program based on Schwab's conception would advocate education for fluid enquiry. What arguments can be made for these divergent recommendations?

Schwab argues that science education ought to be focussed on fluid enquiry because that sort of enquiry is an increasingly dominant aspect of science. He argues that, as a matter of historical fact, science has gone through the *revisionary cycle* — from stable enquiry, through senescence, to fluid enquiry which then reinstates stable enquiry — at increasingly rapid rates. Since the time of this cycle is shortened, the time of stable enquiry is likewise shortened; and fluid enquiry is necessary in greater and greater amounts:

> The bald facts are simply these: the duration of a revisionary cycle has been drastically shortened and the magnitude of the fluid enterprise vastly increased. The extent of the change has been momentous. In many instances the rate of revision is twenty to a hundred times what it was much less than a century ago. The place of fluid enquirers in the scientific polity has been proportionately enhanced.[33]

Schwab presents an account of the growing social role of science as the cause of the increase in the rate of the revisionary cycle. He then argues that, given the prominence of fluid enquiry in the scientific world, it is counter-productive to emphasize stable enquiry in science education, for such emphasis is incongruous with the actual nature of scientific research. To teach science as "dogma"[34] is thus to misrepresent the facts about the nature of scientific enquiry, and so to create an undesirable tension between science as it is practised, and science as it is presented to students:

> The effect of this growing failure of communication between enquiry and the textbook reaches its most pervasive climax in a lapse of relevance, a contradiction, between science as it functions in fact — a fluid enquiry, utilizing changing concepts, producing continuous reorganization and revision of its knowledge — and science as it is taught. It is taught as a nearly unmitigated *rhetoric of conclusions* in which the current and temporary constructions of scientific knowledge are conveyed as empirical, literal, and irrevocable truths.[35]

To teach science as a "rhetoric of conclusions," then, is to misrepresent in the classroom the nature of scientific research. This, Schwab argues, is not the way to produce competent scientists. If science actually depends on fluid enquiry, science education ought to be oriented toward the production of competent fluid enquirers:

> The novelty level of our technical problems requires refreshed scientific knowledge. And this knowledge, in turn, requires new conceptual structures designed to initiate new lines of stable enquiry. It is from fluid enquiries and fluid enquirers that these conceptual structures must come.[36]

We see, then, that even if we grant Kuhn his conception of science as passing through a series of analogues of Schwab's revisionary cycles, as well as his assumption that science education is concerned solely, or mainly, with the production of scientists, his conclusion regarding the virtues of dogmatic, uncritical science education does not follow. Schwab, utilizing the very same assumptions, argues persuasively for a conception of science education in which critical thinking is central. And, given our earlier arguments for the centrality of critical thinking to education, Schwab's portrayal of a critical science education enjoys support not available to Kuhn's anti-critical alternative.

(B) The practical effectiveness of Kuhnian science education

Of course, the Kuhnian need not concede defeat at this point. There are at least three arguments the defender of a Kuhnian science education can make in favor of that approach, and against the Schwabian alternative.

First, the Kuhnian might argue that science education should be concerned primarily with normal science (stable enquiry) because education for revolutionary science (fluid enquiry) is impossible. If scientific revolutions are the result, as Kuhn argues, of gestalt switches and irrational conversions, how can education for these sorts of things possibly be conducted? If education for revolutionary science is impossible, all that is left for science education is training for normal science.

This argument might be more compelling if revolutionary science were indeed as unstructured and uncritical as Kuhn depicts it. But, as suggested earlier,[37] Kuhn's irrationalist portrayal of revolutionary science is highly suspect, and hardly convincing. Insofar as the Kuhnian recommendation for science education rests on Kuhn's discussion of incommensurability, gestalt switches, conversion experiences, and the like, that recommendation is without foundation. I see, moreover, no other reason for taking seriously the view that education for revolutionary science is impossible. Not only has the "unteachability" of revolutionary science not been established, Schwab has provided serious reason for believing that such teaching is possible, and has even sketched how such teaching might be carried out.[38] This argument for Kuhnian science education, based on the alleged impossibility of education for revolutionary science, is thus unpersuasive.

A second argument for Kuhnian science education is that science education should focus on normal science because normal science is more important, or more fundamental, than revolutionary science.[39] This line of argument, however, is at odds with just about everyone's, including Kuhn's and Schwab's, emphasis on the importance of scientific revolutions for the dynamics of science. Kuhn, for example, conceives of normal and revolutionary science as mutually complementary: normal science precipitates the crises which lead to revolutionary science;[40] revolutionary science, in turn, provides a new paradigm under which normal science can flourish. Given this view of the mutual and complementary importance of normal and revolutionary science, it is doubtful that normal science can consistently be maintained to be so much more important, or basic, than revolutionary science that science education should focus only on normal science. Such a view, furthermore, leaves unaddressed Schwab's argument concerning the increasing dominance of fluid enquiry. Reliance on the fundamental status of normal science, therefore, fails to support the recommendation that science education focus on normal science.

Third, and most important, the proponent of Kuhnian science education might argue that that sort of science education is more *effective* than science education which focusses on revolutionary science/fluid enquiry—that is, that science education which emphasizes uncritical normal science/stable enquiry actually produces (more, and) more competent scientists. This line of argument, if successful, would admittedly be very persuasive. However, there are several considerations which render it implausible. For such a claim is an empirical one, and is open to empirical investigation. There is no compelling *a priori* reason to suppose that any particular type of science education would be more effective than another in producing scientists of any particular level of competency. Rather, such considerations must be based on empirical data: clear examples of one or another type of educational orientation; follow-up reports on the students who were the products of these educational programs; statistical analyses; proper experimental design of controlled experiments, etc. A claim that any given educational arrangement actually produces more competent graduates than an alternative arrangement is an empirical one, and must be established as such. As far as I am aware, there are no empirical data which support the claim that Kuhnian science education programs are more effective than non-Kuhnian alternatives. In particular, even if one holds that the goal of science education is the production of competent normal scientists—a goal to be challenged below—the defender of Kuhnian science education must provide evidence that that sort of science education is more effective than a more critical, non-Kuhnian program. In the absence of such evidence, it remains equally (if not more) plausible to maintain that a more critical science education program would produce more competent scientists—even normal scientists.

Indeed, given that the task of ordinary normal research includes the uncovering of anomalies which lead to revolutionary transformations of science, it seems reasonable to suspect that a more critical problem-solver would uncover anomalies more rapidly, and search them out more insightfully, than would a less critical one. On Kuhn's view of ordinary scientific research, for example, the normal scientist plods along with her normal research, taking for granted the boundaries and assumptions of that research, quite oblivious to whatever anomalies are waiting to be uncovered. It is mere chance that anomalies are uncovered; there is no systematic search for them. This is not, it seems, likely to be very effective, in light of the normal scientist's interest in uncovering anomalies. A more critical normal scientist might well be more effective in searching out anomalies, and so be more effective in inducing revolutionary science. An uncritical normal scientist finds anomalies by accident; surely this will not do if, as both Kuhn and Schwab do, we prize the uncovering of anomalies. It appears that even the unquestioning, uncritical normal scientist, then, would be better off, and more effective, if she were more critical. At least, there seems to be no reason to think that an uncritical normal scientist would be a better normal scientist than a critical one.

Similar remarks apply to Kuhnian distortion of the history of science in science education. Kuhn is clear in his insistence that the science student is not to be "encouraged to read the historical classics of his field—works in which he might discover other ways of regarding the problems discussed in his textbook," for in such readings "he would also meet problems, concepts, and standards of solution that his future profession has long since discarded and replaced."[41] Kuhn's suggestion is that these problems, concepts, and standards of solution will hurt the scientific development of the student (and through the student, the development of science itself), since they are not the problems, concepts and standards accepted by the paradigm in which the student is being inculcated. But this takes a rather pessimistic view of the student's critical capabilities. Why should alternative accounts of the problems, concepts and standards of the field confuse the student or otherwise harm the student's ability to master the paradigm of the day? Why wouldn't they, in fact, provide the student with a richer background from which to view, and appreciate, the strengths of the paradigm that has succeeded those from which the alternative accounts come? Alternative accounts of the problems, concepts and standards of solution of the paradigm the student is being taught can be most helpful to the student in gaining a deeper understanding and appreciation of that paradigm and the reasons we regard it as preferable to its historical alternatives. For the alternative accounts, taken from discarded paradigms of the past, can be taught as such—

as earlier attempts to organize and explain a given domain of nature which, for specifiable reasons and shortcomings, have been replaced by a paradigm currently judged to be more adequate to the task. To demonstrate in this way the effectiveness of the new paradigm could greatly enhance the student's comprehension and appreciation of that paradigm. By analogy, it could also serve to demonstrate to the student the fallibility of current scientific theory and thus encourage in the student a critical, improvement-oriented posture toward current theory, and may well facilitate normal scientific activity. Thus it is by no means obvious that Kuhnian distortion of the history of science will prove effective in the production of competent normal scientists.[42]

In short, even granting the Kuhnian that the goal of science education is the production of competent normal scientists, there is no reason to think that an uncritical, distorting science education program will be more effective in such production than a non-distorting, more critically-oriented program.

(C) The morality of Kuhnian science education

Up to now I have been challenging the claim that Kuhnian science education is more effective in the production of competent scientists than a more critical, non-Kuhnian alternative. Even if it were more effective, Kuhnian science education is problematic on a very different score. For such a science education is reprehensible from the moral point of view.

First, the distortion of the history of science Kuhn calls for amounts to nothing less than lying to the science student; to wilfully attempting to get her to believe what we know to be falsehoods concerning the history of the field under study. Distorting science education does not seek to impart to students what we take to be the truth about the history of science; rather, it puts us in the position of manipulating, in an indoctrinary way, historical material, so that the student will draw what we deem to be erroneous conclusions about the history of science. This hardly recognizes the autonomy of the student or the right of the student to bring her own intelligence to bear in the critical assessment of alternative views; rather, it denies the student the rightful status of "equal participant under the judgmental law."[43]

Students are not objects with which we can, as science educators, do as we wish. They are persons, and deserve the respect of their personhood that we demand for ourselves. At the least, such respect requires honesty in our dealings with them. The purposeful distortion of the history of science would in no way meet such a requirement. From the moral point of view, such distortion is repugnant. If we are to meet our moral responsibilities as educators, we cannot wilfully distort the history of science — or anything else — no matter how effective such distortion might be.[44]

These general remarks concerning moral constraints on our dealings with students go beyond the question of distortion. They apply equally as much to the anti-criticality of Kuhnian science education, for discouraging students from questioning or recognizing the fallibility and improvability of current science, however it influences their competence as scientists, fails to recognize their autonomy or personhood. To so recognize is, at a minimum, to encourage students to question, demand reasons and justifications, and submit claims and conceptions to their own independent judgment. None of this goes on in the anti-critical "science-education-for-normal-science" science program advocated by Kuhn. So, with respect to distortion and also with respect to uncriticality, Kuhnian science education faces telling challenges regarding its moral acceptability.

(D) Relativism, dogmatism, and pluralism

Earlier[45] I noted that Kuhn's epistemology is relativistic; that on his conception of science, what counts as scientific knowledge depends on the paradigm one judges from, so that knowledge is relative to paradigm. One might expect, given this epistemology, that Kuhn's recommendations for science education would be similarly relativistic, advocating instruction in a wide variety of alternative theories, paradigms, and methodologies, eschewing the task of judging their relative merits or singling out a "right" one. The extreme relativist might even, as Feyerabend does, argue for the breakdown of the distinction between science and pseudo-science, and so for the inclusion of astrology, witchcraft, creationism, even divination by inspection of entrails, in the science curriculum. There is some irony, then, in Kuhn's plumping for dogmatic, radically non-relativistic science education.

Both of these alternative approaches to science education are problematic. Relativism renders us incapable of making reasoned judgments about the merits of alternative theories and method-ologies, and portrays scientific reasoning, commitment, and judgment as arbitrary. "Absolutism," as we have seen, commits us to a dogmatism which misrepresents the nature of scientific inquiry and its fruits, suggesting indubitable, infallible scientific truths; discourages us from engaging the student in the activity of scientific thinking; and leads us to teach what Schwab aptly calls a "rhetoric of conclusions." We can safely avoid the first alternative, for there is compelling reason for rejecting relativistic epistemology.[46] Can we similarly avoid dogmatic science education? Does an embrace of a non-relativistic, "absolutist" epistemology commit us to dogmatism in science education, since the absolutist holds that science uncovers "the facts," that there is only one set of such facts, and that the well-educated science student is aware of those facts?[47]

Fortunately, the absolutist is not committed to any such conception of science education. The absolutist is committed to the view that knowledge is not relative, but she is not necessarily saddled with the further views that we have all the knowledge there is to have, that such knowledge is certain, that there is only one correct method of obtaining it, that there is therefore no room for ingenuity or creativity in scientific investigation, or that there is therefore no point to any scientific education save the "rhetoric of conclusions" sort. In particular, the absolutist is not committed to the dogmatic approach to science education defended by Kuhn, in which the student is exposed only to the "right"—that is, the currently accepted—theoretical perspective.

The absolutist escapes these pernicious views of science education by distinguishing between relativism and *pluralism*. While rejecting the relativist view that "anything goes," that any particular scientific thesis or methodology is as good as any other, the absolutist can recognize the virtues—both philosophical and pedagogical—of exposure to a variety of methods of investigation and theoretical formulation. Pluralism—a willingness to tolerate and utilize a diversity of ideas and approaches—differs radically from the relativistic view that there is no evaluating the worth of rival ideas and approaches,[48] and the absolutist can perfectly well embrace pluralism while rejecting relativism.

And in fact there are good reasons for embracing a pluralist science education. Philosophically, it recognizes that scientific knowledge is never final or certain, but is always subject to amendment and revision on the basis of additional evidence or novel theoretical considerations; that is, pluralism recognizes the fallibility of scientific knowledge. Moreover, pluralism recognizes the virtue and potential fruitfulness of allowing rival ideas to establish their merits in the free exchange of ideas. This is a point which has pedagogical as well as philosophical appeal. Philosophically, it recognizes the fallibility of scientific knowledge and the goal of improving our ideas as well as the virtues of freedom of thought and expression. Pedagogically, the conflict of ideas can serve to stimulate students, and to spur them on to deeper understanding of the matter at hand. In Schwab's terms, it can help students to become fluid enquirers, which involves the development and appreciation of alternative concepts and frameworks. The non-pluralistic "dogmatic classroom," on the other hand, which fails to develop alternative approaches or conceptions and so avoids pluralism, fails to convey to the student an adequate sense of the tentativeness and struggle, the lurching, weaving, and false starts of actual scientific inquiry, and the tentativeness, dubitability, and fallibility of current scientific knowledge.[49]

A related pedagogical point is made by Michael Martin, who advocates that science students be taught to work with a variety of theories. Borrowing Feyerabend's phrase "proliferation of theories," Martin wrties:

> students of science should be taught a number of different theoretical approaches in a domain of research. If necessary, discarded theories from the history of science should be restructured and re-examined. Students should not only be exposed to different theoretical approaches, but should also learn to work easily with different theories, now seeing the domain from the point of view of one theory, now seeing it from the point of view of another, switching back and forth to get various theoretical perspectives and insights.[50]

Noting that the student is to regard these alternative approaches as working hypotheses, Martin concludes:

> The pedagogical principle of the proliferation of theories could be stated in this way: students should learn to work with many theories as working hypotheses in a given domain of inquiry, even if commitment in the strong sense [i.e. as true or probably true] to an incompatible theory is justified in the domain.
> The rationale for the proflieration of theories approach is this: The more theories one is used to working with in a given domain, the less likely it is that one will be blinded by one's commitments ... to any one of them.[51]

Here Martin is admirably articulating and defending the pluralism discussed above. His defense, in terms of the lowering of the likelihood that one will be blinded or biassed by one's theoretical commitments, is clearly compatible with Schwab's defense of pluralism in terms of fluid enquiry. Moreover, Martin's argument tends to undercut the Kuhnian view that science students, if they are to be successful, must be dogmatically indoctrinated into some particular theoretical perspective, and prevented from entertaining rival perspectives.

We have seen thus far several reasons for taking pluralism to be a valuable approach to science education. It avoids the pitfalls of both relativistic and dogmatic science education. As Schwab suggests, it is compatible with the development of fluid enquirers and is true to the innovativeness of actual scientific inquiry and the tentativeness of the fruits of such inquiry. As Martin suggests, it conforms to our desire to keep the student (and the scientist) from being blinded by her theoretical commitments, thus keeping her open to important new avenues of data and conceptualization. It is on sound epistemological footing in its embrace of a non-relativist, fallibilist conception of scientific knowledge. There is yet another powerful reason for embracing a pluralistic science education: pluralism may reasonably be thought to foster critical thinking in science students. And since we have already noted several considerations which suggest the importance of the educational ideal of critical thinking, a science education compatible with the fostering of that ideal derives additional support from it. Pluralistic science education favors the fostering of critical thinking (since it requires students to judge critically the merits of alternative claims, conceptions, and perspectives); the achievement of the ideal of critical thinking is independently established as a central education aim; consequently, pluralistic science education gains support from the independent justification which the ideal enjoys.

(E) The goals of science education

In fact, there is a tight connection between the goals of science education and the broad aims and ideals of education generally. In helping a student, by way of pluralistic science education, to become a critical thinker with respect to science, one is helping the student to develop a respect for reasons; an inclination to seek reasons and take them seriously as guides to belief and action; an appreciation of objectivity, impartiality, and honesty in the consideration of evidence and argument; and a general commitment to the ideal of rationality as a guide to life. In these respects, as Martin has urged, the propensities and skills we seek to impart to science students are the same that we seek to impart to students more generally[52]; that is to say, science education seeks to foster in students characteristics which will render the student educated—not just in science, but in general. The critical spirit characteristic of science is the critical spirit we seek to impart to students as we help them to become critical thinkers. As Martin puts it, "The aim of science education ought to be to produce people imbued with the spirit of science who manifest that spirit in all relevant contexts."[53] This view of science education is very much in line with the thesis of this book, namely that the fostering of critical thinking, or rationality, in students should be regarded as a fundamental aim of education; moreover, because of the centrality to science education of features which are also central to the ideal of critical thinking—features such as objectivity, impartiality, honesty, and commitment to and respect for evidence—science education has a major curricular role to play in our overall educational effort.[54] The sort of pluralistic approach to science education described above can help to prevent students from being blinded by their theoretical commitments, and can more generally encourage open-mindedness, attention to evidence, and respect for evidence in the assessment of practical and theoretical alternatives. In these respects a pluralistic science education may help to foster the development of rationality and critical thinking, both with respect to science and more generally.[55]

Throughout this chapter I have been granting for the sake of argument the Kuhnian contention that science education is primarily concerned with the production of competent scientists. I have argued that, even if this were the case, anti-critical dogmatic initiation into the presently accepted paradigm is not the most defensible strategy to utilize in that production, for, as has been pointed out, we have no reason to think that an uncritical normal scientist will fare better at the tasks of normal science than a critical one; nor is it clear that a focus on normal science is preferable to a focus on fluid enquiry. So, even given that the sole aim of science education is the production of competent scientists, it does not in the least follow that a Kuhnian science education is the sort we should prefer.

It should now be clear, moreover, that the overarching goal of science education is not the production of competent scientists. For one thing, most science students do not become professional scientists, and we rightly take as an important aim of science education instruction concerning the basic concepts, methods, and features of science, so that non-scientist but well-educated persons have a fundamental grasp of the nature of science and scientific knowledge and therefore are able to utilize scientific information properly in their consideration of personal and public policy matters to which scientific information is relevant.[56] Furthermore, as just argued, science education recognizes goals which go beyond a concern for the production of scientists in that they focus on features of critical thinking which are justifiable independently of the career paths of science students. In addition, we have seen that there are moral constraints on science education which disallow a narrow concern for the production of scientists. Finally, we must acknowledge that the goals of science education are best seen in the light of, and in fact are very closely connected to, the broader goals of education; and in this context there is no place for narrow professionalist concerns, for if we take seriously the ideal of critical thinking, we do not conceive of education as training for future careers. Rather, we conceive of education as the fostering of basic skills, dispositions, and character traits — as the development of certain sorts of persons — who are enabled by their education to direct their own futures. Given the central role that science education can play in the development of such persons, it is impossible coherently to conceive of the goals of science education in careerist terms.

The Kuhnian conception of science education fails even if we aim science education at the production of scientists; that conception fails more decisively still once we recognize the untenability of that narrow view of the aim of science education and the broader aims of a *critical* science education. In addition to the features of a pluralistic science education previously discussed, what else can be said concerning a science education aimed at the development of critical thinking?

4 Critical science education: a focus on reasons in science

We have already noted that pluralistic science education, by utilizing alternative theoretical perspectives, can help to develop in the science student an appreciation of evidence and a commitment to the evaluation of such perspectives on the basis of reasons. How else might the role of reasons in science be emphasized?

One way is to focus on the *philosophy of* science in teaching science. Philosophy of science takes as its subject matter a variety of issues and questions relevant to the nature, role, and assessment of reasons in science. The nature of evidence, the relation between evidence and theory, the evaluation of the strength of evidence, the role of evidence and reason in testing and in theory choice—these are all matters which bear directly on the nature of reasons in science, and which philosophy of science takes as central to its concerns. A science student studying philosophy of science would, in so studying, be more attuned to issues involving scientific reasoning, and to the nature and proper understanding of such reasoning. In studying some episode of theory choice, for example, she might glean an understanding of the way in which a certain piece of evidence supports theory T rather than its rival T': or why that piece of evidence, or some theoretical derivation, supports T decisively rather than only weakly. In studying efforts to construct (and the motivations for constructing) an inductive logic, and efforts to articulate, refine and criticize the variety of confirmationist and falsificiationist "logics of science,"[57] the student stands to gain enormous insight into the character of reasons in science. Studying philosophy of science, therefore, may contribute powerfully to the understanding of reasons in science, and so to the fostering of critical thinking in science, for philosophy of science is profitably and properly seen, in part, as the meta-scientific study of reasons in science.[58]

Another way to utilize philosophy of science so as to impart to the science student a solid understanding of the nature and role of reasons in science is to contrast genuine science with pseudo-science. Studying the differences between science and pseudo-science may serve not only to deepen, in a general way, student understanding of important features of science—e.g. the importance of formulating testable theories, and of considering all relevant evidence—it may also help students to understand, by contrast with pseudo-scientific examples, the constitution and utilization of reasons in science. The contrast between pseudo-science and science may in this way foster critical thinking in science students by highlighting the nature and role of reasons in science.[59]

A critical science education, then, takes as its primary focus the study of reasons in science. Instead of regarding the science curriculum as a "rhetoric of conclusions," it is regarded as a means of helping students to come to understand the nature and role of reasons in the scientific enterprise. The content of contemporary scientific theory plays a significant role in such a curriculum, of course. More significant, however, is a focus on the reasons for regarding current theory as worthy of our attention and embrace. By contrasting science with pseudo-science, by studying philosophy of science, and by examining alternative theoretical perspectives and the reasons for regarding some as superior/inferior to others—and so, by being exposed to the general problem of the reasoned evaluation of alternatives—the student's study of science is never far from consideration of the nature and role of reasons in science. Here we see a version of McPeck's call for subject area curricula paying attention to the "epistemology of the subject." Moreover, if our earlier discussion concerning the relationship between the goals of science education and the goals of education more broadly is on target, we see that a critical science education contributes to, and is part and parcel of, the general effort to put education in the service of critical thinking.

5 A postscript on generality

I have argued in this chapter for a critical science education rather than a Kuhnian anti-critical one. I have also argued that the goals of science education are in important respects isomorphic to the goals of education more generally, and that critical thinking is a central goal in both contexts; and, most recently, that a desirable science education has much to gain from the incorporation of philosophy of science, pseudo-science, and the consideration of alternative theoretical perspectives into the curriculum, for these all have much to teach concerning the nature, role and assessment of reasons in science. This last point can and should be generalized to other curricular areas.

To be a critical thinker with respect to science, one needs to understand the nature and function of reasons in science, and such understanding, I have suggested, might be furthered by exposure to philosophy of science, pseudo-science, and alternative theoretical perspectives. Science is not special or unique, however; the general point applies to all or most curricular areas. In history, literature, mathematics, and so on, familiarity with the philosophy of that subject may reasonably be expected to enhance students' critical thinking in that subject, since the philosophies of the subjects all take as part of their domain the proper analysis of reasons in that subject. While critical thinking is not identifiable with philosophy (as McPeck points out), a critical-thinking oriented curriculum will likely give philosophy a larger role than is customary, because of the role of "philosophies of" in analyzing the nature, function and assessment of reasons in the various disciplines.[60] Similarly, attention to work which is regarded as so grossly inadequate that it fails to qualify as work in the discipline—the analogues of pseudo-science in math, history, literature, etc.—will also serve well in the working out of a critical education in that discipline, since it will highlight, by contrast, the features of work in the area which meet minimal disciplinary standards. Finally, the consideration of alternative theoretical perspectives, and of the problem of the evaluation of these alternatives, promises much to the effort of helping students come to an adequate grasp of reasons in the area in question. Thus for any curricular area X, the study of philosophy of X, the contrast between geniune- and pseudo-X, and the consideration of alternative theoretical perspectives both within and with regard to X and the problem of the evaluation of those alternatives, all promise to aid in the effort to make the curriculum in X contribute to a critical education in X. (For example, in the study of a literary work we may urge students to consider analyses of the work from a variety of critical perspectives, consider the criteria which distinguish that sort of work from work which is not of that sort, and investigate various questions in the philosophy of literature and language; similarly for social studies, math, etc.) And since the goals of education in these varied curriculum areas are related to the broader goals of education, organizing subject curricula in these ways serves the general educational effort of fostering critical thinking. In this way, then, I hope the discussion in this chapter can be seen as illustrative of the way in which the curriculum of any area can be conceived and organized so as to reflect the ideal of critical thinking and to foster critical thinking skills, abilities and attitudes in students.

Finally,[61] it must be acknowledged that all of these suggestions are couched in a relentlessly abstract way, and fail to take into account even the most rudimentary considerations regarding human learning and its psychology, the social and political context in which education takes place, the bureaucratic structure of schools, etc. I trust that it is clear that any serious educational efforts we make on behalf of critical thinking must take these more concrete dimensions of education into account if we are to have any reasonable prospect of success. If we want students to learn about critical thinking, and to become critical thinkers, we must create educational environments in which such learning, and such becoming, can take place. In neglecting such considerations here, I do not mean to leave the impression that they are unimportant to our educational efforts. On the contrary, attention to them is crucial and necessary. I have provided, at best, a general framework for conceiving of the ways in which curricular efforts can be informed by, and can further, the ideal of critical thinking. Detailed curricular plans are beyond the scope of the present effort, and the competence of the present author. Nevertheless, such detailed plans, and attention to questions about the psychology of learning, the structure of schools, the social and political context in which educational efforts take place, and so on, are of the first importance in the effort to help our students to become critical thinkers. I hope that my own efforts here prove useful in providing some sort of theoretical perspective from which to view questions concerning the nature and desirability of education for critical thinking. In the formulation of concrete educational programs aimed at the fostering of critical thinking, however, the philosopher's concerns are, of practical necessity, only some among many, and far from the whole story.

CHAPTER 7

Minimum competency testing

Parents usually educate their children in such a manner that, however bad the world may be, they may adapt themselves to its present conditions. But, they ought to give them an education so much better than this, that a better condition of things may thereby be brought about in the future.[1]

1 The aims of the chapter

In this chapter I wish to illustrate the relevance of critical thinking to educational policy and practice by considering the phenomenon of minimum competency testing (henceforth MCT). This widespread[2] practice has, like most educational panaceas, generated a storm of debate, and various criticisms and defenses of the practice can be heard: that it unfairly treats minority students; that it is a boon to educational efficiency and accountability; that establishing minimum competency mastery levels is arbitrary; and more. There is one sort of consideration relevant to the assessment of MCT, however, that is conspicuously absent from public debate. That sort of consideration is largely philosophical, having to do with our educational aims and ideals.

The debate concerning MCT is typical, I think, of most debate concerning the pros and cons of various educational policies and practices: it neglects to consider the extent to which such policies and practices either further or frustrate our efforts to achieve our educational ideals. I wish here, then, to consider MCT from the point of view of the ideal of critical thinking: does MCT help or hinder our efforts to inculcate the skills and attitudes of the critical thinker? My aim is two-fold: first, to argue that MCT is a foe, not a friend, of critical thinking; second, to argue that this first result is of fundamental importance for the assessment of MCT, and, more generally, that it is folly to neglect philosophical considerations concerning the aims of education in considering the desirability of educational policies and practices. This folly is, unfortunately, a popular one, as educational practitioners and policymakers seem loathe to raise questions regarding educational aims and ideals. I hope, then, to make the general point that such questions must be faced by responsible policymakers and practitioners—that philosophical considerations are essential to the proper assessment of educational policies and practices, and that it is irrational to pursue policies and practices which are incompatible with our best-defended educational ideals—in addition to the more specific point that, from the point of view of those ideals, especially that of critical thinking, MCT is *not* a defensible educational practice.

I will attempt to make my argument by way of a detailed analysis of the recent debate concerning MCT's alleged arbitrariness. I will argue that MCT can avoid the charge of arbitrariness only by exposing its inadequacy from the point of view of well-established educational ideals, in particular that of critical thinking. The general points to be made are that MCT, like all educational practices, must be conceived and conducted with an eye to philosophically defensible educational ideals; that MCT's failings are directly attributable to its inadequacy from the point of view of such ideals; and that educational policies and curricular designs which are conceived and implemented without regard for such ideals are bound to be inadequate, both philosophically and practically.

I begin with a consideration of MCT and its alleged arbitrariness.

2 Minimum competency testing

MCT is a loosely defined set of educational practices which include the testing of students at various grade levels to determine the extent of their "mastery" of some set of "competencies." The specific competencies tested for vary from program to program, and are conceived of either as "school subject" (basic skill) competencies such as reading and mathematical computation, or as "life skill" (functional literacy) competencies such as balancing a checkbook or successfully answering an employment advertisement. The student is expected to demonstrate a certain specifiable level of mastery of the competency; if the student fails to so demonstrate, either retesting, remediation efforts, failure to be promoted to the next grade, failure to receive a graduation diploma, or some combination of these is the result. The MCT movement is widely held to be largely supported by politicians and the public at large rather than by educators,[3] and is generally held to be motivated both by an effort of state legislatures to wrest educational control from local school systems, and by the public's dismay at lowered standards and seeming abundance of high school graduates who are "functionally illiterate."[4] Arguments frequently given in support of MCT involve enhanced accountability, the need to stop the downward slide of test scores, and the need to provide students with the competencies necessary for functional participation in society.[5]

I will not attempt here any systematic review of the many arguments advanced in favor of or opposed to MCT.[6] Rather, I will focus on one central consideration regarding the worth and justifiability of MCT, namely the debate concerning MCT's alleged arbitrariness. This debate will, in due course, afford a clear view of the relationships between MCT and both critical thinking and our educational ideals more generally.

3 The arbitrariness of standards

Perhaps the most philosophically pregnant dispute regarding MCT is that concerning MCT's alleged arbitrariness. Critics have repeatedly pointed out that a significant degree of arbitrariness is unavoidable in MCT, because there appears to be a non-arbitrary way of determining cut-off scores, or mastery levels, to differentiate those students who have attained minimum competency from those who have not. The most vocal of these critics, Gene V. Glass, states the position forcefully:

> I have read the writing of those who claim the ability to make the determination of mastery or competence in statistical or psychological ways. They can't. At least, they cannot determine "criterion levels" or standards other than arbitrarily.[7]

Glass argues that the difficulty of individual test items is largely unmonitored and typically fluctuates considerably,[8] and that cut-off scores are chosen more on the basis of the "tough-" or "tender-mindedness" of the test constructor than on any evidence that a particular cut-off score actually indicates mastery of the skill or subject matter being tested. In fact, Glass suggests that such a non-arbitrary cut-off score is *in principle* unattainable, since there is no non-arbitrary way of establishing a point at which demonstrable non-mastery turns into demonstrable mastery:

> For most skills and performances, one can reasonably imagine a continuum stretching from "absence of the skill" to "conspicuous excellence." But it does not follow from the ability to recognize absence of the skill (e.g., this paraplegic can type zero words per minute at 0 percent accuracy) that one can recognize the highest level of skill below which the person will not be able to succeed (in life, at the next level of schooling, or in his chosen trade). What is the minimum level of skill required in this society to be

a citizen, parent, carpenter, college professor, keypunch operator? Imagine that someone would dare to specify the highest level of reading performance below which no person could succeed in life as a parent. Counter-examples could be supplied in abundance of persons whose reading performance is below the "minimal" level yet who are regarded as successful parents. And the situation is no different with a secretary or electrician—in case one wished to argue that minimal competence levels are possible for "training," if not for "education." What is the lowest level of proficiency at which a person can type and still be employed as a secretary? Nearly any typing rate above the trivial zero-point will admit exceptions; and if one were forced nontheless to specify a minimal level, the rate of exceptions that was tolerable would be an arbitrary judgment.[9]

As this passage indicates, Glass holds that the arbitrariness endemic to MCT is so widespread, misleading, and potentially dangerous to students that MCT (and criterion-referenced testing generally) ought to be removed, root and branch, from the schools, and replaced with norm-referenced testing.

While Glass's case for the inherent arbitrariness of the standard setting required for MCT is powerfully made—and in fact, even his critics grant that in some sense he is right on that score—there are two difficulties with Glass's position. First, it is not clear that his suggestion regarding reliance on norm-referenced testing actually helps to avoid the arbitrariness problem. Glass's defense of norm-referenced testing is straightforward: comparative judgments, or measurements of change of performance, are not arbitrary, or at least not as capriciously arbitrary, as "absolute" judgments or measurements of criterion-referenced mastery:

Perhaps the only criterion that is safe and convincing in education is change. Increases in cognitive performance are generally regarded as good, decreases as bad. Although one cannot make satisfactory judgments of performance (is this level of reading performance good or masterful?), one can readily judge an improvement in performance as good and a decline as bad. My position on this matter is justified by appeal to a more general methodological question in evaluation. Is all meaningful evaluation comparative? Or do there exist absolute standards of value? I feel that in education there are virtually no absolute standards of value. "Goodness" and "badness" must be replaced by the essentially comparative concepts of "better" and "worse". . . Absolute evaluation in education . . . has been capricious and authoritarian. On the other hand, the value judgments based on comparative evidence impress one as cogent and fair.[10]

Unfortunately, comparative evaluation does not so easily escape the charge of arbitrariness as Glass suggests. Granted that increase in cognitive performance is good, how much improvement is good enough to warrant, say, promotion from grade to grade, or graduation from high school? Surely zero-level change is insufficient; consequently here, just as in the case of criterion-referenced testing, a decision must be made, a point must be picked, which designates the minimum improvement necessary for promotion or graduation. And this decision appears to be every bit as arbitrary as the decisions concerning mastery levels Glass argues against so cogently. So the move to comparative evaluation does not escape the charge of arbitrariness.[11]

The difficulty just noted concerns Glass's solution to the problem of the arbitrariness of MCT. A more serious difficulty with his position is one raised by several of his critics, most notably W. James Popham and Michael Scriven, who claim that Glass's case for the arbitrariness of MCT is itself weak, and that MCT standard setting need not be as arbitrary as Glass suggests. Popham notes that there are two senses of "arbitrary"—judgmental, and capricious—and argues that, while mastery levels are abitrary in the first sense, they need not be arbitrary in the second, more pernicious sense:

> The cornerstone of Glass's attack on the setting of performance standards is his assertion that such standards are set *arbitrarily*. He uses the term in its most pejorative sense; that is, equating it with mindless and capricious action. But while it can be conceded that performance standards must be set *judgmentally*, it is patently incorrect to equate human judgment with arbitrariness in this negative sense.[12]

Popham suggests here that standard setting, while necessarily judgmental, need not be capriciously judgmental. This distinction is an important one, but it does not in any way rebut Glass's indictment of the arbitrariness of MCT, for Glass is claiming not simply that standard-setting requires judgment, but that there can be no good reason for choosing one cut-off point over another. Let us distinguish, with Popham, between grounded and capricious judgment. Glass's charge is that standard setting is always a matter of capricious or ungrounded judgment. This is the thrust of Glass's criticisms of test item construction which fails to pay close attention to the difficulty of the item, and of the setting of cut-off scores according to whether or not the test constructor is "liberal" (e.g. 65 or 70 per cent) or "tough-minded" (e.g. 90 per cent).[13] Popham suggests that a grounded, non-capricious judgment of minimum competency standards can be had by educators—such judgments "can refer to the lowest level of proficiency *which they consider acceptable* for the situation at hand."[14] But, Glass must retort, on what basis is such consideration made? Is 90 per cent proficiency considered acceptable because the educator is "tough-minded"? Is 70 per cent considered acceptable because the educator in question is a "liberal guy"? And how difficult should the test items be? Unless such considered judgments are grounded somehow, they are indeed capricious, and Popham's distinction between judgmental arbitrariness and capricious arbitrariness seems not to protect MCT from Glass's criticism. Popham provides no reason for thinking that the minimum competency levels educators "consider acceptable" are groundedly rather than capriciously so considered.

Michael Scriven pushes the rebuttal of Glass's criticism of MCT further, by suggesting that judgments concerning mastery levels can be grounded in empirical research. Scriven argues that *needs assessment* is the key which will provide the possibility of setting non-arbitrary standards of mastery:

> We can only set mastery levels—other than as a first approximation—in light of needs assessment, and typically a bi-level one that addresses both the needs of those being tested for the skills and so forth being tested, and the needs of certain clienteles (which may or may not include the testees) for the mastery test.[15]

Presumably Scriven has in mind something like this: To establish mastery levels for the competent automobile mechanic, one studies the needs of those clienteles in need of mechanics—e.g. frustrated automobile owners, dealership service managers, gas station operators, etc.—and the needs of aspiring mechanics. If it turns out, say, that the needs of various clienteles are for mechanics who can tune engines, troubleshoot and repair failures in electrical systems, and replace exhaust systems, then the needs of aspiring mechanics are for those skills and abilities which would enable the student mechanic to satisfy those needs of the clienteles—e.g. to "read" properly the "scope" utilized for electronic tune-ups, to follow with understanding the manufacturer's repair manual, to possess a good working knowledge of automobile electrical systems, to have a significant amount of manual dexterity with regard to screwdrivers, wrenches, ratchets, air compressors, and pneumatic hand tools, and so on. In this way, by tentatively setting up mastery standards, researching the efficacy of those standards, monitoring the needs of both students and clienteles, and adjusting standards in light of such research, non-arbitrary standards of mastery can be established.

There is much to be said for Scriven's realistic, commonsense approach to the standard-setting problem. Nevertheless, there is a crucial difficulty with it. For the needs assessment approach to standard setting for MCT to be successful, it must be the case that becoming educated is in the relevant respects like becoming a mechanic—that is, that in the former case as in the latter, research concerning needs assessment of students and of the various clienteles of educational testing will turn up specifiable needs which, if met, would certify the student who met those needs as a well educated or successfully educated person. However, as I will now attempt to show, such a parallel between specific occupations (like mechanic or typist) and education is dubious. Any philosophically defensible view of the aims of education—and especially the view that critical thinking is an important educational aim—will preclude conceiving of education along the occupational training lines that the needs assessment approach assumes.[16]

How do we determine what specific skills and abilities a student will need in the future, when the student's future is undetermined? Scriven writes: "When you know how graduates need to perform on the job (the needs assessment) and you have a test you can use on pregraduates which has some predictive validity against job performance, you can set cutting scores (or bands)."[17] This makes sense, however, only if we *do* know what job the student will need to perform well at. But while for technical training (e.g. auto mechanics school) we do know this, for the typical public school student we do not. Our ignorance on this point is not simply a matter of too little research, moreover. On the contrary, we do not seek to determine students' futures, for we generally regard that as in large part, if not solely, the prerogative of the student, and we recognize that, except for the rare student, the years of public education end far too quickly for such determination. Indeed, if we take seriously that component of the ideal of critical thinking which emphasizes the student's achievement of self-sufficiency and autonomy, we note that the student's future is essentially always open. We educate so as to enable the student to *create* her future, not to submit to it. Unless "education" is to mean "training and socialization into predetermined adult roles and jobs," we cannot specify in advance what a student's future will be—and so we cannot specify in advance the needs of students which testing will serve, nor the needs of the various clienteles of educational testing. For the job of life—the only job which all students must engage in—needs assessment seems a hopeless task. Education is not geared to any particular job performance; consequently, Scriven's needs assessment approach will not help our efforts to set non-arbitrary standards for MCT. It depends on identifying in advance the job performance an educated person needs to pursue, and it pushes too hard the weak analogy between becoming (say) a mechanic and becoming an educated person.

4 A second locus of arbitrariness

There is, moreover, a related problem concerning the notions of "life skill" and "functional literacy" which bedevils most discussions of MCT. Thus far we have considered one charge of arbitrariness levelled at MCT, namely the charge that, given specific skills or subject matter, setting mastery levels is arbitrary. There is another sort of arbitrariness to be considered as well, concerning the determination or constitution of those skills, abilities, and items of knowledge, mastery of which are necessary for the achievement of functional literacy. How do we determine what counts as functional literacy? Here is a second locus of arbitrariness, one not always sufficiently distinguished from the first:

1 *First Level Arbitrariness*: given specified skills, etc., which constitute functional literacy, what constitutes mastery?
2 *Second Level Arbitrariness*: what constitutes functional literacy? What skills, etc., are to be specified?

Many critics of MCT have noted the arbitrariness of selecting the skills and abilities which are to constitute functional literacy or life skills. However, such arbitrariness is typically conflated with first level arbitrariness. Glass, for example, notes that "No one knows how well a person must read to succeed in life or what percent of the graduating class ought to be able to calculate compound interest payments."[18] Here Glass runs together both first and second level arbitrariness. The first case, specifying how *well* a person must be able to read in order to "succeed in life," queries the *level* of reading ability necessary for mastery. This is first level arbitrariness. The second case, however, suggests that some members of the graduating class may succeed in life perfectly well, even though they are unable to calculate compound interest payments. What is being questioned here is whether or not that ability is a part of functional literacy, or a "life skill," *at all*. This is second level arbitrariness. For discussion of the arbitrariness of MCT to be conducted fruitfully, these two levels of arbitrariness must be distinguished and considered separately.

As argued earlier, Glass has provided a strong case for the

unavoidability of first level arbitrariness. While that case is perhaps not conclusively made, it easily survives the criticisms offered by Popham and Scriven.[19] Glass has noted the problem of second level arbitrariness as well, but because he has failed adequately to distinguish the two levels, he has not offered any reason for taking second level arbitrariness to be either avoidable or unavoidable. Glass's arguments for the unavoidability of arbitrariness all speak to first-level standard-setting arbitrariness. Scriven's suggestion for avoiding arbitrariness via needs assessment similarly founders on a conflation of the two levels, for at best it offers a way of avoiding first level arbitrariness in relatively narrow, job-related training programs, while failing to take into account both second level arbitrariness (Does being able to "perform on the job" make one functionally literate? Can one be trained for some specific occupation, unquestioningly accept that occupation as one's lot in life, and be counted as one whose education or life is a "success"?) and the fact that becoming an educated person is in crucial respects very much unlike becoming a typist or mechanic, thus misconstruing the nature of the problem of avoiding first level arbitrariness. In order to settle the question, "Is MCT unavoidably arbitrary?", then, we must specifically address the problem of second level arbitrariness, and inquire further into the notion of "functional literacy" (or "life skill").

5 The notion of functional literacy

What constitutes functional literacy? Can we specify an acceptable conception of functional literacy? How might such a conception be grounded? In his paper on curricular implications of MCT,[20] Harry Broudy notes that functional literacy can be defined narrowly, as "the ability to read utility bills and classified ads, to write a letter of application, do simple sums,"[21] or broadly as "being able to use language in all its forms to enlarge knowledge, clarify thought, enrich the imagination, and guide judgment."[22] The narrow definition offers at best a minimal conception of functional literacy; we may indeed doubt whether one whose skills and knowledge are limited to those specified by the narrow conception (and their ilk) is either functional or literate. As Broudy argues, "Literacy itself presupposes more than mechanical mastery of the three R's . . . To be genuinely functional, literacy requires all strands of the curriculum."[23] Yet many proponents of MCT would reject the broad conception of functional literacy—as Popham notes, "The public is screaming for minimum warranties, not an enlightened conception of functional literacy."[24] Have we then unavoidable arbitrariness at the second level? Can we ground our judgments about the skills and knowledge a functionally literate person must possess?

I believe that we can. Such judgments may, and indeed must, be grounded ultimately in a philosophical conception of the aims of education. What counts as functional, as literate, and as functionally literate depends on considerations concerning the traits and talents of well-educated persons. If, as I have been arguing, critical thinking is an important educational ideal, then the narrow conception of functional literacy will not do. If our educational aim is to foster in students the features of the critical thinker, and if critical thinking involves much more than the narrow conception of functional literacy takes account of—which it does—then a student who is minimally competent must be a student who is at least minimally *critical*, not "functional" as narrowly construed. In so far as minimum competence is conceived in terms of narrow functional literacy, MCT is doomed to be an unjustifiable educational practice, since it would at best promote an educational scheme sorely lacking in attention to those aspects of a student's education that are crucial to the achievement of critical thinking.

It seems, then, the MCT is not unavoidably arbitrary. While first level arbitrariness may be unavoidable, second level arbitrariness may be avoided by appealing to philosophical considerations concerning the aims of education and the skills, abilities, knowledge and understanding, dispositions, and character traits of well-educated persons. This conclusion should provide little comfort to the proponents of MCT, however, for once we move to avoid second level arbitrariness, we are immediately confronted by the huge disparity between the conception of education offered by the ideal of critical thinking, and that embodied in MCT programs. For the latter, education is a matter of getting students to master the mechanics of linguistic and computational skills, and sufficient occupational skills for holding a place in the current economic order. For the former, education goes far beyond such considerations, by seeking to inculcate the skills, dispositions, habits of mind, and character traits constitutive of the critical thinker, and, therefore, the autonomy to control one's life and life-decisions. From the point of view of critical thinking, MCT is not arbitrary—it is rather colossally inadequate and indefensible—as educational practice, and as an embodiment of a serious conception of education.[25]

6 Philosophical ideals and educational practices

I have been arguing that MCT fails to deal seriously with or be informed by philosophical considerations concerning the aims of education and our conception of a well-educated person, and that, once these considerations are raised, MCT appears grossly inadequate as an educational practice. I have defended the ideal of critical thinking for the last several chapters, and in this chapter I have argued that MCT fails to measure up to that ideal. I hope, however, that the arguments of the present chapter have broader force, for I think that any defensible view of the aims of education would include features of critical thinking—skills of reasoning, appropriate habits of mind, autonomy, and self-sufficiency, for example—and that these features go far beyond the narrow conception of functional literacy tacitly adopted by MCT. Thus, MCT would be deficient from the point of view of *any* defensible view of the aims of education, not simply that of critical thinking. And, indeed, most of the criticisms of MCT offered above would stand independently of their connection with critical thinking.[26]

There is a final, larger point to be made, which concerns the role of philosophical considerations in establishing educational policies and practices. There is a great tendency on the part of policymakers and practitioners to shy away even from raising questions concerning the aims of education when considering policy and practice alternatives. This tendency is no doubt related to the often-noted fondness for fads education regularly exhibits. Fads are frowned upon primarily because they are not serious or well-founded. Neither, I want to suggest, are educational practices (like MCT) which fail meaningfully to raise questions regarding their own aims. What is it that we as educators are trying to accomplish? What would the ideally educated person be like? Without at least tentative answers to such questions in hand—ends-in-view, to use Dewey's phrase—which serve to guide educational practice, that practice is blind. Such questions demand careful philosophical reflection, and educational policy and practice will remain ineffective and inconstant until it is guided by such considerations. Thus, educational practice and philosophical reflection are wed. Without the guidance of the latter, the former can only be folly.

Nowhere is this more clear than with regard to MCT. As I have argued, MCT does not foster and is not compatible with critical thinking, or indeed with any defensible conception of the aims of education. I hope it is clear that MCT is simply one example illustrative of a more general point regarding the relation between educational policies and practices and philosophically informed educational ideals, for that general point involves all such policies and practices, not only MCT. And if the previous articulation and defense of the ideal of critical thinking is thought plausible, then the arguments of this chapter should suggest how brightly that ideal can illuminate the domain of educational policy and practice.

Towards a theory of rationality

The whole concept of argument ... rests upon the ideal of rationality—of discussion not in order to move or persuade, but rather to test assumptions critically by a review of *reasons* logically pertinent to them.[1]

1. Critical thinking, rationality, and the theory of rationality

There is, I have been arguing, an intimate connection between the notions of critical thinking and rationality. The former, I have suggested, is best thought of as the educational cognate of the latter; and to hold that critical thinking is a fundamental educational ideal is to hold that education ought ideally to foster the rationality of students. It is not clear to me that there is much more to be said about the notion of critical thinking as such, but there is very much more to be said about that of rationality.

Indeed, the theory of critical thinking—in so far as it involves more than the spelling out of the educational ramifications of an intellectual ideal—depends fundamentally on the theory of rationality. Theorists of critical thinking must perforce turn to the development of the theory of rationality, for it is that latter theory which undergirds the former one. To be a critical thinker, I have suggested, is to be appropriately moved by reasons. But what are reasons? How is their force determined and assessed? How do they justify beliefs and actions? Here what is called for is a philosophical, specifically epistemological, account of reasons and rationality. The theory of critical thinking must be deepened by a philosophical theory of rationality, and theorists of critical thinking can best pursue their theoretical activity by pursuing the theory of rationality.[2]

As it happens, the notion of rationality is a central focus of investigation throughout philosophy. In the philosophy of science, for example, much blood has been shed over the last three decades over the rationality of theory choice; the nature, and indeed the existence, of scientific method; and other, related questions involving the nature of the rationality of science.[3] Action theory has been concerned since its inception with the distinctive features of rational action. The relationship between rationality and morality, and the nature and force of moral reasons, have long been problems at the heart of moral theory. Rational decision theory, a domain which reaches beyond philosophy into economics, mathematics, and other disciplines, sees many philosophers struggling mightily over questions concerning the special nature of rational decisions, and of particular conundrums which raise those questions, e.g. the Prisoner's Dilemma and Newcomb's problem. Philosophy of religion has long been concerned to come to grips with the tension between reason and faith. And contemporary epistemology abounds with discussions of the nature of reasons and of justification, the relation (if any) between reason and truth, the extent (if any) to which human rationality can be studied empirically, and other issues centrally concerned with rationality. It seems fair to say that the notion of rationality constitutes a thread which runs through the entire domain of philosophy; and controversies surrounding that notion lay at the heart of contemporary as well as traditional philosophical problems. Insight into the nature of rationality thus promises to shed light in a variety of areas of philosophy—not just philosophy of education. Indeed, such insight seems to be required for progress on many philosophical problems, including those in the philosophy of education. Consequently, the development of a deeper understanding of the notion of rationality is a task which confronts virtually the whole of philosophy; a general theory of rationality is fundamental to philosophy. Such a theory is also basic to the further theoretical refinement of the notion of critical thinking, at least in so far as that notion is conceived, as I have, as the educational cognate of rationality.

2 Problems in the theory of rationality

I have already noted some problems with which theorists of rationality have been trying to cope: the nature of rational action and rational decision; the relationships between rationality and morality, reason and faith, justification and truth; the legitimacy of the special claim to rationality of science; and so on. I should like here to mention several other problems for the theory of rationality, problems that are especially relevant to the theory of critical thinking.

(A) The notion of rationality and the epistemology of reasons

The most basic problem, I suppose, concerns the exact constitution or conception of rationality. Of the many competing conceptions available, which is the most independently satisfactory, or the most satisfactory for the theory of critical thinking? For example, by far the most prevalent conception of rationality in the philosophical market-place is that of the rational person as a means-end reasoner, a maximizer of expected utility or of subjective preference. The idea here is simply that one determines what one wants, what one's ends or objectives are, or what the expected utility of the outcomes of the several options open to one are, based on one's subjective preference for the various possible outcomes; then one chooses so as to achieve most efficiently those ends, or to maximize utility or the satisfaction of preference. If one wants to get from point A to point B quickly, and route X is more likely to get one from A to B quickly than route Y, then it is rational to opt for route X. Similarly, if one's ends involve the achieving of a certain level of professional status, which in turn requires the unfair treatment of one's competitors, then, given those ends, the rational thing to do is to engage in the unfair treatment of one's competitors, for to do so is most efficiently to achieve one's ends.

Despite the widespread acceptance of this means-ends conception of rationality, and despite the obvious and important truth that efficiency is not unrelated to rationality, there are difficulties with this conception which render it problematic for several areas of philosophy, including philosophy of education and the theory of critical thinking.

The means-ends conception of rationality seems inappropriate for the study of the connection between rationality and morality, for example, for it abolishes both the distinction between morality and prudence and the possibility of specifically moral reasons. It may, for instance, be prudent for my career to assassinate falsely the character of a colleague who is my competitor for a single tenured slot in my department. Given my aim of achieving tenure, and the high degree of expected utility and subjective preference such achievement enjoys over its alternatives, it is surely rational on the means-ends conception to assail the character of my colleague, so long as it is indeed likely to enhance my chances of attaining tenure myself. But, however "rational" such character-assassination is in terms of its efficiency in gaining me tenure, its rationality is problematic in other ways. For one thing, it overlooks moral constraints on rational choice—it may be immoral for me to treat my colleague in this way, and if, as many philosophers have held, moral considerations are properly thought of as moral *reasons*, then, in ignoring those reasons I am not only immoral but *irrational* in so treating my colleague. Prudential reasons, in short, may not be the only sort of reasons there are. To the extent that the means-ends conception obliterates the distinction between prudential and moral reasons, then, it obscures the fundamental problem of the relationship between rationality and morality.[4]

The means-ends conception's denial of the distinction between prudence and morality, and so of the possibility that moral constraints on choice can constitute (non-prudential) reasons for choice, is problematic and more contentious than is generally realized. There is a further difficulty with the means-ends conception which renders it problematic for the clarification of the relationship between rationality and morality. The means-ends account takes ends as given, and judges rationality solely in terms of the efficiency of means in achieving ends. But we would do well to preserve the possibility of judging the rationality of our ends themselves, as well as the means to those ends. To consider our example further, my end is to attain tenure, even at the cost of unfairly ruining my colleague's career. Is it rational to have this as my end? Is it reasonable to regard tenure as *that* important? Aren't there reasons for regarding that end of mine as faulty, at least in the absence of other counterbalancing ends concerning the role of others in my life and the way they, and I, should be treated? The means-ends conception rules out such consideration, but it is not at all clear that such considerations, concerning the rationality of ends as well as means, should not be even possible on our best conception of rationality. In this regard, too, then, the means-ends conception seems a deficient conception of rationality.[5]

A similar difficulty renders the means-ends conception problematic for a proper understanding of the rationality of science as well. Most discussion of the problem of science's rationality takes for granted the unproblematic nature of the ends of scientific inquiry, and strives to understand the rationality of science strictly in terms of those (allegedly unproblematic) ends. If, for example, one takes the end of scientific inquiry to be the maximization of explanatory power, or the solving of problems, or the ability to predict or control nature, or the discovery of truth, then rational theory choice is a matter of choosing the theory that affords maximal explanatory power, or problem-solving ability, or predictive power, etc. But if these goals conflict, as they sometimes do, then the means-ends account will not help to determine the rationality of theory choice. Nor will it help settle disputes about the legitimacy of these several alternative putative goals of scientific inquiry. In short, the means-ends account of rationality, because of its inability to assess the rationality of ends, is inadequate for the resolution of outstanding questions regarding the rationality of science.[6]

I have been belaboring the weaknesses of the means-ends conception of rationality for the clarification of central problems concerning rationality with respect to moral theory and the philosophy of science. Most important in the present context, however, is the fact that the weaknesses with the means-ends account adumbrated thus far render it deficient as an account helpful for the development of the theory of critical thinking. First, it is clear that all *bona fide* reasons are relevant to the critical appraisal of belief and action, yet the means-ends conception threatens to rule out some sorts of reasons in favor of prudential or efficiency considerations. That "This is the most effective way to achieve my goal, or maximize my expected utility" is a perfectly respectable sort of reason I do not question. But it is important to see that it is not the only sort of reason there is, and that other sorts of reasons, e.g. "This course of action violates someone's rights," or "This way of operating fails to treat others with respect," are not only legitimate sorts of reasons themselves, but may in some instances override or outweigh the first sort of reason.[7] So too may considerations which challenge the rational legitimacy of one's ends; a reason like "The goal I am intent on pursuing is itself not rationally justifiable and (on the basis of reasons) should not be pursued" can also override the first sort of reason mentioned. In short, the theory of critical thinking and, more generally, of rationality, must both take into account the panoply of legitimate reasons and provide insight into their status as reasons, and also allow for the possibility of the rational evaluation of ends. The means-ends conception of rationality appears unable to do either.

A further weakness of the means-ends conception, at least in so far as critical thinking is concerned, is its inability to account for the values and character traits associated with the critical thinker, for those features of critical thinking cannot be accounted for in terms of the efficient orientation of means to ends. Rather, they specify or constitute ends, which enjoy rational justification but on bases other than that of the efficient achievement of (still other) ends. As argued earlier, the values and character traits of the critical thinker are absolutely central to a full conception of critical thinking; in so far as the means-ends conception is unable to account for these features of critical thinking, that conception of rationality is inadequate for the further development of the theory of critical thinking.

At a minimum, then, we need a better account of rationality than the means-ends account if we are to further our understanding of rationality and of the many philosophical problems which center on that notion. We need an account of rationality which recognizes various sorts of reasons and which provides insight into the nature and epistemic force of reasons, and which affords the possibility of the rational scrutiny of ends. We need, in short, a deeper conception of rationality than the means-ends conception, and an epistemology of reasons alongside it.

(B) The justification of rationality

Another problem for the theory of rationality which has implications for the theory of critical thinking concerns the justification of rationality itself. It is clear that, in order to justify a commitment to critical thinking, we must be committed to rationality and the value of reasons. How are that latter commitment and value themselves justified? Why, in short, should we be rational?

This is a classic philosophical problem. Some philosophers have held that the value of rationality is obvious; others, that rationality has positive disvalue and that we should strive not to be rational. Still others have held that the question is an illegitimate one; that the demand for a rational justification of the commitment to rationality is a bogus demand.[8] In my view, none of these putative solutions or objections succeed. The demand for justification is a legitimate one, if our commitment to rationality is not to be arbitrary. And if that commitment is to be justified, we must produce a non-question-begging reason for committing ourselves to rationality.

I believe that the demand can be met—that we can say why we should be rational.[9] A full answer would require another book, and would take us far afield, but briefly, we meet the demand by seeing that rationality is *self-justifying*. By this I mean that, in order seriously to question the worth of rationality, one must already be committed to it. For to ask "Why be rational?" is to ask for *reasons* for and against being rational; to entertain the question seriously is to acknowledge the force of reasons in ascertaining the answer. The very raising of the question, in other words, commits one to a recognition of the force of reasons. To recognize that force is straightaway to recognize the answer to the question: we should be rational because (for the reason that) reasons have force.[10]

This is of course just the barest bones of a full treatment of the question; *much* more needs to be said. This is as it should be, since the justification of rationality is perhaps the most basic problem which a full theory of rationality must face. Here I wish to urge two points: first, that the challenge can be met, in the manner indicated; second, that the challenge is fundamental to the theory and practice of critical thinking, for if we cannot say why we should be rational, we cannot justify efforts at fostering critical thinking.

(C) The limits of rationality

Yet another question which is basic to the theory of rationality and which has ramifications for the theory of critical thinking concerns the bounds, or limits, of rationality. Do reasons settle every question? Are we ever justified in "setting reasons aside"?

Here again we confront a fundamental and classic philosophical problem. Here again, full treatment of it would take us far afield and is not possible in the present context. However, I do want to urge that nothing said thus far commits us to the view that reasons can never be rightfully overriden—although when they can, it will typically be for other, more powerful reasons.

It does not follow from what has been said that we should engage in a mindless or slavish devotion to reason. It makes perfect sense to "shut reason off" and ignore the demands of reason in some circumstances—for example, in playing a musical instrument or when making love. This poses no problem for the theory of rationality or of critical thinking, I think, for what we have here are cases in which it is, we might say, "rational to be irrational"; that is, there are meta-reasons for ignoring object-level reasons. If my mental health requires me to take a break from paying attention to reasons, or if my piano-playing will benefit from ignoring reasons for striking a certain key at a certain time and rather playing "by feel" or automatically, or if my love-making will benefit in quality and intensity by "shutting my mind off," or if my performance as a soldier in battle, and my chances of survival, are likely to benefit from refraining from critically assessing the orders of my superior officer—these may all be good (meta-) reasons for ignoring reasons which are otherwise relevant to my beliefs and actions. In such cases reasons are ignored or set aside, but for good reason. Thus reason may rule the roost—we should be rational—without our becoming "rational automata," moved solely and slavishly by devotion to reasons, with no critical insight into our relationship to reasons at various levels. Such insight is not only possible and desirable; we should strive to make it a part of the equipment of the critical thinker/rational person. The critical thinker should, that is, be critical about being critical.[11]

(D) The alterability of principles of reason assessment[12]

As pointed out at the outset of chapter 2, there is a close connection between reasons and principles. One of the aims of a theory of rationality is the articulation and justification of principles by which reasons are assessed. Rationality presupposes principles which are general and impartial, and which can serve as criteria for the assessment of reasons. Such principles arise, however, in the context of the development of rational traditions; and as traditions evolve, principles governing the assessment of reasons in the traditions' domains evolve and change as well. (In chapter 3 I argued that one of the justifications for taking critical thinking to be a fundamental educational ideal is the centrality of education's task of initiating students into the rational traditions.)

The evolutionary character of these traditions appears to raise a problem for the theory of rationality. As Scheffler notes:

> rationality cannot be taken simply as an abstract and general ideal. It is embodied in *multiple evolving traditions*, in which the basic condition holds that issues are resolved by reference to *reasons*, themselves defined by *principles* purporting to be impartial and universal.[13]

The principles *purport* to be impartial and universal, and rational judgment is judgment which accords with extant principles "as crystallized at the time in question"[14] by and in the relevant tradition. Yet the principles by which reasons are defined and assessed themselves evolve and change as their defining traditions evolve and change, and they are differently formulated or "crystallized" at different evolutionary stages of their defining rational tradition. How, then, can principles serve to define and constitute criteria for the assessment of reasons—which definition and constitution both require that the principles purport to be and are taken to be impartial and universal—when principles must also be acknowledged to evolve and change? There appears to be a significant tension between the fact that principles evolve and change, on the one hand, and the requirement that they purport to be and are taken to be impartial and universal in order to fulfill their function of governing the definition and assessment of reasons within a rational tradition, on the other. If they evolve and change, how can they be impartial and universal? If impartial and universal, how can they change?

I suspect that the tension outlined is only apparent. Consider an analogy with biological evolution.[15] In order to survive, a species must occupy an ecological niche, and must meet the criteria for survival more fully than rival potential occupiers of that niche. Those criteria may change over time: one generation may need to avoid a particular predator, or digest certain foods, in order to succeed in that niche, while the next generation may face entirely different challenges which must be met in order to succeed. The criteria for survival change, yet those criteria, which are defined by the specific features of the niche and change as the character of the niche changes, apply impartially and universally to all potential occupiers of the niche: given the characteristics of this niche at this time, this is what (members of) a species must be able to do in order to survive here now. In this instance evolution and change are compatible with impartiality and universality.

Similar remarks apply, I think, regarding reasons, principles, and rational traditions. Principles embody rationality and define and assess reasons in a tradition at a time. As the tradition evolves, so do the principles which define and assess reasons. So what counts as a good reason in a tradition may change over time; today's compelling reason may be seen as less than compelling tomorrow—just as powerful jaws may aid survival, or slowness of foot condemn to extinction, in one generation but not in another. Still, the principles which determine the compellingness of reasons at a time apply to all putative reasons impartially and universally; moreover, such principles still serve to embody rationality. As time goes on, the qualities which secure evolutionary success for a species in a niche may change, for the character of the niche may change, but evolutionary success remains the same—survival and flourishing of the species. Similarly, as time goes on, the qualities which secure the legitimacy and force of reasons in a tradition may change, for the principles which define reasons and determine their force may change, but rationality remains the same—judgment and action in accord with reason, as determined by principles (which are themselves justified) crystallized at a time in a rational tradition.

I have no doubt that there is much more to be said, and that, as before, what I have offered here is the merest beginning of a solution to a pressing problem for the theory or rationality. Nevertheless, it appears that the principles which embody rationality in a tradition and define and assess the force of reasons in that tradition can be understood both to evolve and to purport to be impartial and universal. The alterability of principles of reasons assessment need not constitute an overwhelming difficulty for the theory of rationality.[16]

3 The theory of rationality and the theory of critical thinking

I have noted several problems in the theory of rationality which are directly relevant to the theory of critical thinking: the inadequacy of the means-ends conception of rationality and the need to develop a more adequate conception; the need for a full development of an epistemology of reasons; the problem of the justification of the commitment to rationality; the delineation of the limits of rationality; and the problematic nature of the alterability of principles of reason assessment. No doubt there are others. All of these problems are relevant to critical thinking and its theory. But they all far outstrip that theory, and must be pursued as independent philosophical problems with lives of their own, whose solutions are independent of their ramifications for critical thinking.

This suggests two facts about the theory of critical thinking. First, that theory is itself no philosophically deep, but rests upon the philosophical theory of rationality. Second, consequently, critical thinking theory and practice requires taking stances on, and certainly recognizing the importance of, deep philosophical questions.[17] (For example, our aspirations for critical thinking education will surely be affected by answers to questions concerning the limits of rationality, the justification of rationality, the alterability of principles of reason assessment, and the constitution of rationality itself.) This second fact is enormously important, I think, for theorists of critical thinking, for it means that they have no choice but to pursue these philosophical questions on their own merits. The theory of critical thinking cannot be conceived of as insulated from the broader philosophical context in which it is embedded.

This is of course not to say that that is all the critical thinking theorist must do. There are a host of empirical matters which require the expertise of psychologists, educators, and educational researchers, and such specialists are rightly welcomed into the community of critical thinking theorists.[18] There are, among these empirical matters, a subset of specifically pedagogical matters which outstrip philosophical expertise but are central to critical thinking activities.[19] There is of course more to critical thinking than philosophy (and vice versa). My point, however, is that the theory of critical thinking is ultimately dependent upon the philosophical theory of rationality and other philosophical matters, and that theorists of critical thinking do well to recognize that dependence and take up the pursuit of relevant philosophical matters as their own—or at least recognize the commonalities of purpose between themselves and philosophers independently pursuing such matters.

4 A concluding note

I close with an admission and with one final argument. Throughout this effort I have warily avoided pinning down precisely how important an educational ideal critical thinking is, by using "weasel words" such as "fundamental," "central," "basic," etc. Is critical thinking the *only* educational ideal? Is is *basic* in that it overrides other legitimate ideals? Is it simply one among many other equally legitimate ideals (e.g. creativity, or citizenship, or happiness)?

I have refrained from detailed examination of these questions, and have been content to establish that critical thinking is, at least, a very important educational ideal, one which must be given its due in educational deliberation and practice, and which educators wrongly downplay or ignore. I do not deny that other putative ideals ought also to have a role in shaping educational affairs.

My final (transcendental) argument, however, is for the proposition that critical thinking is, at a minimum, "first among equals" in the pantheon of educational ideals. Why should critical thinking be the ultimate, if not the only, educational ideal? Consider a case in which that ideal conflicts with some legitimate other. In such a case, one might argue that the other should override critical thinking in this instance. And perhaps so it should. But it requires rational argument, and appeal to reason, in order to make the case for the preferability of the rival ideal to that of critical thinking. And such appeal is, of course, an appeal to, and an honoring of, the latter ideal itself. Consequently, an overriding of critical thinking by a rival educational ideal at one level requires acknowledgment of the reign of critical thinking at the next highest level. In this way critical thinking must preside over and authorize the force of its rivals. In so far, critical thinking is rightfully seen as first among equals, or, more dramatically, as the ultimate educational ideal. It must be seen so for reasons which parallel those which secure the place of rationality at the head of intellectual ideals more generally.

Notes

Introduction

1 Scheffler, *Reason and Teaching*, p. 1.

2 As J. Anthony Blair has forcefully pointed out to me, it is misleading to speak of the Informal Logic Movement as a monolithic group with universally shared viewpoints. On the contrary, philosophers who identify themselves with the Movement differ widely on virtually every matter of group interest. Indeed, the very identification of the Movement and its members is problematic. Roughly, I have in mind those persons who: read the journal *Informal Logic*; before to the Association for Informal Logic and Critical Thinking (AILACT), which is affiliated with the American Philosophical Association; attend conferences on critical thinking and/or informal logic held periodically at Sonoma State University, the University of Windsor, and elsewhere; and teach courses in informal logic and/or critical thinking. The diversity of opinion among such a wide collection of persons is, I agree with Blair, very great. Nevertheless, some generalizations, such as the ones which appear in this paragraph, seem to me appropriate.

3 Paul, "An Agenda Item for the Informal Logic/Critical Thinking Movement," p. 24.

4 It is perhaps worth noting that there is nothing necessary about the connection between the Informal Logic Movement's defining characteristic—a preference for informal rather than formal techniques—and a pedagogical concern regarding critical thinking. One can, for example, be an enthusiastic proponent of the educational goal of improving students' reasoning ability without having an opinion as to the relative merits of formal versus informal methods of argument analysis. Indeed, it seems a good bet that most of the members of the various educational, political, and public policy commissions and groups calling for increased emphasis on the development of reasoning abilities are blithely unaware of what is, after all, a relatively arcane professional dispute amongst logicians. Similarly, one can have strong opinions as to the relative merits of formal versus informal techniques without ever considering the educational advantages of couching "everyday reasoning" in formal or informal terms—that is, one can be an enthusiastic proponent of formal or informal techniques for a variety of reasons, none of which

need have anything to do with educational or pedagogical concerns. There is therefore no reason why members of the Movement must perforce construe it as an educational movement which speaks to practical educational matters. Nevertheless, many do. To cite just one more example of this attitude, Blair and Johnson, in their influential volume which for all intents and purposes inaugurated the Movement, offer as one of the attitudes which might be shared by many members of the Movement the following: "An orientation that treats the teaching of reasoning skills as a key part of education, integral ... to preparation of youth for responsible social and political roles." J. Anthony Blair and Ralph H. Johnson, 'Introduction', in Blair and Johnson, eds, *Informal Logic: The First International Symposium,* p. x.

Chapter 1 Three conceptions of critical thinking

1 I. Scheffler, *Reason and Teaching*, p. 22, emphasis in original.
2 Scheffler, *op. cit.*, pp. 142–3.
3 R.H. Ennis, "A Concept of Critical Thinking."
4 Ennis, *op. cit.*, p. 83.
5 Ennis notes in this paper (p. 85), as he does in his later papers, that a complete set of criteria for critical thinking cannot be established, and that "intelligent judgment" is also required.
6 And, as noted earlier, the "intelligent judgment" required for correct assessment.

Ennis has pointed out to me (in correspondence) that it is possible to read his 1962 paper in a way which avoids the objection just noted. In analyzing critical thinking as the correct assessment of statements, Ennis need not commit himself to the view that a person with the ability to assess statements correctly is thereby a critical thinker. All he is committed to, rather, is (as he puts it) that "someone who has the ability to assess statements correctly has the ability to think critically." On this reading of his paper—which Ennis endorses—it is a mistake to interpret his 1962 account of critical thinking as a "pure skills" account; rather, that account is a "pure skills" account of the *ability* to think critically. Actually being a critical thinker then goes beyond having the requisite skills, and involves the utilization of those skills.

I happily concede Ennis's point. While it should be noted that the 1962 paper does not explicitly discuss either the tendency to utilize skills or the actual utilization of skills (and so my characterization of the 1962 position as a "pure skills" position seems to me justified by the text), Ennis is right that his earlier position is compatible with what I call below the "skills plus tendencies" position, according to which actually *being* a critical thinker involves both having the requisite skills *and* utilizing them. The point is perhaps only of secondary interest, since (as discussed below) in his later writings Ennis explicitly adopts the "skills plus tendencies" view, and so explicitly rejects the "pure skills" view I have attributed to his 1962 piece. In any case I am grateful to Ennis for his help in clarifying my thinking on this (and many other) matter(s).

7 More exactly, who assess statements relevant to such actions as buying cars and voting for politicians poorly, as judged by the criteria for correct assessment which Ennis articulates. The relation between critical thought and critical action is of course contentious, though I am inclined to go along with Ennis (who in turn goes along with Max Black) in denying a sharp separation between theoretical and practical reasoning. Cf. Ennis, "A Conception of Rational Thinking," p. 4.

8 Ennis, *op. cit.*, p. 17; also Ennis, "Rational Thinking and Educational Practice," p. 182.

9 Ennis, "A Conception of Rational Thinking," p. 17; also "Rational Thinking and Educational Practice," p. 182.

10 Cf. Ennis, "Problems in Testing Informal Logic/Critical Thinking/Reasoning Ability."

11 In fairness to Ennis it must be noted that the task appears daunting; moreover, ethical considerations (involving consent, subject awareness, right to privacy, etc.) may impinge upon the testing for the tendency in ways which do not hamper testing for the proficiencies. Nevertheless, anyone familiar with the complexity of testing for the proficiencies will recognize that difficulty will not distinguish the two sorts of testing; in any case, difficulty has not stopped Ennis before. Inquiry into testing for the tendency, furthermore, is not sufficiently advanced for confident judgment regarding either the avoidability or the seriousness of possible ethical objections to such testing.

12 As Perry Weddle has pointed out to me, it is perhaps more reflective of the limitations of the process of paper-pencil testing than of Ennis's conception of critical thinking that his work on devising critical thinking tests has focussed much more heavily on proficiencies and skills than on tendencies and dispositions. I suspect that Weddle is right about this, although I think that the dearth of effort in constructing tests for tendencies makes the judgment premature.

13 Ennis, "Rational Thinking and Educational Practice," p. 165.

The reader will have noted by now my sliding back and forth between the locutions "critical thinking" and "rational thinking." In chapter 2 I argue that "critical thinking" is best regarded as the *educational cognate* of "rational thinking," because critical thinking is simply thinking (and acting) which is appropriately moved by reasons. In this note I wish only to sort out Ennis's use of the two terms. Ennis's working group was originally called the "Illinois Critical Thinking Project," but, as Ennis explains at the outset of his "A Conception of Rational Thinking" (p. 3), the group felt this to be limiting, since it regarded "critical thinking" as denoting solely the evaluation or assessment of statements (as Ennis defined it in "A Concept of Critical

Thinking"). Project members found themselves studying other thinking-related phenomena, such as observing, inferring, and so on, and, seeking to include these "contributory thinking activities" ("A Conception of Rational Thinking," p. 3) into their conceptualization of their work, which they saw as involving good thinking and rational action—and so as broader than the assessment of statements—they renamed the group the Illinois Rational Thinking Project (*ibid.*). At this point, then, Ennis used "critical thinking" to refer to statement assessment, and "rational thinking" to refer to the entire panoply of activities constitutive of good thinking and rational action. Notice that on this delineation of the two terms, critical thinking does not, but rational thinking does, include the tendency to utilize proficiencies.

More recently, however, Ennis has grown less enchanted by this treatment of the two terms. In his "Problems in Testing Informal Logic/Critical Thinking/Reasoning Ability," he remarks that he "use[s] the terms 'critical thinking' and 'informal logic' and 'reasoning' roughly interchangeably as labels for an area of concern" (p. 3); and in his "Goals for a Critical-Thinking/Reasoning Curriculum" he offers as a working definition of thinking critically "reasonably going about deciding what to believe and do" (p. 1), and as involving both competencies and tendencies. He here thus broadens his conception of critical thinking to include what he earlier regarded as constitutive of rational, but not critical, thinking. And in a footnote (p. 5) he explicitly acknowledges this point: "The term: 'rational thinking,' as used in [Rational Thinking and Educational Practice] is what I mean here by 'critical thinking/reasoning'. In deference to popular usage and theoretical considerations as well, *I have abandoned the more narrow appraisal-only sense of 'critical thinking' that I earlier advocated*" (emphasis added).

Thus in my sliding back and forth in the text between "critical thinking" and "rational thinking," I am simply reflecting Ennis's own collapsing of the two terms. As noted, in chapter 2 I explicitly address the relationship between critical thinking and rationality, and argue that the former is best understood as the educational cognate of the latter.

14 While Ennis is clearly concerned to incorporate dispositions into his conception of critical thinking, his recent "working definition" of critical thinking as "reasonable reflective thinking that is focussed on deciding what to believe and do" ("A Conception of Critical Thinking—With Some Curriculum Suggestions," p. 14; "Taxonomy of Critical Thinking Dispositions and Abilities," p. 10) fails to capture the dispositional nature of critical thinking, for I might reasonably and reflectively go about deciding (and on that basis decide) what do believe or do, yet fail to believe or do it. Unless deciding to do A automatically results in the doing of A—a dubious proposition, which has been largely discredited since Aristotle's criticism of Plato's articulation of it—the dispositional

character of critical thinking cannot be analyzed as a matter of deciding, however reasonable the decision. I believe that the "reasons" conception of critical thinking to be developed in the next chapter handles this problem, by making critical thinking a function, not of deciding to believe or act, but rather of actually believing or acting; that is, of being (appropriately) *moved* to belief or action by reasons.

15 Because of the close conceptual link between critical thinking and rationality (which I urge in chapter 2), justifying critical thinking as an educational ideal indirectly involves the justification of rationality. "Why Be Rational?" is one of philosophy's oldest questions, and it must be answered if the justification of critical thinking is to succeed. I address this matter in the Postscript. Ennis raises the question briefly ("A Conception of Rational Thinking," p. 26), but does not attempt to answer it. He hints at how he might answer it elsewhere, in terms of "the works of the world's great philosophers, the legal tradition, and the progressive development of the methodology of disciplines organized for the pursuit of knowledge" ("Rational Thinking and Educational Practice," p. 146, note 1), but this just re-raises the question, and does not answer it.

16 Ennis, "A Conception of Rational Thinking," p. 5.

One might also ask where Ennis's criteria for determining the rationality of given pieces of reasoning come from, and how they are themselves justified. To ask these questions is to point out the need, for Ennis's project, for an underlying conception of rationality. (This need is pointed out by Nel Noddings in her response to Ennis's paper (Noddings, "Response to Ennis," pp. 31–2).) My own view is that they stem from and are justified by epistemological considerations; that is, from the theory of evidence, which in this context may be thought of as the theory of good reasons. This view is connected, of course, to the "reasons" conception of critical thinking, presented in chapter 2. (Ennis's lists of proficiencies should then be seen as lists of (types of) good reasons.) On this view, the theory of critical thinking rests ultimately upon epistemology. This is discussed further in the Postscript; cf. also my "Educating Reason: Critical Thinking, Informal Logic, and the Philosophy of Education. Part Two: Philosophical Questions Underlying Education for Critical Thinking."

17 *Ibid.*

18 Paul's account rests heavily on empirical claims regarding the typical student and her psychology, the effect of "atomistic" critical thinking instruction, etc. While I do not belabor the point below, it seems worth noting Paul's reliance on these empirical claims, many of which have not been subjected to empirical testing. I am grateful to Stephen Norris for correspondence concerning this point.

It also seems worthwhile to underline at this point the motivational force for Paul's theorizing provided by his underlying practical, pedagogical concerns. For this suggestion I am grateful to Brad Bowen.

19 R.W. Paul, "Teaching Critical Thinking in the 'Strong' Sense: A Focus on Self-Deception, World Views, and a Dialectical Mode of Analysis," p. 3, emphasis in original.

20 *Ibid.*

21 *Ibid.*

22 Notice that Ennis's list of proficiencies is made up of "atoms" very much like standard lists of fallacies. For example, Ennis's consideration of when one should accept the opinion of expert authority is a refinement of standard treatments of the fallacy of appeal to authority. So Paul's challenge of "atomic" approaches to critical thinking challenges Ennis's approach as much as it does standard "fallacies" approaches.

23 *Ibid.*, emphasis Paul's. Note that Paul, like Ennis, here connects critical thinking with rationality. The nature of this connection will be considered explicitly in the next chapter.

24 *Ibid.*

25 By this I mean that the relativistic implications of Paul's discussion of "world views" (which are exposed and criticized below) are not a necessary component of the "strong sense" conception of critical thinking. The heart of the strong sense conception is the Socratic dictum, central to Paul's analysis, regarding the importance of knowing oneself and critically examining one's own basic beliefs and presuppositions. This essential component of the strong sense view is easily articulated without recourse to talk of world views—as Socrates showed. So in criticizing Paul's discussion of world views, I do not mean to be criticizing the strong sense conception in general. On the contrary, I endorse that conception. But I believe it is better to articulate it without recourse to talk of world views. It is the relativistic implication of talk of world views which I am claiming is unnecessary to the satisfactory presentation of Paul's strong sense conception of critical thinking. I am grateful to Perry Weddle and Denis Phillips for conversation/correspondence on this point.

26 In commenting on this passage, Paul has emphasized the distinction between a bit of reasoning's *being* fallacious and its being *seen as* fallacious. In conversation he has assured me that his view is not the relativistic one that criteria are relative to world view, but rather that such criteria, which he takes to be world view neutral, are *applied* by actual persons from the perspective of their world view. Thus relativity to world view is a property, not of criteria of critical thinking, but of the application of such criteria. I welcome this clarification of Paul's view, and welcome its rejection of relativism with respect to the epistemological issue of the status of criteria of evaluation of reasoning and claims.

Paul distinguishes (as I do) between the philosophical question "Are the standards of reason assessment world view neutral?" and the psychological question "Can persons escape or transcend their world views and *apply* such standards neutrally?" His answer to the first question is "Yes." His answer to the second is "It is difficult, and perhaps impossible, to do so." In his own writing he is mainly concerned with facilitating critical thinking in actual persons, and so is concerned to focus attention on the psychological difficulty many people have in transcending or gaining a critical perspective on their own world views. To the extent that his relativistic-sounding remarks concern the application of criteria rather than the criteria themselves. Paul should not be considered an epistemological relativist—the sort of relativist I criticize below. Paul's writing does suggest (to me least) a relativist stance, however; this reflects (I think) his deep concern for the psychology of actual reasoning, as opposed to my primarily epistemological concern. (We obviously differ on the extent to which the two can be separated.) My hope is that the present discussion will prod Paul to clarify in print his stands on relativism, and on the relationship between psychology and epistemology in the theory of critical thinking.

As always, I have learned a lot from discussions on these matters with Paul, and I am grateful to him for conversation concerning the issues considered here.

27 For discussion of the parallel issue with respect to Kuhn and the evaluation of "paradigms," cf. my "Objectivity, Rationality, Incommensurability, and More."

28 Further discussion of relativism may be found in chapter 4. A systematic analysis of epistemologial relativism and its difficulties is offered in my *Relativism Refuted: A Critique of Contemporary Epistemological Relativism.*

29 Though not all are convinced that a notion of critical thinking relativized to world view or "form of life" is untenable. For consideration of this question with special attention to Kuhn and Wittgenstein, cf. my exchange with Jon Fennell and Rudy Liveritte, full references to which can be found in my "Rationality, Talking Dogs, and Forms of Life."

Paul claims (in conversation) to reject both absolutism and relativism. It is difficult to see how this is possible, however, at least if they are taken in their usual philosophical meanings, to be not simply contraries but contradictories. Cf. my *Relativism Refuted.*

30 The criteria are to be thought of in this way, of course, only in so far as they are sanctioned as legitimate by the theory of critical thinking (actually, the theory of rationality). I make no claims here about the legitimacy of the putative criteria mentioned in the text, although I strongly suspect that they are legitimate criteria of world view appraisal and would be sanctioned by the theory of rationality. Fallibilism towards that latter theory requires that we keep open the possibility of criticizing the very criteria of legitimate criticism we utilize. If the

argument in the text is correct, though, some such "atomistic" criteria will be sanctioned by the theory, simply because of the necessity of avoiding the relativistic implications of the absence of such criteria. Indeed, fallibilism—the thesis that all our knowledge-claims are open to revision and are possibly mistaken—is itself best thought of as a particularly important requirement ("atomistic" criterion) of the theory of rationality, which is itself fallible but is very strongly sanctioned by our best efforts at articulating the theory of rationality. It is a cornerstone of contemporary epistemology. I am grateful to Dennis Rohatyn for pointing out to me the need for this note.

31 Indeed Paul himself seems to embrace it when, in a critical thinking research assignment (described in Paul, *op. cit.*, p. 6) he asks his students to "Give good reasons for rejecting and/or accepting whatever aspects of the two world views [being considered] you reject or accept," thus suggesting that one can offer atomistic appraisal of world views. However he confounds matters by suggesting that "good reasons" are themselves relative to world views when he continues his directions in this way: "Make clear to the reader how your position reflects your world view." In another paper, "Critical Thought Essential to the Acquisition of Rational Knowledge and Passions," Paul more clearly seems to embrace the second option, rejecting relativism and acknowledging atomistic appraisals of world views. He writes: "There is only one way to test whole frames of reference without begging the question and that is by setting them dialectically against each other. By this I mean that the logical strength of one must be tested against the logical strength of the contending others, by appeal to standards not peculiar to either" (pp. 2–3). This last sentence clearly rejects relativism. But what constitutes the "logical strength" of a frame of reference or world view? The only criterion Paul offers here (though it is entirely in keeping with the others mentioned in the text) is that of "answering the objections framed from the opposing point of view" (*ibid.*). Non-question-begging assessment of the ability of a point of view to do this requires taking this criterion as a non-framework-relative, atomistic criterion.

32 I should note that my discussion has neglected Paul's emphasis on the importance of *reciprocity*, that is of sympathetically entering into the world view of one's "opponent." I agree with Paul concerning the importance of reciprocity in critical thinking, and the importance of encouraging it in critical thinking education. But reciprocity will not solve the epistemological problem concerning relativism. For having sympathetically entered into another world view, the critical thinker must still appraise the adequacy of the world view she has sympathetically entered into, at which point the question about the status of criteria of evaluation of world views is raised anew.

I hope it is clear that I am not claiming that Paul is in fact committed to relativism; as the preceding notes suggest, he is not. My point is simply that his characterization of critical thinking in terms of "world views" needlessly suggests an objectionable relativism.

33 Paul, "Teaching Critical Thinking in the 'Strong' Sense," p. 5, emphasis in original.

34 R. Paul, "Critical Thinking: Fundamental to Education for a Free Society," p. 5.

35 "Naive falsificationism" is the view that a hypothesis is conclusively falsified—shown to be false—by a single bit of negative evidence. According to this view, one wrong prediction forces the rejection of the hypothesis or theory on which the prediction is based. The view is widely regarded as untenable by philosophers of science, for several reasons. First, no experimental or observational result is sacrosanct. A bit of putatively negative evidence may turn out to be only *apparently* negative. Second, given negative evidence, it is often not clear which of a series of hypotheses is the refuted one. In fact, on at least one influential view, there is no fact of the matter as to which hypothesis is falsified by "recalcitrant experience," and the scientist always has considerable latitude in deciding which hypothesis to "blame" for the failed prediction. (This view is widely associated with Quine, and is related to the famous "Duhem-Quine Thesis" according to which hypotheses, to paraphrase Quine, "face the tribunal of experience not singly but only as a corporate body.") Finally, the history of science is full of examples of scientists who stubbornly maintained their theories in the face of negative evidence, only to be vindicated in the end. The literature here is vast. For examples of the last sort of case mentioned, cf. my "Brown on Epistemology and the New Philosophy of Science," p.80. The general point to be noted is that it is far from easy to distinguish legitimate, reason-based acceptance/rejection of hypotheses from illegitimate, uncritical acceptance/rejection, and it is doubtful that the notions of egocentrism, sociocentrism, and self-deception will be useful in drawing the distinction.

36 This criticism, which assumes the legitimacy of distinguishing between the nature of critical thinking and the pedagogy of teaching for critical thinking, raises the perennial philosophical problem of the relation between theory and practice. This problem is considered, in connection with the philosophy of education, in my "The Future and Purpose of Philosophy of Education" and "How 'Practical' Should Philosophy of Education Be?" I say a bit more about the pitfalls of conflating the epistemology with the pedagogy of critical thinking towards the end of my "Educating Reason: Critical Thinking, Informal Logic, and the Philosophy of Education. Part Two: Philosophical Questions Underlying Education for Critical Thinking."

37 Paul, "Critical Thinking: Fundamental to Education for a Free Society," p. 5, emphasis added.

38 I am grateful to conversation and correspondence with Ralph Johnson and Stephen Norris regarding Paul's conception of critical thinking. Of course the analysis of Paul's conception offered above is my responsibility alone.

39 J.E. McPeck, *Critical Thinking and Education.*

40 *Ibid.*, p. 3.

41 *Ibid.*, p. 5.

42 *Ibid.*, p. 4.

43 Cf. Stephen P. Norris's excellent discussion of this issue in his "The Choice of Standard Conditions in Defining Critical Thinking Competence", and similar criticism in Richard Paul's, Perry Weddle's and Trudy Govier's reviews of McPeck's book.

44 McPeck, "Response to H. Siegel," p. 74, emphasis in original.

45 As Trudy Govier has pointed out, logicians generally do not claim that logic is sufficient for argument evaluation. So McPeck may be after a straw opponent here. Of course, were anyone seriously to hold that logic is sufficient, McPeck would be entirely in the right in countering that subject-specific information is generally also necessary for argument assessment. Cf. Govier, Review of John E. McPeck, *Critical Thinking and Education*, p. 172.

46 "Response to H. Siegel," p. 75, emphasis in original.

47 McPeck, *Critical Thinking and Education*, p. 6.

48 *Ibid.*, p. 7, emphasis in original.

49 *Ibid.*, pp. 7–8.

50 *Ibid.*, p. 8.

51 *Ibid.*, p. 8.

52 *Ibid.*, p. 9.

53 *Ibid.*, p. 9. This makes clear McPeck's idea that critical thinking is not general, but is subject-, field-, or area-*specific.*

54 As Passmore puts it, a critical thinker "must be alert to the possibility that the established norms themselves ought to be rejected, that the rules ought to be changed, the criteria used in judging performances modified." "On Teaching To Be Critical," p. 197.

55 *Ibid.*, p. 13.

56 The "reasons" conception of critical thinking will be presented in more detail in chapter 2. I should note that Robert W. Binkley also holds something like this two-part conception of critical thinking/good reasoning. Cf. his "Can the Ability to Reason Well Be Taught?"

57 McPeck, *op. cit.*, p. 19. Cf. also pp. 17–18.

58 *Ibid.*, p. 22.

59 *Ibid.*, p. 22.

60 *Ibid.*, p. 23.

61 In correspondence, McPeck assures me that he claims not that logic is *always* irrelevant to reason assessment, but only that it is *largely* or *mostly* irrelevant. This is, at least as far as I am concerned, a welcome

clarification. As McPeck points out, simply showing that logic is *sometimes* relevant to reason assessment is not sufficient to justify general critical thinking courses. But in this circumstance the justification of such courses rests clearly on empirical information: how frequently logical knowledge is useful in reason assessment; how generalizable it is; how easy it is for students to pick up such knowledge elsewhere, etc. It is clear that McPeck thinks that such knowledge is not so useful as to justify such courses, and that educational intervention whose purpose is the improvement of critical thinking ability is better aimed at the improvement of traditional subject instruction by placing more emphasis on the epistemology of each subject, etc. But the difference here between McPeck and the defender of general critical thinking courses can be resolved, I think, by finding out how useful such courses are. Various members of the Informal Logic Movement (perhaps most especially Ennis) are engaged in just that task, and in the allied project of using information regarding critical thinking testing in order to design courses which do a better job of imparting critical thinking skills. So far as I am aware, McPeck has offered no empirical support for his claim that critical thinking courses are less useful than other sorts of educational interventions. Moreover, it must be pointed out that the empirical claim McPeck makes does, perhaps despite his intentions, often appear in his book in the guise of an *a priori* necessary truth concerning the nature of critical thinking (cf., e.g., the citation at note 59 above).

62 My indefiniteness here simply reflects the fact that *any* role for logic in reason assessment is sufficient to undermine McPeck's strong claim that logic is entirely irrelevant to reason assessment, and so to critical thinking. To the extent (however great) that logic is relevant to reason assessment, to that extent standard informal/critical thinking courses which seek to impart knowledge of and skill in logic are not misconceived, contrary to McPeck's charge against the standard informal logic/critical thinking course.

63 The two distinctions McPeck draws are closely related; logic is to be distinguished from critical thinking precisely because it is not logic, but (subject-specific) information, which is relevant to reason assessment. They are of a piece. Nevertheless, it serves clarification more fully to separate the distinctions and discuss them in turn.

64 McPeck, *op. cit.*, p. 23.

65 *Ibid.*, p. 28.

66 *Ibid.*, p. 56.

67 *Ibid.*, p. 64.

68 *Ibid.*, pp. 23–4.

69 It is worth noting that the stronger claim undermines McPeck's own efforts, for McPeck is offering reasons for his view of critical thinking. To what specialized field are these reasons assigned? What specialized,

technical knowledge is necessary for their proper evaluation? It appears
that McPeck's account of critical thinking is just the sort that that
account itself holds to be impossible—that is, a general, subject- or
field-neutral account. It thus undercuts itself. This point is briefly
returned to in chapter 2. Govier notes it as well in her review of
McPeck's book, p. 173.

70 *Ibid.*, p. 12, emphasis in original.
71 *Ibid.*, p. 13.
72 I. Scheffler, *Conditions of Knowledge*, p. 107. Further discussion both
of Scheffler's work and of the relation between critical thinking and
rationality may be found in chapter 2.
73 L. Laudan, *Progress and Its Problems*, p. 123. Critical discussion of
Laudan's application of this point to the problem of the rationality of
science may be found in my "Truth, Problem Solving and the
Rationality of Science."

Chapter 2 The reasons conception

1 L. Laudan, *Progress and Its Problems*, p. 123.
2 I. Scheffler, *Reason and Teaching*, p. 62, emphasis in original. Cf. also
Popper's remarks on the "attitude of reasonableness," in *The Open
Society and Its Enemies*, Volume 2, p. 225.
3 N. Burbules, "A Theory of Power in Education," p. 113, emphasis in
original.
4 I. Scheffler, *Conditions of Knowledge*, p. 107. Cf. also Scheffler,
Reason and Teaching, pp. 62-3. It should already be apparent, though
it will become even more so as we proceed, that the theory of critical
thinking thus rests ultimately on the theory of rationality. This point
will be pursued further in the Postscript.
5 Throughout I should be taken to mean that the critical thinker accepts
the convicting force of *good* reasons, i.e. of reasons which actually have
convicting force and which warrant conviction. I have not added
"good" before each occurrence of "reason," because I take it to be
implied by "appropriate" in "appropriately moved by reasons." To be
appropriately moved is to be moved to just the extent that the reasons
in question warrant. I am grateful to several correspondents, especially
Emily Robertson, for suggesting this clarification.
6 R.S. Peters, "Reason and Habit: The Paradox of Moral Education,"
p. 248, bracketed phrase added. Cf. also Peters, *Reason and
Compassion*.
7 I. Scheffler, "Philosophical Models of Teaching," p. 76, emphasis in
original. I would add to this conception of the rational person only that
the principles freely chosen themselves admit of rational justification.
Cf. *op. cit.*, p. 79.
8 As Peters says, "Reason ... is the anthithesis of arbitrariness" (*Reason
and Compassion*, p. 77); as Scheffler puts it, "Reason stands always in

contrast with inconsistency and with expediency" ("Philosophical Models of Teaching," p. 76).

9 Any view which rejects such standards is thus incompatible with critical thinking. For further discussion, cf. chapter 4. Articulating and justifying the standards are tasks for the theory of rationality (cf. Postscript). The point now being argued in the text is simply that critical thinking and rationality require, and so presuppose, such standards; this requirement in turn helps to delineate what is to count as critical and/or rational thinking.

10 Of course it may be the case that one sort *is* more important educationally, either because one sort is more utilized in the life of a critical thinker, or is more difficult to master, and so on. Here it seems clear that the matter can be settled only empirically. Cf. further discussion in chapter 1.

11 J.E. McPeck, *Critical Thinking and Education*, for example, pp. 22–4 and 155–7.

12 *Op. cit.*, p. 157.

13 *Op. cit.*, p. 155.

14 *Ibid.* I suspect that the problem McPeck faces here stems in part from his view that the goodness of reasons is "discovered" by "collective human experience" (*ibid.*), as if justification is a "natural fact" about the world, rather than something established by epistemological argument. But I cannot pursue the point here. Critical discussion of "naturalized epistemology" may be found in my "Justification, Discovery and the Naturalizing of Epistemology," and my "Empirical Psychology, Naturalized Epistemology, and First Philosophy."

15 It is worth noting that these difficulties with McPeck's discussion of "the epistemology of the subject" stem, at least in part, from his uncritical acceptance of Stephen Toulmin's views on field-dependence. McPeck cites Toulmin (*op. cit.*, pp. 32–3, 79–80) to the effect that criteria of argument assessment are intra-, not inter-field; but fails to consider the obvious self-reflexive question regarding the generality or field-specificity of the criteria by which Toulmin's claim is itself to be evaluated. I believe that McPeck is far too uncritical of Toulmin's views on logic, rationality, and epistemology. For critical discussion of McPeck's appeal to Toulmin, cf. Govier's review of McPeck's book, pp. 171–2; for critical discussion of Toulmin's most recent foray into the area of critical thinking/informal logic, cf. Ralph Johnson's thorough review, "Toulmin's Bold Experiment"; for consideration of Toulmin's views on rationality and epistemology, cf. my "Truth, Problem Solving and the Rationality of Science." I am grateful to Dennis Rohatyn for discussion of McPeck's use of Toulmin.

The sort of generality which I am here arguing is necessary for a satisfactory account of the relationship between epistemology and critical thinking is analogous to Walton's and Woods' demands for generality in the theory of fallacy. Cf. Blair and Johnson's "Introduction," in their *Informal Logic: The First International Symposium*, regarding Walton's and Woods' papers.

16 It should be clear that I am not here attempting to formulate specific principles of reason assessment. Many philosophers, informal logicians, and critical thinking theorists have done a far better job of articulating such principles than I could hope to do. My aim has rather been to say something about the place of such principles in a general conception of critical thinking.

17 On the relation between rationality and character, cf. Scheffler, *Reason and Teaching*, pp. 28, 64, and *passim*; also Scheffler, "In Praise of the Cognitive Emotions," p. 142 and *passim*.

18 I am assuming here that it is possible that reasons and self-interest might conflict, and so that a thoroughgoing rational egoism is impossible—that is, that acting immorally is contrary to reason. The question of the relation between rationality and morality is an old and deep one. I cannot raise it here, although I briefly mention it in the Postscript. I offer some reasons for the assumption noted in "Is It Irrational to Be Immoral? A Response to Freeman," and "Rationality, Morality, and Rational Moral Education: Further Response to Freeman." I am grateful to Emily Robertson for correspondence on this point.

19 R. Binkley, "Can the Ability to Reason Well Be Taught?" p. 83. Further insightful discussion of critical spirit may be found in Passmore, "On Teaching To Be Critical"; also in Paul, "Critical Thinking: Fundamental to Education for a Free Society."

Scheffler notes, in *The Language of Education*, chapter 5, a systematic failure to distinguish, in curricular contexts, between what he calls "norm-acquisition" and "skill-acquisition," which results in a failure to recognize that we often want our students to develop, not just skills and abilities, but dispositions and habits of mind and action:

> we talk of "citizenship" as if it were a set of skills, whereas our educational aim is, in fact, not merely to teach people *how* to be good citizens but, in particular, to *be* good citizens, not merely *how* to go about voting, but *to* vote. We talk about giving them "the skills required for democratic living," when actually we are concerned that they acquire democratic habits, norms, propensities. To take another example, *we talk of giving pupils the "ability to think critically" when what we really want is for them to acquire the habits and norms of critical thought*. (pp. 98–9, last emphasis added).

Here, in a nutshell, is why it is necessary to incorporate a critical spirit component (along with a reason assessment component) into a full conception of critical thinking. We want students to *be*, and be *disposed* to be—not just be *able* to be—critical thinkers.

20 Notice that the attitudes, dispositions, habits of mind, and character traits constitutive of the critical spirit are general and subject-neutral. The disposition to demand reasons, for example, is the same whether one is demanding reasons for a claim in physics, photography or philosophy. Thus the critical spirit offers a variety of characteristics of critical thinking which are general, and so stand as counter-examples to McPeck's claim that features of critical thinking are uniformly subject-specific. I am grateful to Robert Floden for pointing this out to me.

21 Another time-honored distinction which needs to be exploded is that between critical and creative thinking. The relationship between critical thinking and creativity is a complex one, but it is not one of mutual exclusion. The critical thinker, for example, needs to be creative in developing reasons, arguments, examples, etc., as well as critical in assessing those creations. While I cannot argue the point in any detail here, I would suggest that critical thinking involves creativity, and that creative thinking involves criticality. The distinction between boring, automatic critical thinking and wild, unconstrained, undisciplined creative thinking is untenable, and assumes an indefensible conception of creativity. For fine discussions of the weaknesses of the standard view of creativity, and an argument for the indispensability of disciplined, principled critical thinking to an adequate conception of creativity, cf. S. Bailin, "Creativity and Quality," and Bailin, *Achieving Extraordinary Ends: An Essay on Creativity*. On the interconnectedness of critical and creative thinking, cf. Passmore, "On Teaching To Be Critical"; also Ennis, "A Conception of Critical Thinking—With Some Curriculum Suggestions," p. 14–15. I want to emphasize that nothing about the reasons conception of critical thinking forces a sharp split between critical and creative thinking, or the view that creativity, properly conceived, is not part of the repertoire of the critical thinker. I am grateful to Francis Schrag, Edward Mooney, and especially Sharon Bailin for correspondence/conversation concerning this point.

22 As Denis Phillips reminds me, what is usually meant here is that certain emotions (e.g. hatred, envy, anger, etc.) ought not to interfere with or inappropriately override the exercise of reasoned judgment. This is of course correct. The point in the text is simply that a wholesale bifurcation between reason and emotion is untenable.

23 Cf. Scheffler, "In Praise of the Cognitive Emotions"; Peters, "Reason and Passion" and *Reason and Compassion*, especially Lecture Three; and Paul, "Critical Thought Essential to the Acquisition of Rational Knowledge and Passions."

24 Scheffler, *op. cit.*, p. 141.

25 Paul, *op. cit.*, p. 23, emphasis in original.

26 Peters, *op. cit.*, p. 75. For a provocative attempt to connect care with critical thinking in a different way, cf. H. Alderman, "Dialectic as

Philosophical Care," who suggests that care for argument is related in a more direct way with care for persons. Popper (*The Open Society*, p. 236) notes that Socrates also made this link.

27 *Op. cit.*, p. 79.

28 Although, as noted in note 22 above, it goes without saying that critical thinking requires the monitoring of certain emotions, and the prevention of particular emotions from overriding the proper exercise of reasoned judgment. One must care enough about truth, for example, to have one's concern for truth outweigh and nullify any feeling (e.g. of envy or hatred) which might tend to distort one's judgment about the truth of some claim.

29 *Op. cit.*, p. 101.

30 A related point is made by Scheffler, in *Conditions of Knowledge*, p. 90. Cf. also T.F. Green's related remarks about "psychic freedom," in his "Indoctrination and Beliefs," pp. 38–9. This psychological make-up is something to be striven for, and developed to varying degrees, over time, not something to be accomplished once and for all. I am grateful here for discussion with Robert Floden and Dennis Rohatyn.

31 Assuming here that acts of thinking are acts, the present point is simply that acts of thinking are not the only sort of acts there are.

32 In the philosophy of action a distinction is frequently drawn between what are called the "internalist" and "externalist" perspectives. The rationality of an action can be appraised externally, by inquiring as to whether there are (were) good reasons for performing the action; or internally, by inquiring as to whether the agent has (had) good reasons for performing the action, and acts (acted) for those reasons. Full consideration of this matter would take us far afield. It is clear, however, that critical thinking is to be understood in an internalist way, in so far as the critical thinker acts in accordance with reasons she has. An excellent and thorough discussion of the internalist/externalist literature and its relevance to education may be found in Emily Robertson's "Practical Reasons, Authority, and Education." I am grateful to Robertson for correspondence and conversation on these and related matters.

33 Cf. Passmore, *op. cit.*, pp. 195ff.

34 Of course achieving the ideal—*being* a critical thinker—is a matter of degree. Taking critical thinking as an ideal means fostering the features of critical thinking to the greatest extent possible. But there is no magic point or threshold at which the non-critical thinker turns into a critical thinker. Presumably most people have the capacity to be at least minimally critical, and presumably no one is perfectly critical. Critical thinking must be taken as an ideal which we strive for, and approximate to to varying degrees. I am thankful for discussion with Robert Floden, Emily Robertson, and Dennis Rohatyn on this point.

35 These points are developed more fully in Israel Scheffler, "Moral

Education and the Democratic Ideal." Cf. also Scheffler, *The Language of Education*, chapter 5, esp. pp. 94–5.

36 Gilbert Ryle, *The Concept of Mind*.

37 For it is of course not the case that we have the "ultimate" or final criteria in our pockets. The refinement and improvement of criteria is an ongoing part of rational inquiry. Cf. Scheffler, *Reason and Teaching*, pp. 78–80, regarding the improvability of principles and criteria of reason assessment; also the Postscript below.

38 Scheffler, *The Language of Education*, p. 57, emphasis in original.

39 Scheffler, *Conditions of Knowledge*, p. 107. Further discussion of the critical manner of teaching as initiating the student into the rational life can be found on pp. 11, 90, and 106–7; also in Scheffler, *Reason and Teaching*, pp. 1–3 and 76–80. Similar points, in a different context, concerning the manner of teaching are made by Leonard Waks, "Knowledge and Understanding as Educational Aims," pp. 109–10. Cf. also Passmore, "On Teaching to Be Critical," pp. 198ff.

40 C. J. B. Macmillan suggests ("Love and Logic in 1984") that there are limits to the relationship between teaching and rationality which render problematic the deep connection between the two suggested here. But I think that the limits Macmillan points to are themselves problematic, and reflect too uncritical an acceptance of Wittgensteinian assumptions.

There is clearly much more to say concerning the relationship between critical thinking and teaching, teacher education and teacher evaluation. I regret that space—and competence—prevent my saying more here. I hope that the present work will encourage others to join me in exploring the enormous ramifications that critical thinking, taken as an educational ideal, has for our conception of teaching and for our institutional education and treatment of teachers.

41 For a useful discussion of the analogous role of regulative ideals in science, cf. Kordig, *The Justification of Scientific Change*, pp. 111–13.

Chapter 3 The justification of critical thinking as an educational ideal

1 Scheffler, *Reason and Teaching*, p. 64.

2 G. K. Chesterton, "A Defense of Nonsense," p. 317.

3 As I argue below, even if it were the case, a justification would still be called for. I must note, however, that some philosophers would disagree, claiming rather that a justification is called for only when the view to be justified is challenged or a demand for a justification issued. I am grateful to J. Anthony Blair for discussion of this point.

4 For discussion, cf. my "Creationism, Evolution, and Education: The California Fiasco," and my "The Response to Creationism."

5 *Ibid*.

6 For a critique of the work of one such scholar, cf. my "Genderized Cognitive Perspectives and the Redefinition of Philosophy of Education."

7 Cf., e.g., J. Culler, *On Deconstruction: Theory and Criticism After Structuralism*; or J. Searle's devastating "The World Turned Upside Down."

8 Cf. my *Relativism Refuted*.

9 P. Feyerabend, *Against method,* p. 180.

10 Dostoyevsky, *The Brothers Karamazov*, p. 407. Note the assumption, challenged in chapter 2, of a sharp distinction between reason and emotion. Nevertheless, there is some point to Dostoyevsky's remark, for its raises a profound question regarding the *limits* of rationality. This matter will be considered a bit in the Postscript below.

11 The following paragraphs were prompted by the good questioning and criticism of those who attended my presentation on these matters at the Eastern Division Meeting of the American Philosophical Association (Association for Informal Logic and Critical Thinking Session) in December 1984. I am especially indebted to Mark Weinstein for his probing questions.

12 As Denis Phillips reminds me, the line taken here—of justifying the ideal to those who are already committed to reason—runs the risk of "preaching to the converted," since those who are open to rational persuasion have already committed themselves to the ideal. What, however, of those who are not yet persuaded? How will reasoned argument work on them, if they are not already committed to reason? What is called for here is a "transcendental argument" for the justification of rationality. Whether or not rationality can be transcendentally justified is one of philosophy's most basic questions. I return to it in the Postscript.

13 Notice that, if a philosophical justification can be given, then the ideal is justified even if it turns out that the ideal issues have no positive pragmatic ramifications. To paraphase Morris Cohen's remark regarding Dewey (referred to in Scheffler, *Reason and Teaching*, p. 59), critical thought may well have dignity and worth even in the absence of (pragmatic) value.

14 McPeck, *Critical Thinking and Education*, p. 34.

15 *Ibid.*, p. 37. McPeck's argument occurs on pp. 34-7. I wish here to point out a confusion in the argument to which space forbids further attention. McPeck confuses the relationship between a belief and its evidence, on the one hand, and that between a belief and its compatibility with the believer's existing belief system, on the other. While McPeck's argument utilizes the latter relationship, it is the former which is the key. My reconstruction reflects this point.

16 *Ibid.*, p. 34. Cf. also McPeck's surprising comments regarding schools and education, pp. 152-3.

17 As William Dray pointed out in his classic response to R. S. Peters' analysis of the concept of education. Cf. Dray's "Commentary," pp.34-9.

18 McPeck, in correspondence, correctly points out that the ideologue

(etc.) might well accept a conceptual connection between education and knowledge, differing only in what passes for knowledge. I agree, but only if her conception of knowledge does not involve rational justification. Given that involvement (which McPeck accepts), the ideologue (etc.) not only can, but must, give up the conceptual connection in question.

McPeck also claims, again correctly, that in these last pages I have run together education and schooling—a basic distinction in philosophy of education. I plead guilty, but do not think it affects the point at issue, for the ideologue (etc.) would and should hold that what is involved in schooling for ideological purity (etc.) constitutes education.

Here, as throughout, I am grateful to McPeck, whose correspondence and conversation have forced me to clarify my thinking.

19 Indeed, on a Deweyan reading of "reason," reason is to be *identified* with autonomy. Cf. R. F. Ladenson, "A Theory of Personal Autonomy," esp. pp. 43–7. I am grateful to Ralph Page for calling this article to my attention.

20 Cf. Scheffler, *The Language of Education*, pp. 58–9.

21 But it is a consistent theme in the writing of Israel Scheffler, cf. *The Language of Education*, pp. 58–9; and *Reason and Teaching*, pp. 155–6, chapter 11, and *passim*.

22 Cf. Kant, *Foundations of the Metaphysics of Morals*. An excellent contemporary discussion of Kant's conception of human dignity and the respect such dignity requires may be found in Hardy Jones, *Kant's Principle of Personality*. Cf. also Joel Feinberg, *Social Philosophy*, pp. 84–97, and references to Vlastos and Williams therein; Scheffler, *Reason and Teaching*, chapters 5 and 6; and Scheffler, *Of Human Potential*.

23 It seems plausible that teaching in the critical manner might help to develop the critical spirit. To demand the impartial evaluation of claims, for example, and to encourage students to question, challenge, and sharpen their evaluative and judgmental skills, which respect for persons entails, might well serve to aid in the development of a student's willingness and predisposition to question, challenge, and demand reasons. Teaching in the critical manner, that is, might serve to help develop the critical spirit. But this is an empirical question which cannot be decided on *a priori* grounds. Even if it turned out that such teaching did not foster the critical spirit, teaching in the critical manner would still be justified in terms of the general obligation to treat students with the respect due to them as persons.

It is clear that this first justification of critical thinking, in terms of respect for students as persons, succeeds only if one accepts the Kantian principle. Justification of *that* principle extends far beyond the scope of the present work (as well as my competence). But it does seem to me both that the principle can be justified, and also that it is widely acknowledged, in one form or another, by contemporary moral theorists of various persuasions. Cf. Scheffler's discussion of the "moral point of view," *Reason and Teaching*, pp. 140ff., and references therein. For a different but related argument to the effect that education bears an obligation to foster students' rationality, cf. A. Brinton, "Values and the Ideal of Objectivity."

24 Both these terms are suggested by Scheffler, *Reason and Teaching*, chapter 9, esp. pp. 123–5. Further discussion of the relation between critical thinking and preparation for adulthood may be found in M. S. Katz, "Critical Literacy: A Conception of Education as a Moral Right and a Social Ideal," pp. 201–2.

25 Cf. Scheffler, *Of Human Potential*.

26 Further discussion of self-sufficiency, especially as it relates to the justification of curriculum decisions, can be found in Scheffler, *Reason and Teaching*, chapter 9.

27 Scheffler, *Reason and Teaching*, p. 143.

28 *Ibid.*

29 Coupled, of course, with the competence of judgment just mentioned.

30 *Ibid.*, pp. 143–4.

31 Cf. R. S. Peters, "Education as Initiation."

32 This is very close to McPeck's view, whose debt to Peters is obvious. Cf. McPeck, *Critical Thinking and Education*, pp. 155–8. To underscore the closeness of the views of McPeck and Peters, witness the following McPeckian sentiment expressed by Peters: "there are as many brands of 'critical thinking' as there are disciplines, and in the various disciplines such as history, science, and philosophy, there is a great deal to be known before the peculiar nature of the problem is grasped" (Peters, "Education as Initiation," p. 104).

33 Scheffler, *Reason and Teaching*, p. 79, emphasis in original.

Much more needs to be said here concerning the nature of reasons and the warrant they confer. For consideration of the contribution philosophy, and specifically epistemology, has to make to the proper understanding of reasons over and above that which is involved in the several (other) rational traditions, cf. my "Justification, Discovery and the Naturalizing of Epistemology" and my "Empirical Psychology, Naturalized Epistemology, and First Philosophy."

Scheffler's discussion here raises an important problem, namely that of reconciling the fact that principles (according to which reasons are judged) evolve and change, with the fact that they purport to be and are to be taken to be "impartial and universal." This seems to me a fundamental problem for the theory of rationality. It is considered briefly in the Postscript.

34 Of course one could deny that we ought to regard education as involving initiation into the rational traditions. It seems to me difficult to maintain such a denial coherently, however, for one would need to

embrace at least some of these traditions in simply articulating and defending the denial, and such embracing lends credibility to the legitimacy of the role of the traditions in education. It seems clear that education rightly involves at least *some* initiation into the rational traditions; in so far the ideal of critical thinking derives support. My own view is that such initiation is central to education, but I cannot develop the point further here. I am not aware of many who would deny the relevance of initiation to education completely, though some argue strenuously for the due recognition of other ingredients of education. For further defense of initiation, cf. the references to Peters and McPeck above, and Scheffler, *Reason and Teaching*, esp. pp. 2, 60–2; for an example of one who argues for the importance of other ingredients, cf. the references to Jane R. Martin in my "Genderized Cognitive Perspectives and the Redefinition of Philosophy of Education."

35 Scheffler, "Moral Education and the Democratic Ideal," p. 137. This classic essay constitutes *the* basic discussion of the fundamentality of critical thinking to democracy; I regret that my brief attention to the topic in the text does not do it justice. Cf. also Scheffler, *Of Human Potential*, pp. 122–6, esp. the citation of Ralph Barton Perry on p. 123; Katz, "Critical Literacy," pp. 210–11; and P. Thagard and R. E. Nisbett, "Rationality and Charity," pp. 263–4, who stress the centrality of logic (and statistics) to education for democracy.

36 Cf. Paul's discussion of education and society, and his citations of Sumner, who writes that "Education in the critical faculty is the only education of which it can be truly said that it makes good citizens," in Paul's "Critical Thinking: Fundamental to Education for a Free Society," p. 10.

Of course this line of argument supports critical thinking only if we are antecedently committed to democracy. This is, needless to say, a contentious issue. I cannot here endeavor to defend the "democratic ideal" (as Scheffler calls it, *ibid.*), although I do believe that it is defensible. I shall rest content, here, with the conditional: *if* democracy, *then* critical thinking.

One argument for democracy, however, I cannot refrain from mentioning. If the first three justifications of critical thinking are acceptable, so that critical thinking *is* rightly regarded as an educational ideal, then that fact offers strong support for democracy: it is that social arrangement which most clearly manifests and values the several aspects of critical thinking which are independently justified. In this way the fourth justification may be logically posterior to the first three (or not, if democracy can be independently justified), but nevertheless important.

Chapter 4 The ideology objection

1 I. Scheffler, *Reason and Teaching*, p. 23.

2 H.A. Giroux, *Ideology Culture and the Process of Schooling*, p. 57.

3 R.I. Simon, "Signposts for a Critical Pedagogy: A Review of Henry Giroux's *Theory and Resistance in Education*," p. 382, emphasis added.

4 C.A. Bowers, "Emergent Ideological Characteristics of Educational Policy," p. 35.

5 I.A. Snook, "'Ideology' in Educational Theory," p. 12.

6 Personal communication.

7 N.C. Burbules, "A Theory of Power in Education," p. 106.

8 M.W. Apple, *Ideology and Curriculum*, p. 20.

9 Geertz, "Ideology as a Cultural System," cited in Apple, *Ideology and Curriculum*, p. 20.

10 The label "pejorative" is Geuss's; he contrasts this sense of ideology with the "purely descriptive" and the "positive" senses. In general, Geuss provides an excellent clarificatory discussion of the several main senses of "ideology." Cf. Geuss, *The Idea of a Critical Theory*, pp. 4–26.

11 For discussion of this "pejorative" sense of ideology, cf. Mannheim, *Ideology and Utopia*, p. 62; Harris, *Education and Knowledge*, p. 64; Apple, *Ideology and Curriculum*, p. 20; Giroux, *Ideology Culture and the Process of Schooling*, pp. 19–22.

12 The concatenation of "legitimate" and "unjustifiable" may strike the reader as oxymoronic. It is not, for "legitimate" and "legitimation" are often used ambiguously in the literature on ideology. To legitimate a belief (etc.) may mean actually to demonstrate a belief's worthiness, i.e. to show that the belief in question is deserving of belief, e.g. on the basis of evidence. But it may also mean to make a belief *seem* worthy when it isn't, for example when a suspect ideology props up a belief contrary to a more perspicacious or less tainted reading of the evidence. Thus "legitimating a belief" may mean showing that the belief is legitimately believed, *or* that the belief is *falsely portrayed* as legitimate. It is the latter sort of case the phrase "to legitimate unjustifiably" refers to. Evidence legitimates in the first sense; ideology (it is often claimed) legitimates in the second.

13 Wirth offers this characterization in the name of Mannheim. Cf. Wirth, "Preface" to Mannheim, *Ideology and Utopia*, p. xxi. Cf. also Harris, *Education and Knowledge*, p. 47; Apple, *Ideology and Curriculum*, p. 20.

14 Giroux, *op. cit.*, p. 137.

15 Cf. Giroux, *op. cit.*, p. 148, who writes of ideologies as "social reconstructions" which retain their critical edge to the extent that they are oppositional to the dominant, hegemonic ideology. Cf. also Harris, *op. cit.*, p. 65; and Geuss, *op. cit.*, p. 5.

16 Cf. Geuss, *op. cit.*, pp. 5ff.

17 Harris, *op. cit.*, pp. 86–93.

18 Cf., e.g. Giroux, *op. cit.*; also M.R. Matthews, *The Marxist Theory of Schooling*, pp. 120–1.

19 As Geuss points out, we should not be surprised by the wide variety of accounts of ideology, since different accounts are often intended by their developers to speak to very different sorts of questions and issues. Cf. Geuss, *op. cit.*, p. 4.

20 The several theorists to be cited do not all explicitly articulate the objection; indeed, as will be noted, many of them explicitly reject the objection and engage in the project—forbidden by the objection—of rationally criticizing ideologies. I cite them here only to suggest the sorts of considerations that could, and sometimes do, give rise to the objection.

21 Here understood as the study of the nature and force of reasons and evidence, i.e. as the development of the theory of evidence. Cf. my *Relativism Refuted*.

22 P. Freire, *The Politics of Education*, p. 102. Cf. Freire's *Pedagogy of the Oppressed*; also *Education for Critical Consciousness*.

23 Giroux, *Ideology Culture and the Process of Schooling*, p. 129. For critical discussion of Freire's treatment of the "everything is political" theme, cf. P.J. Crittenden's excellent analysis, "Neutrality in Education."

24 J. Kozol, "A New Look at the Literacy Campaign in Cuba," p. 364. Cf. also p. 363.

25 Kozol, *op. cit.* Cf. also Kozol, *The Night Is Dark and I am Far from Home*, pp. 95–6.

26 Bowers, "Emergent Ideological Characteristics of Educational Policy," pp. 52–4.

27 Harris, *Education and Knowledge*, p. 2.

28 *Ibid.*, pp. 94, 47.

29 Mannheim, *Ideology and Utopia*, pp. 125–6; quoting Marx's remark from the latter's *A Contribution to the Critique of Political Economy*.
   I am duty bound to point out that Mannheim precedes the just-quoted passage with the following remark: "the fact that our thinking is determined by our social position is not necessarily a source of error. On the contrary, it is often the path to political insight" (p. 125). Here then, he denies that the thoroughgoing sociology of knowledge he espouses leads to any sort of serious relativism, an implication he seems to be committed to elsewhere (e.g. pp. 78ff., where he unsuccessfully distinguishes "relationalism" from relativism). But, as I shall argue below, his denial is not so easily maintained, for how is one to evaluate the quality of insight afforded by the recognition that our thinking is determined by our social position once it is recognized that this recognition is *itself* determined by our social position? Mannheim's position does lead, despite his disclaimer, to a vicious sort of relativism which undercuts the very point concerning the social determination of thought that he (and Marx in the cited passage) is most concerned to make.

Nor should it be thought that Mannheim espouses here an anachronistic version of an outdated relativist position. Relativism—in some ways more thoroughgoing than Mannheim's in that it embraces the relativity of scientific, mathematical and logical knowledge, as well as political and social knowledge—is decidedly on the ascendancy at present. Cf. my "Relativism, Truth and Incoherence" or *Relativism Refuted* for further discussion and references.

Finally, I should note that the Marx citation is used here simply to illustrate the thesis that ideology shapes consciousness. As noted above, Marx's sense of "ideology" is not this one, but rather that ideology distorts reality and is to be overcome. Thus Marx, despite the cited passage, is not correctly thought of as a proponent of the ideology objection. He may be, and usually is, regarded as a friend, not a critic, of ideology-free critical thinking. I am grateful here to Lenore Langsdorf for conversation regarding this point.

30 Harris, *Education and Knowledge*, p. 94. Harris goes on to consider how we might get ourselves from a less adequate to a more adequate ideology, conceiving of adequacy in terms of progressiveness and the satisfaction of legitimate interests, apparently not realizing that this possibility is precluded by the thoroughgoing ideological determinism he espouses; for judgments of ideological adequacy or progressiveness will necessarily be, given such determinism, themselves ideologically biassed or tainted. On this point cf. R. Small's good discussion, "Knowledge and Ideology in the Marxist Philosophy of Education," esp. pp. 31–3. I shall return to this point below.

31 Even if we restrict ideological determination to sociopolitical thoughts, the problem for educational ideals remains, since they are at least partly sociopolitical in nature.

32 I am grateful to Jim Giarelli for forcefully reminding me not to "straw man" the opposition by painting everyone as crazy ideological determinists. Giarelli is surely correct that most writers on ideology are not as extremely deterministic as the Mannheim, Marx and Harris passages cited above suggest. I regret that space and competence prevent me from a more serious consideration of the complex of views, espoused by the tradition of critical theory, which offer an alternative conception of rationality according to which judgment can be both contextually grounded and rational, and which explore the extent to which historical, sociopolitical and ideological context interferes with, distorts or inhibits rational thought. While I think that this reconceptualization of rationality is doomed to failure on grounds of reflexivity—to wit, the reconceptualization must be offered a-contextually if it is to avoid begging questions, but if offered in this way it refutes itself—by chapter's end I will have offered far too cursory a sketch of the alternative position to claim to have shown it to be doomed to failure. In particular, the work of Habermas and his

colleagues requires far more attention than I can give it here. Nevertheless, I hope to raise some difficulties for the reconceptualization of rationality as contextual when, near the end of the chapter, I raise the general issue of the relationship between rationality and ideology, and argue that theories of ideology, rationality, undistorted communication, and the like presuppose an a-contextual conception of rationality in the very articulation and pursuit of their contextualist alternatives.

33 An excellent discussion of the multifarious and complex nature of the "everything is political" claim, with specific reference to Freire, may be found in Crittenden, "Neutrality in Education."

34 Cf. chapter 3 for further discussion, including some caveats, concerning the justification of the principle of respect for persons. Those caveats do not materially affect the present point concerning the distinction between the two senses of "everything is political."

Remarks similar to those just made in the text could be made concerning at least some of the other considerations offered in chapter 3 in support of the ideal of critical thinking.

Finally, the position here defended is compatible with another common claim, namely that moral education and political education cannot, in practice, be neatly separated.

35 The argument against ideological determinism just rehearsed is of course an adapted version of the well-known *reductio* argument against epistemological relativism. My claim, then, is that determinism fails for the same reasons that relativism does. For the detailed case against relativism, cf. my "Relativism, Truth and Incoherence," or chapter 1 of *Relativism Refuted*. With respect to ideology, cf. the exchange between Tony Stigliano ("Remarks on C. A. Bowers's 'Curriculum as Cultural Reproduction: An Examination of Metaphor as a Carrier of Ideology'") and C. A. Bowers ("Metaphor and the Problem of Epistemological Relativism: A Response to Tony Stigliano's Comments"); also Bowers, "The Reproduction of Technological Consciousness: Locating the Ideological Foundations of a Radical Pedagogy," pp. 555–6. Note also Mannheim, who unsuccessfully attempts to avoid relativism, *Ideology and Utopia*, pp. 85–6.

36 An analogous point concerning the wisdom of regarding education, and its ideals of inquiry and rationality, as autonomous from, and capable of evaluating, alternative social goals—rather than regarding education and educational institutions as functioning so as to achieve predetermined social goals—is persuasively made by Scheffler, *Reason and Teaching*, pp. 134–5.

37 Harris, *Education and Knowledge*. Cf. Small's critical discussion of Harris, "Knowledge and Ideology in the Marxist Philosophy of Education."

38 Cf., e.g., Giroux, "Public Philosophy and the Crisis in Education." This

insistence upon evaluating ideologies, upon criticizing some and defending others, on the basis of reasons and arguments, is (in my view happily) ubiquitous in Giroux's work.

39 Bowles and Gintis, *Schooling in Capitalist America.*
40 Burbules, "A Theory of Power in Education," pp. 107ff.
41 Bowers, "Linguistic Roots of Cultural Invasion in Paulo Freire's Pedagogy," pp. 936-8.
42 Bowers, *op. cit.* Cf. also Bowers, "The Reproduction of Technological Consciousness: Locating the Ideological Foundations of a Radical Pedagogy," esp. pp. 534ff.
43 Bowers, "The Problem of Individualism and Community in Neo-Marxist Educational Thought," pp. 380-2 and *passim.*
44 Bowers, "Emergent Ideological Characteristics of Educational Policy," p. 53.
45 *Op. cit.*, p. 54.
46 After all, perhaps the most fundamental question asked by the rationalist tradition is the self-reflexive question "Why be rational?" Thus this tradition, or "ideology" (if one insists), can and does raise questions about its own adequacy. Cf. the Postscript below.
47 For the parallel case regarding relativism, cf. my "Relativism, Truth and Incoherence."
48 Dennis Rohatyn raises the following (ugly) possibility. Suppose "ideology" and "rationality" were substituted for each other in my argument. Then wouldn't I be forced to conclude that rationality presupposes ideology, rather than the reverse, and that "we are all—necessarily—ideologues here"?

I am pleased to be able to report that these conclusions would not be forced upon us, for there is an asymmetry in the relationship between rationality and ideology; in a way it is this asymmetry I have been appealing to throughout the development of my argument. I have been arguing that making claims concerning ideology requires appeal to standards of rationality—otherwise one could not be said to be making claims, for making claims amounts to offering theses which one (tacitly) asserts are warranted, and so presupposes standards of warrant or justification. That is, making claims presupposes an appeal to rational standards of appraisal. Thus making claims about ideology presupposes a commitment to rational standards, i.e. to rationality.

The reverse, however, is not the case. Making claims about rationality does not presuppose any appeal to ideology—except, perhaps, in the harmless sense I have been illustrating the harmlessness of in the text. Thus the ugly conclusions are I think safely avoided.

I should note that the ideologue can argue not that rationality presupposes ideology *in principle*, but rather that in practice "enlightened rationality" functions as an ideology in certain ways and influences, if not determines, our judgments. This I suspect is the case.

But it is important to see that this "in practice" dependence of rationality upon ideology is very different in kind from the "in principle" dependence of ideology upon rationality I have been belaboring in the text. The relationship between the two simply is not symmetrical in the way required to get the ugly conclusions out of a substitution of the one for the other in the argument.

I am most grateful to Dennis Rohatyn for his lengthy and challenging commentary on this chapter.

49 Although they frequently put the point in terms of "personal development," which is not rightly regarded as equivalent to liberation. Still, I think a sympathetic reading reveals that the latter is what Bowles and Gintis have in mind. Cf. Bowles and Gintis, *Schooling in Capitalist America*, chapter 2, pp. 264–6, and *passim*.

50 Burbules, "A Theory of Power in Education," pp. 112–113.

51 Cf., e.g., Bowers, "The Reproduction of Technological Consciousness: Locating the Ideological Foundations of a Radical Pedagogy," pp. 555–6.

52 Dewey, *Experience and Nature*, p. 222. Cf. also William Proefriedt's effort to wed this Deweyan concern for critical thinking with a concern for ideology and socialist social change in "Socialist Criticisms of Education in the United States: Problems and Possibilities," esp. pp. 475–8.

Chapter 5   The indoctrination objection

1 B. Russell, *Education and the Social Order*, quoted in P. Smart, "The Concept of Indoctrination," p. 33. Russell's comment continues: "also at some stage during education an attempt should be made to free boys and girls as far as possible from the influence of propaganda by teaching them methods of arriving at impartial judgements."

2 J. Wilson, "Indoctrination and Rationality," p. 23.

3 A similar situation is considered in D. C. Phillips, "The Anatomy of Autonomy."

4 Snook puts it this way: "A person indoctrinates P (a proposition or a set of propositions) if he teaches with the intention that the pupils or pupil believe P, regardless of the evidence." I. Snook, *Indoctrination and Education*, cited in P. Smart, "The Concept of Indoctrination," p. 39. Cf. also Wilson, "Indoctrination and Rationality," pp. 18–20, who endorses the idea that indoctrination is necessarily intentional. But Wilson seems to hold in these pages that indoctrination is also, necessarily, a matter of method and content as well.

5 Cf. Smart, *op. cit.*, pp. 35, 42–3; also Wilson, *op. cit.*, p. 19.

6 Cf. the discussion of the relation between indoctrination and truth in T. F. Green, "Indoctrination and Beliefs," *passim*. A. Flew conflates the first and third views mentioned when he writes that indoctrination is "a matter of trying to implant firm convictions of the truth of doctrines

which are in fact either false or at least not known to be true," cited in
D. Benedict-Gill, "Some Philosophical Directions in a Controversy
Over Public Moral Education," p. 104. The citation is taken from
Flew's "What is Indoctrination?" Finally, cf. once again Wilson, *op. cit.*,
pp. 19–20.

7 T. F. Green, "Indoctrination and Beliefs," p. 37. Green, putting the point
in terms of aims, writes that "Indoctrination aims simply at establishing
certain beliefs so that they will be held quite apart from their truth,
their explanation, or their foundation in evidence" (p. 25); he explicates
the notion of "non-evidential belief" in this way: "When beliefs are held
without regard to evidence or contrary to evidence, then we may say
they are held non-evidentially. It follows that beliefs held non-
evidentially cannot be modified by introducing evidence or reasons or
by rational criticism" (p. 33). Cf. pp. 34–5; also Green, *The Activities of
Teaching*, pp. 48–51. Here too Green characterizes indoctrination in
terms of aim or intention. Intention is not the key, however; if I do not
intend to establish beliefs irrespective of the evidence for them, but
nevertheless my students wind up with non-evidential styles of belief,
then we should still say that they have been indoctrinated, and that I
(however unwittingly) indoctrinated them by fostering such styles.
Uncriticality, not intention, is the mark of indoctrination. Cf. note 8
below and the text to the end of this section.

8 We see here, incidentally, that while intentions, methods, and content
are neither necessary nor sufficient for indoctrination, they all can tend
to promote non-evidential belief. This is what is insightful about the
three views of indoctrination noted, an insight incorporated by the view
that indoctrination is a matter of non-evidential—or, as I am about to
call it in the text, *non-critical*—belief.

This, as noted, is not the place for a full analysis of indoctrination.
However, I believe that what has been said thus far is sufficient to
suggest a fourth view of indoctrination, according to which
indoctrination is not a matter of intentions, aims, methods, or content,
but rather a matter of the *results* or *upshot* of the aims, intentions,
methods, or content of instances of belief inculcation. I regret that
space does not allow the further development of what might be called
the "upshot conception" of indoctrination.

9 As Wilson puts it, in his excellent phrase, indoctrinated beliefs are those
which have been accepted when the indoctrinated person's "will and
reason have been put to sleep," *op. cit.*, p. 18.

10 Wilson, *op. cit.*, p. 21.

11 This is very much like the position argued for by B.B. Suttle, "The Need
For and Inevitability of Moral Indoctrination."

12 P. Wagner, "Moral Education, Indoctrination and the Principle of
Minimizing Substantive Moral Error," p. 192.

13 Cf. also B.B. Suttle, *op. cit.* These questions and related ones concerning

indoctrination and moral education are fruitfully pursued in the exchange between E.L. Pincoffs ("On Avoiding Moral Indoctrination") and K. Baier ("Indoctrination and Justification").

14 Green, "Indoctrination and Beliefs," pp. 44–5.

15 Green, *op. cit.*, p. 33.

16 Note that this solution has the ramification—positive, if one favors consistency with ordinary language—of preserving the pejorative connotation of "indoctrination."

I hope it is clear, however, that considerations of ordinary usage play virtually no role in my argument. The important thing is not to offer a conception that adequately captures our intuitions about indoctrination or our uses of "indoctrination." The important thing, rather, is adequately to determine that which our educational institutions ought to be about. Hard philosophical work concerning the aims of education and their justification (and harder empirical work aimed at making those philosophical aims and ideals reality) far outstrips the analysis of ordinary language that still, alas, strangles much contemporary analytic philosophy of education.

17 As Denis Phillips points out, this implies that if a person has been indoctrinated, that indoctrination cannot be undone *by appealing to reasons*, since she has a non-evidential style of belief. Counteracting indoctrination, I think, requires not the alteration of specific beliefs, but the development of an evidential style of belief. This must be the aim of "dedoctrination."

18 Suttle, *op. cit.*, p. 155. Despite our disagreement over the inevitability of indoctrination, our views concerning both moral education and the place of rationality in education are in many respects quite close. I am grateful to Suttle for extensive and very helpful correspondence and conversation on these and related issues.

19 R.S. Peters, "Reason and Habit: The Paradox of Moral Education," p. 252.

20 Cf. Suttle, *op. cit.*, pp. 156–7; Wagner, *op. cit.*

21 Peters, *op. cit.*, p. 253.

22 Consequently, it does not matter much to my argument whether Aristotle, Dewey and Peters are right concerning the role of habit in the resolution of the paradox of moral education. I believe that they are, but the argument for the possibility of inculcating beliefs (and, possibly, habits) *sans* rational justification without that inculcation constituting indoctrination goes through even if habit is not the key to the resolution of the paradox.

Note also that we are here considering how one *becomes* a critical thinker, rather than what it is to *be* a critical thinker. These two matters being distinct, I hope it is clear that my Kantian answer (in chapters 2 and 3) to the latter does not conflict with my (weakly) Aristotelian answer to the former. Here again I am grateful to Dennis Rohatyn.

23 As Smart puts it (*op. cit.*, p. 45):

> to be indoctrinated is to become enmeshed within a web of
> doctrines from which there can be no escape. One cannot extricate
> oneself because one sees no need for doing so. Usually we change
> our opinions in the light of experience or because of inconsistencies
> which arise from commitment to particular beliefs. But if we are
> presented with a set of beliefs which can explain away alleged
> inconsistencies and maintain that experience is irrelevant there
> remains nothing which can challenge our beliefs.

24 Dennis Rohatyn reminds me that the critical thinker is also a prisoner,
in a sense. She is a "prisoner" of the dispositions, values, habits, etc., of
critical thinking. However, there are several reasons for thinking that
being a "prisoner of critical thinking" is different from—and better
than—being a prisoner of uncritical convictions. First, the critical
thinker is aware of her own circumstances; she is self-aware in a way the
other sort of prisoner is not. Second, with that awareness comes at least
the possibility of liberation. If the critical thinker comes to the view that
her critical thinking is less desirable than some alternative, or is
obsessive, she can, at least in principle, work to change herself—though
it is difficult to see why she would come to feel that way about critical
thinking. The critical thinker might be "doomed" to critical thinking,
but being so doomed is preferable to being doomed to uncriticality, for
the same reasons that critical thinking is itself preferable to its
alternatives. And of course she is not really doomed, since, being a
critical thinker, she is able to think about, evaluate, and work to alter
her habits and commitments.

In some sense paternalism is forced upon us by the very nature of
childhood. Paternalism in the direction of the enhancement of critical
thinking is nevertheless fundamentally preferable to its alternatives,
since such a paternalism seeks explicitly to minimize its control over the
child and to get the child to the point at which further paternalism is
unnecessary, and prior paternalism, if deemed by the child unhappy,
undone.

These considerations clearly raise the question of the justification of
rationality, for the person who feels herself a prisoner of critical
thinking is questioning the justifiability of rationality/critical thinking,
and the wisdom of a commitment to it. However, such justifiability and
wisdom appear unassailable, for one cannot seriously ask "Why should
I value rationality?" without already valuing rationality, for to ask the
question seriously is to seek, and to commit oneself to, reasons which
might answer the question. This shows, I think, that rationality is in an
important sense *self-justifying*; to ask about its rational status is *eo ipso*
to commit oneself to it. I shall say a bit more about the problem of

justifying rationality in the Postscript.

25 As Wilson puts it (*op. cit.*, p. 22), "To indoctrinate is ... to take over [the child's] consciousness."

26 As I suggest in "The Response to Creationism," pp. 360–2 (from which pages the present paragraph in the text is drawn), much fundamentalist religious education fits this indoctrinative, immoral picture, and children have a right to be protected from being victimized by such an education, even though it may be private rather than public education—and we have a concomitant obligation so to protect them. Green suggests a similar view of the character of fundamentalist religious education, *op. cit.*, pp. 40–1.

27 There is a neat self-referential problem with the last belief mentioned, which solution may require that that particular belief *cannot*, in principle, be the object of indoctrination. We need not settle the question here.

28 This sentence, and other ideas of this and the preceding paragraph, are taken from my "Rationality, Morality, and Rational Moral Education: Further Response to Freeman," pp. 41–2.

Chapter 6 Science education

1 B. Russell, *A History of Western Philosophy*, p. 527, emphases in original.

2 My own view is that, while the traditional image of the scientist as the dispassionate seeker of truth is rightly exploded, it nevertheless remains that science *is* properly regarded as a pre-eminently rational activity. I argue for this view, and offer a characterization of the rationality of science, in "What Is the Question Concerning the Rationality of Science?" Cf. also my "Truth, Problem Solving and the Rationality of Science."

3 The *locus classicus* here is of course Kuhn's incredibly influential *The Structure of Scientific Revolutions*. A critical discussion of Harold Brown's helpful presentation of the "new philosophy of science" may be found in my "Brown on Epistemology and the New Philosophy of Science."

4 Before launching into a discussion of Kuhn, a caveat is in order. In what follows I offer a particular interpretation of the Kuhnian position. It is an interpretation which many readers of Kuhn share, and which I try to defend in the text. However, as is well known, interpreting Kuhn is a tricky business, and many readers of Kuhn read him in very different ways. Consequently, it is important to keep in mind the purpose of this chapter, and the role that the discussion of Kuhn plays in it. As I interpret Kuhn, his view forces upon us a conception of science education which is antithetical to a science education which takes seriously the ideal of critical thinking. This interpretation of Kuhn is then set out against a conception of a more critical science education.

We should not be distracted, however, by hermeneutical questions concerning Kuhn interpretation. If I have misinterpreted him, and he is best interpreted as being more sympathetic to a critical science education, then he and I should be seen alike—as friends of critical science education, and enemies of anti-critical science education. The important question is not "Is Kuhn really an opponent of critical science education?" Rather, the important question is "Should science education be critical; and, if so, what would a critical science education be like?" Our focus is not Kuhn, but the nature of science education. My discussion of Kuhn is intended only as a useful way to get at the question concerning science education just mentioned. I am grateful here to Dennis Rohatyn, whose challenge to my reading of Kuhn has reminded me of the importance of reminding the reader that the issues to be considered here concern not Kuhn and the proper interpretation of the Kuhnian corpus, but science education and its relation to critical thinking.

5 A fuller articulation of Kuhn's conception of science is offered in chapter 3 of my *Relativism Refuted*. Consideration of the most controversial aspects of Kuhn's view, concerning science's rationality, objectivity, and the relativity of scientific knowledge and truth, may be found in that chapter, and in my "Objectivity, Rationality, Incommensurability, and More."

6 Kuhn, *The Structure of Scientific Revolutions*, p. viii.

7 *Ibid.*, p. 10.

8 *Ibid.*, pp. 148–50.

9 *Ibid.*, pp. 150–151.

10 I hasten to reiterate that the above account is too quick and simple-minded to do justice to the nuances of Kuhn's discussion. For a more detailed presentation, and a defense of this "irrationalist" interpretation of Kuhn, cf. the references cited in note 5 above.

11 Kuhn, "Logic of Discovery or Psychology of Research?", p. 6.

12 J. W. N. Watkins, "Against 'Normal Science,'" p. 27.

13 *Ibid.*, p. 37; the enclosed citation is of course from Kuhn, cf. note 11 above.

14 Popper, "Normal Science and Its Dangers," pp. 52–3.

15 The reader might think, as Fennell and Liveritte do ("Kuhn, Education and the Grounds of Rationality," p. 119), that I have erred in taking Kuhn's *de*scription of normal science as *pre*scription; that is, in taking Kuhn to be *endorsing* the anti-criticalness of normal science rather than simply describing it. It is true that Kuhn takes himself here to be describing normal science. But he also thinks that the achievement of normal science—complete with its anti-criticalness—is a prerequisite for the development of science, and that the furthering of science and scientific knowledge requires the achievement of the anti-critical normal scientific stage. (Indeed, for Kuhn the pre-normal scientific, i.e. pre-

paradigmatic, stage, is pre-scientific.) Thus Kuhn both describes normal science as anti-critical, and prescribes it as such. His appreciation of science requires no less. This becomes especially clear in light of his views concerning the desirability of indoctrinating science students into the dogma of the current paradigm, and of distorting the history of science so as to facilitate such indoctrination, for both of these educational policies are intended to foster the development of competent (anti-critical) normal scientists. Cf. the discussion of these educational matters in this chapter, sections 2(D) and 2(E) below; also my "Rationality, Talking Dogs, and Forms of Life." Kuhn himself explicitly acknowledges that he is both describing and prescribing in "Reflections on My Critics," p. 237.

I should note here as well that many have disputed the Kuhnian conception of normal science on factual, descriptive grounds. Cf., e.g., Toulmin, *Human Understanding*; or Lakatos, "Falsification and the Methodology of Scientific Research Programmes."

16 It is reviewed in considerable detail in my "Objectivity, Rationality, Incommensurability, and More."

17 "Know" appears here in scarce quotes for the obvious reason: the claims just adumbrated cannot all be known, for they are not all true, and it is an epistemological commonplace that truth is a necessary condition of knowledge—what is not true cannot be known. Kuhn disavows the idea that science seeks truth (*The Structure of Scientific Revolutions*, p. 170); it appears that incommensurability commits him to the claim that scientific claims cannot be known, except relatively to paradigms. Thus he appears to be committed either to relativism or to skepticism. Cf. my *Relativism Refuted*, chapter 3, for consideration of these aspects of Kuhn's view.

18 Again, for more careful articulation, and criticism, of the Kuhnian position, cf. *Relativism Refuted*.

19 Kuhn, "The Function of Dogma in Scientific Research," p. 351.

20 Kuhn, *The Structure of Scientific Revolutions*, pp. 165–6.

21 Note that the label "indoctrination" is perfectly justified here, since the Kuhnian science student is inculcated into the currently dominant paradigm in such a way that the paradigm does not come into question or itself stand in need of justification; that is, the normal scientist is to have a non-evidential style of belief, at least with respect to the paradigm she is inculcated into. This sort of education, given the discussion of chapter 5, surely qualifies as indoctrinative.

22 Kuhn, *The Structure of Scientific Revolutions*, p. 137.

23 *Op. cit.*

24 Kuhn, "The Essential Tension: Tradition and Innovation in Scientific Research," p. 344.

25 *Ibid.*, p. 352. It must in fairness be pointed out that Kuhn in this essay allows "divergent" thinking also to play a role in scientific practice.

Nevertheless, his insistence on the inculcation in the student of an "unequivocal tradition" is clear, and the establishment of the illusion of such a tradition requires the systematic distortion of the history of science.

26 I note in passing that Kuhn is not clearly entitled to appeal to any notion of scientific progress, since incommensurability appears to rule out the possibility of any such notion. Cf. *Relativism Refuted*, chapter 3, or "Objectivity, Rationality, Incommensurability, and More," for further consideration of this problem for Kuhn.

27 Kuhn, *The Structure of Scientific Revolutions*, pp. 137–8, emphases added.

28 Below (section 3(E)) I return to the question of whether the production of competent scientific researchers is rightly thought of as the main or sole goal of science education, as Kuhn presupposes. In the remainder of the present section I argue that, even if we grant Kuhn this view of the aim of science education, and also grant his view of the nature of science, a commitment to un- or anti-critical science education for normal science still does not follow.

29 Schwab, *The Teaching of Science As Enquiry*, p. 5.

30 *Ibid.*, pp. 15–16.

31 *Ibid.*, p. 16.

32 *Ibid.*, pp. 16–17.

33 *Ibid.*, p. 18.

34 It is interesting to note that Schwab characterizes education for stable enquiry as education into "dogma" (in *ibid.*, p. 21). Kuhn, as we have seen, similarly characterizes education for normal science as dogmatic. Of course, Schwab uses the term pejoratively, while Kuhn's use of the term is salutary.

35 *Ibid.*, p. 24, emphasis in original.

36 *Ibid.*, p. 38.

37 Cf., e.g., *Relativism Refuted*, chapter 3.

38 Cf. Schwab's depiction of the "enquiring classroom," in Schwab, *The Teaching of Science As Enquiry*, pp. 65ff.

39 Several of Kuhn's remarks suggest this. See his "Logic of Discovery or Psychology of Research?" and his "Reflections on My Critics."

40 Cf., e.g., *The Structure of Scientific Revolutions*, p. 166.

41 Kuhn, "The Essential Tension," p. 344.

42 Cf. also my "Rationality, Talking Dogs, and Forms of Life," pp. 137–8.

43 The reference of course is to Kant. Cf. chapters 2 and 3 above.

44 Cf. my "Rationality, Talking Dogs, and Forms of Life," pp. 137–8.

45 In section 2(C) above.

46 Cf. *Relativism Refuted*.

47 Cf. Nelson Goodman's similar suggestions concerning the epistemological "fundamentalist," and my reply, in my "Goodmanian Relativism."

48 Cf. Michael Scriven's discussion of this distinction with respect to moral education in his "Cognitive Moral Education."

49 Cf. Ennis, "Research in Philosophy of Science Bearing on Science Education," p. 152.

50 Martin, *Concepts of Science Education*, p. 125.

51 *Ibid.*, p. 126.

52 *Ibid.*, pp. 157–60.

53 *Ibid.*, p. 158.

54 Here I echo D.C. Phillips, "Can Scientific Method Be Taught?", who argues that science education should be viewed as central to a liberal education. It goes without saying that other curricular areas, e.g. literature and language arts, mathematics, and history, can also contribute to the development of critical thinking. But, as I argue in "What is the Question Concerning the Rationality of Science?", science is uniquely qualified for this task in that its method is focussed squarely on the production and recognition of evidence (both empirical and theoretical) and good reasons on which to base belief and action. This view of the place of science in education is of course Dewey's as well. Cf., e.g., Dewey, *Democracy and Education*, pp. 189, 228.

55 An excellent discussion of some controversies regarding the way in which science manifests rationality, with specific attention to science education, may be found in Gerald Holton, "Science, Science Teaching, and Rationality," and in Ernest Nagel's reply to Holton, "In Defense of Scientific Knowledge."

56 Cf. my "On the Distortion of the History of Science in Science Education," esp. the discussion of the Project Physics Course.

57 Cf. Martin, *Concepts of Science Education*, chapter 1.

58 Cf. Scheffler, *Reason and Teaching*, p. 75 and chapter 3, esp. pp. 35–6, for related discussion; also Scheffler, "Philosophies-of and the Curriculum." Cf. also Martin, *Concepts of Science Education*, whose discussion both exemplifies and argues for the virtues of a science education informed by philosophy of science.

59 Cf. Martin's discussion of pseudo-science in the science curriculum in *Concepts of Science Education*, pp. 40–2.

My own favorite example of pseudo-science, for purposes of contrast with genuine science, is that of "scientific" creationism. Cf. my "Creationism, Evolution, and Education: The California Fiasco," and "The Response to Creationism." An excellent discussion may also be found in D. Moshman, "A Role for Creationism in Science Education." A provocative alternative view, which denies the science/pseudo-science distinction but nevertheless upholds standards of good science, is P. Kitcher's "Good Science, Bad Science, Dreadful Science, and Pseudo-science."

60 This suggestion is similar to McPeck's call for teaching the "epistemology of the subject" in subject area courses. It differs,

however, in its attention to philosophical treatment of area concerns, as opposed to McPeck's "informationist" slant on subject epistemology. Cf. chapter 1 above.

61 I am grateful here for hours of memorable conversation with Barbara and Don Arnstine, who have forcefully reminded me of the importance of the points mentioned in this paragraph.

Chapter 7 Minimum competency testing

1 The words are Immanuel Kant's, and appear in his *Education*. The citation is taken from M. Greene, "Response to 'Competence and Excellence: The Search for An Egalitarian Standard, the Demand for a Universal Guarantee,' by Jenne K. Britell," p. 47.

2 Cf. C. Pipho, "Minimum Competency Testing in 1978: A Look at State Standards." My understanding is that MCT is at present even more widely practised, and more firmly entrenched, than it was at the time of Pipho's report.

3 *Op. cit.*, p. 586.

4 *Ibid.*; cf. also A. E. Wise, "Minimum Competency Testing: Another Case of Hyper-Rationalization."

5 The educational literature here is voluminous. A good place to start is Pipho, *op. cit.*, and the articles collected in Jaeger and Tittle, *Minimum Competency Achievement Testing*.

6 In "Critical Literacy and Minimum Competency Testing," I consider three other reasons for regarding MCT as inadequate from the point of view of critical thinking: MCT's reliance on testing; its tendency to reduce "maxima" to "minima"; and its conception of teachers as automata.

7 G. V. Glass, "Standards and Criteria," p. 237.

8 For examples, cf. *op. cit.*, pp. 238–9.

9 *Op. cit.*, pp. 250–1.

10 *Op. cit.*, p. 259.

11 Glass recognizes this problem, but does not offer any solution, *op. cit.*, pp. 259–60. I am indebted to Judy Rule for helpful discussion on this point.

12 W. J. Popham, "As Always, Provocative," p. 298, emphasis in original. Cf. also Popham, *Criterion-Referenced Measurement*, p. 168.

13 Glass, *op. cit.*, pp. 238–9; cf. also Glass, "Minimum Competence and Incompetence in Florida," p. 604.

14 Popham, *op. cit.*, p. 298, emphasis in original. Popham contrasts this "lowest acceptable performance" conception of MCT with the conception Glass utilizes, namely a "requisite for the future" conception. But this distinction does not establish Popham's defense of MCT, because the arbitrariness charge Glass levels at MCT applies equally well to either of these conceptions.

15 M. Scriven, "How to Anchor Standards," p. 274.

16 Of course Scriven can deny that he is speaking of education here at all, but has in mind rather something like licensing or certification. This would indeed avoid the objection I am about to develop in the text, but at a cost, for such a move would render MCT much less central an *educational* matter. This is manifestly not how MCT is generally conceived or practised. When fourth graders are tested for minimum arithmetical competency, for example, neither certification or licensing are at issue. Education is.

17 *Op. cit.*, p. 275.

18 Glass, "Minimum Competence and Incompetence in Florida," p. 603; cf. also his discussion of "survival skills," p. 605.

19 How serious a problem first level arbitrariness is remains open to debate. My own view is that it is not as serious as second level arbitrariness, and that the latter can be avoided, although not in a way which strengthens the case for MCT; cf. below.

20 H. Broudy, "Impact of Minimum Competency Testing on Curriculum."

21 *Op. cit.*, p. 113.

22 *Op. cit.*, p. 115.

23 *Op. cit.*, p. 116.

24 W.J. Popham, "Curriculum and Minimum Competency: A Reaction to the Remarks of H.S. Broudy," p. 122.

25 I have thus far confined my critical remarks to MCT, but some of my criticisms may apply with equal force to testing for critical thinking as well. It may well be that testing for critical thinking is antithetical to the spirit of that ideal, and, more concretely, that such testing may be counter-productive to the effort to develop the dispositions constitutive of the critical thinker. At a minimum, we need to know more about the conditions for learning and for the acquisition of dispositions before we commit ourselves to testing for critical thinking, for it might turn out that, if we want to foster critical thinking skills and dispositions, we are ill-advised to test for them: the testing itself may frustrate rather than further that fostering. I am grateful to Denis Phillips, Dennis Rohatyn, and especially Barbara Arnstine for conversation concerning this point.

26 One might think (as Denis Phillips has pointed out to me) that what I am objecting to is not MCT as such, but rather to particular *instantiations* of it. Thus I might be opposed to MCT programs as presently constituted, but have given no reason to reject all possible MCT programs. Indeed, were an MCT program to emphasize testing for minimum competency with respect to critical thinking, one might think that, given my commitment to the latter, I should endorse such a program. I do not, however, for the reasons given in the text and in the previous note. I believe that there *are* competencies a critical thinker possesses; but that in no way implies that *testing* for such competencies is either desirable or helpful in fostering them. If it could be shown that such testing was useful in fostering critical thinking, then I would of

course welcome it as an important tool to be utilized in the educational effort of fostering critical thinking. But I suspect that testing would not be such a tool; or, if such a program could be devised, it would be unrecognizable as an MCT program.

Postscript: Towards a theory of rationality

1 Scheffler, *Reason and Teaching*, p. 22, emphasis in original.
2 Cf. my "Educating Reason: Critical Thinking, Informal Logic, and the Philosophy of Education. Part Two: Philosophical Questions Underlying Education for Critical Thinking," especially the penultimate section, "Critical Thinking and Epistemology"; cf. also chapter 1 above. R. Roemer also argues that work in the theory of rationality is required if rationality (and so critical thinking) is to be unproblematically regarded as an educational ideal. For discussion of this requirement, and of some of the pitfalls awaiting critical thinking theorists, cf. Roemer, "Pedagogy and Rationality."
3 Cf. my "What Is the Question Concerning the Rationality of Science?"
4 I don't mean to suggest that the distinction between prudential and moral reasons is obviously legitimate; it is contentious. My point is just that the means-ends conception of rationality wrongly settles the question by fiat, by ruling out the possibility of reasons which are not prudential.
5 For further discussion of this point, cf. my "Is It Irrational to be Immoral? A Response to Freeman," pp. 53–6.
6 Cf. especially my "What Is the Question Concerning the Rationality of Science?"; also "Truth, Problem Solving and the Rationality of Science."
7 Cf., e.g., K. Baier, *The Moral Point of View*.
8 The literature here is vast. Cf., e.g., Trigg, *Reason and Commitment*, or Kekes, *A Justification of Rationality*.
9 In saying that we *should* be rational, I am apparently committed (as Harold Alderman has pointed out to me) to the view that it is immoral to be irrational. (I have already suggested earlier that it is irrational to be immoral.) I accept the commitment, and would if pressed analyze the immorality, in Kantian fashion, in terms of duties to self. I am grateful to Alderman for his challenging and very helpful comments on this chapter.
10 Many writers have urged similar views. Cf., e.g., Martin, *Concepts of Science Education*, p. 157. The basic form of argument can be traced back at least as far as Aristotle; cf. D. Rohatyn, *Naturalism and Deontology*, chapter 2.
11 I am grateful to Emily Robertson for correspondence concerning this point, and have shamelessly borrowed some of the examples in the text from this correspondence.
12 This problem is perhaps best seen not as a problem independent of those already noted, but rather as one aspect of the problem of

providing an epistemology of reasons.

I have considered this problem in the context of reason assessment in science in "Truth, Problem Solving and the Rationality of Science."

13 Scheffler, *Reason and Teaching*, p. 79, emphases in original.

14 *Ibid.*

15 As both Harold Alderman and Dennis Rohatyn have pointed out to me, the analogy between biological evolution and the evolution of principles of reason assessment is problematic. I completely agree. (For critical discussion of the analogy, with specific reference to Toulmin's evolutionary epistemology, cf. my "Truth, Problem Solving and the Rationality of Science.") I do not mean to suggest any substantive analogy between the two sorts of evolution. My discussion is intended *only* to suggest a way in which principles of reason assessment can be thought both to evolve and change, and also to be impartial and universal.

16 For further discussion of the compatibility of universality and impartiality with the changing character of principles of reason assessment, cf. Thagard and Nisbett, "Rationality and Charity," esp. pp. 252, 260.

17 Cf. my "Educating Reason: Critical Thinking, Informal Logic, and the Philosophy of Education. Part Two: Philosophical Questions Underlying Education for Critical Thinking." I am grateful to Harold Alderman for conversation and correspondence on this matter.

18 Cf., e.g., Perkins, "Post-primary Education has Little Impact on Informal Reasoning"; Perkins, "The Nature of Shortcomings in Everyday Reasoning"; Cornbleth, "Critical Thinking and Cognitive Processes"; Resnick, "Education and Learning to Think".

19 Cf. my "Educating Reason: Critical Thinking, Informal Logic, and the Philosophy of Education. Part Two: Philosophical Questions Underlying Education for Critical Thinking."

Bibliography

Alderman, H., "Dialectic as Philosophical Care," *Man and World*, 6, no. 2, May, 1973, pp. 206–20.

Apple, M. W., *Ideology and Curriculum*, London, Routledge & Kegan Paul, 1979.

Baier, K., *The Moral Point of View: A Rational Basis of Ethics*, Ithaca, Cornell University Press, 1958.

Baier, K., "Indoctrination and Justification," in Doyle, ed., *Educational Judgments*, pp. 74–89.

Bailin, S., "Creativity and Quality," in E. E. Robertson, ed., *Philosophy of Education 1984: Proceedings of the Fortieth Annual Meeting of the Philosophy of Education Society*, Normal, Illinois, The Philosophy of Education Society, 1985, pp. 313–21.

Bailin, S., *Achieving Extraordinary Ends: An Essay on Creativity*, Dordrecht, Martinus Nijhoff, 1987 (forthcoming).

Benedict-Gill, D., "Some Philosophical Directions in a Controversy Over Public Moral Education," in C. J. B. Macmillan, ed., *Philosophy of Education 1980: Proceedings of the Thirty-Sixth Annual Meeting of the Philosophy of Education Society*, Normal, Illinois, Philosophy of Education Society, 1981, pp. 103–13.

Binkley, R. W., "Can the Ability to Reason Well Be Taught?" in Blair and Johnson, eds, pp. 79–92.

Blair, J. A. and Johnson, R., eds, *Informal Logic: The First International Symposium*, Inverness, California, Edgepress, 1980.

Bowers, C. A., "Emergent Ideological Characteristics of Educational Policy," *Teachers College Record*, 79, no. 1, September, 1977, pp. 33–54.

Bowers, C. A., "Metaphor and the Problem of Epistemological Relativism: A Response to Tony Stigliano's Comments," *Teachers College Record*, 83, no. 2, Winter, 1981, pp. 292–9.

Bowers, C. A., "The Reproduction of Technological Consciousness: Locating the Ideological Foundations of a Radical Pedagogy," *Teachers College Record*, 83, no. 4, Summer, 1982, pp. 529–77.

Bowers, C. A., "Linguistic Roots of Cultural Invasion in Paulo Freire's Pedagogy," *Teachers College Record*, 84, no. 4, Summer, 1983, pp. 935–53.

Bowers, C. A., "The Problem of Individualism and Community in Neo-

Marxist Educational Thought," *Teachers College Record*, 85, no. 3, Spring, 1984, pp. 365–90.

Bowles, S. and Gintis, H., *Schooling in Capitalist America*, New York, Basic Books, 1976.

Brinton, A., "Values and the Ideal of Objectivity," *Journal of Educational Thought*, 16, no. 1, April, 1982, pp. 29–34.

Broudy, H. S., "Impact of Minimum Competency Testing on Curriculum," in Jaeger and Tittle, eds, pp. 108–17.

Burbules, N. C., "A Theory of Power in Education," *Educational Theory*, 36, no. 2, Spring, 1986, pp. 95–114.

Chesterton, G. K., "A Defense of Nonsense," reprinted in H. Peterson, ed., *Fifty Great Essays*, Washington Square Press, 1954.

Cornbleth, C., "Critical Thinking and Cognitive Processes," in *Review of Research in Social Studies Education, 1976–1983*, Bulletin 75, ERIC Clearinghouse for Social Studies/Social Science Education, pp. 11–63.

Crittenden, P. J., "Neutrality in Education," *Educational Philosophy and Theory*, 12, no. 1, June, 1980, pp. 1–18.

Culler, J., *On Deconstruction: Theory and Criticism After Structuralism*, Ithaca, New York, Cornell University Press, 1982.

Dewey, J., *Democracy and Education*, New York, The Free Press, Macmillan, 1916.

Dewey, J., *Experience and Nature*, Chicago, Open Court, 1926.

Dostoyevsky, F., *The Brothers Karamazov*, New York, Random House, 1955.

Doyle, J. F., ed., *Educational Judgments*, London, Routledge & Kegan Paul, 1973.

Dray, W., "Commentary," in R. S. Peters, ed., *Philosophy of Education*, Oxford, Oxford University Press, 1973, pp. 34–9.

Ennis, R. H., "A Concept of Critical Thinking," *Harvard Educational Review*, 32, no. 1, 1962, pp. 81–111.

Ennis, R. H., "Research in Philosophy of Science Bearing on Science Education," in P. D. Asquith and H. E. Kyburg, Jr., eds, *Current Research in Philosophy of Science*, East Lansing, Michigan, Philosophy of Science Association, 1979, pp. 138–70.

Ennis, R. H., "A Conception of Rational Thinking," in J. R. Coombs, ed., *Philosophy of Education 1979: Proceedings of the Thirty-Fifth Annual Meeting of the Philosophy of Education Society*, Bloomington, Illinois, Philosophy of Education Society, 1980, pp. 3–30.

Ennis, R. H., "Rational Thinking and Educational Practice," in J. F. Soltis, ed., *Philosophy and Education: Eightieth Yearbook of the National Society for the Study of Education, Part 1*, Chicago, Illinois, The National Society for the Study of Education, 1981, pp. 143–83.

Ennis, R. H., "Problems in Testing Informal Logic/Critical Thinking/Reasoning Ability," *Informal Logic*, 6, no. 1, 1984, pp. 3–9.

Ennis, R. H., "Goals for a Critical Thinking/Reasoning Curriculum," unpublished draft, June 21, 1985.

Ennis, R. H., "A Logical Basis for Measuring Critical Thinking Skills," *Educational Leadership*, October, 1985, pp. 45-8.

Ennis, R. H., "A Conception of Critical Thinking—With Some Curriculum Suggestions," in J. Hoagland, ed., *Conference '85 on Critical Thinking: Proceedings of the April 11-12 Conference on Critical Thinking at Christopher Newport College*, Newport News, Virginia, Christopher Newport College Press, 1986, pp. 13-40.

Ennis, R. H., "A Taxonomy of Critical Thinking Dispositions and Abilities," in J. Baron and R. Sternberg, eds, *Teaching for Thinking*, New York, W. H. Freeman, 1987, pp. 9-26.

Feinberg, J., *Social Philosophy*, Englewood Cliffs, New Jersey, Prentice-Hall, 1973.

Fennell, J. and R. Liveritte, "Kuhn, Education and the Grounds of Rationality," *Educational Theory*, 29, no. 2, Spring, 1979, pp. 117-27.

Feyerabend, P., *Against Method*, New York, Free Press, 1975.

Flew, A., "What is Indoctrination?" *Studies in Philosophy and Education*, 4, no. 3, 1966, pp. 281-306.

Floden, R. E., "The Role of Rhetoric in Changing Teachers' Beliefs," *Teaching and Teacher Education*, 1, no. 1, 1985, pp. 19-32.

Freire, P., *Pedagogy of the Oppressed*, New York, Seabury Press, 1973.

Freire, P., *Education for Critical Consciousness*, New York, Seabury Press, 1978.

Freire, P., *The Politics of Education*, South Hadley, Massachusetts, Bergin & Garvey, 1985.

Geuss, R., *The Idea of a Critical Theory*, Cambridge, Cambridge University Press, 1981.

Giroux, H. A., *Ideology Culture and The Process of Schooling*, Philadelphia, Temple University Press, 1981.

Giroux, H. A., "Public Philosophy and the Crisis in Education," *Harvard Educational Review*, 54, no. 2, May, 1984, pp. 186-94.

Glass, G. V., "Standards and Criteria," *Journal of Educational Measurement*, 15, Winter, 1978, pp. 237-61.

Glass, G. V., "Minimum Competence and Incompetence in Florida," *Phi Delta Kappan*, 59, May, 1978, pp. 602-5.

Govier, T., Review of John E. McPeck, *Critical Thinking and Education*, *Dialogue*, 22, 1983, pp. 170-5.

Green, T. F., "Teaching, Acting, and Behaving," reprinted in Scheffler, ed., *Philosophy and Education*, pp. 115-35. Originally published in *Harvard Educational Review*, 34, no. 4, Fall, 1964, pp. 507-24.

Green, T. F., *The Activities of Teaching*, New York, McGraw-Hill, 1971.

Green, T. F., "Indoctrination and Beliefs," in Snook, ed., *Concepts of Indoctrination*, pp. 25-46.

Greene, M., "Response to 'Competence and Excellence: The Search for an Egalitarian Standard, the Demand for a Universal Guarantee,' by Jenne K. Britell," in Jaeger and Tittle, eds, pp. 40–8.

Harris, K., *Education and Knowledge: The Structured Misrepresentation of Reality*, London, Routledge & Kegan Paul, 1979.

Holton, G., "Science, Science Teaching, and Rationality," in S. Hook, P. Kurtz, and M. Todorovich, eds, *The Philosophy of the Curriculum*, Buffalo, NY, Prometheus Books, 1975, pp. 101–18.

Jaeger, R. M., and Tittle, C. K., eds, *Minimum Competency Achievement Testing*, Berkeley, McCutchen, 1980.

Johnson, R., "Toulmin's Bold Experiment," *Informal Logic Newsletter*, 3, no. 2, 1981, pp. 16–27, and 3, no. 3, pp. 13–19.

Jones, H., *Kant's Principle of Personality*, Madison, University of Wisconsin Press, 1971.

Kant, I., *Foundations of the Metaphysics of Morals*, trans. L. W. Beck, New York, Bobbs-Merrill, 1959. The Original *Grundlegung Zer Metaphysik Der Sitten* was published in 1785.

Katz, M. S., "Critical Literacy: A Conception of Education as a Moral Right and Social Ideal," in R. B. Everhart, ed., *The Public School Monopoly: A Critical Analysis of Education and the State in American Society*, Cambridge, Massachusetts, Ballinger, 1982, pp. 193–223.

Kekes, J., *A Justification of Rationality*, Albany, The State University of New York Press, 1976.

Kitcher, P., "Good Science, Bad Science, Dreadful Science, and Pseudoscience," *Journal of College Science Teaching*, 14, no. 3, December 1984/January 1985, pp. 168–73.

Kordig, C. R., *The Justification of Scientific Change*, Dordrecht, D. Reidel, 1971.

Kozol, J., *The Night Is Dark and I Am Far from Home*, New York, Continuum, 1975.

Kozol, J., "A New Look at the Literacy Campaign in Cuba," *Harvard Educational Review*, 48, no. 3, August, 1978, pp. 341–77.

Kroman, N., "Epistemology as the Locus of Teacher Competence," *Journal of Educational Thought*, 11, no. 2, 1977, pp. 119–29.

Kuhn, T. S., "The Function of Dogma in Scientific Research," in A. C. Crombie, ed., *Scientific Change*, London, Heinemann, 1963, pp. 347–95.

Kuhn, T. S., "The Essential Tension: Tradition and Innovation in Scientific Research," in C. W. Taylor and F. Barron, eds, *Scientific Creativity: Its Recognition and Development*, New York, Wiley, 1963, pp. 341–54. Reprinted as the title essay in T. S. Kuhn, *The Essential Tension*.

Kuhn, T. S., *The Structure of Scientific Revolutions*, second edition, enlarged, Chicago, University of Chicago Press, 1970. First edition published in 1962.

Kuhn, T. S., "Logic of Discovery of Psychology of Research?", In Lakatos and Musgrave, eds, pp. 1–24.

Kuhn, T.S., "Reflections on My Critics," in Lakatos and Musgrave, eds, pp. 231–76.

Kuhn, T.S., *The Essential Tension*, Chicago, University of Chicago Press, 1977.

Ladenson, R.F., "A Theory of Personal Autonomy," *Ethics*, 86, no. 1, October, 1975, pp. 30–48.

Lakatos, I., "Falsification and the Methodology of Scientific Research Programmes," in Lakatos and Musgrave, eds, pp. 91–196.

Lakatos, I., and A. Musgrave, eds, *Criticism and the Growth of Knowledge*, Cambridge, Cambridge University Press, 1970.

Laudan, L., *Progress and Its Problems*, Berkeley, University of California Press, 1977.

Macmillan, C.J.B., "Love and Logic in 1984," in E.E. Robertson, ed., *Philosophy of Education 1984: Proceedings of the Fortieth Annual Meeting of the Philosophy of Education Society*, Normal, Illinois, Philosophy of Education Society, 1985, pp. 3–16.

McPeck, J.E., *Critical Thinking and Education*, New York, St Martin's Press, 1981.

McPeck, J.E., "Response to H. Siegel," in D. Nyberg, ed., *Philosophy of Education 1985: Proceedings of the Forty-First Annual Meeting of the Philosophy of Education Society*, Normal, Illinois, Philosophy of Education Society, 1986, pp. 73–7.

Mannheim, K., *Ideology and Utopia*, New York, Harcourt, Brace & World, 1936.

Martin, M., *Concepts of Science Education*, Chicago, Scott Foresman, 1972.

Matthews, M.R., *The Marxist Theory of Schooling: A Study of Epistemology and Education*, Sussex, Harvester Press, 1980.

Moshman, D., "A Role for Creationism in Science Education," *Journal of College Science Teaching*, 15, no. 2, November, 1985, pp. 106–9.

Nagel, E., "In Defense of Scientific Knowledge," in S. Hook, P. Kurtz, and M. Todorovich, eds, *The Philosophy of The Curriculum*, Buffalo, NY, Prometheus Books, 1975, pp. 119–26.

Noddings, N., "Response to Ennis," in J.R. Coombs, ed., *Philosophy of Education 1979: Proceedings of the Thirty-Fifth Annual Meeting of the Philosophy of Education Society*, Bloomington, Illinois, Philosophy of Education Society, 1980, pp. 31–4.

Norris, S.P., "The Choice of Standard Conditions in Defining Critical Thinking Competence," *Educational Theory*, 35, no. 1, Winter, 1985, pp. 97–107.

Norris, S.P., "Synthesis of Research on Critical Thinking," *Educational Leadership*, May, 1985, pp. 40–5.

Norris, S.P., "Evaluating Critical Thinking Ability," *The History and Social Studies Teacher*, 21, no. 3, March, 1986, pp. 135–46.

Passmore, J., "On Teaching To Be Critical," in R.S. Peters, ed., *The Concept of Education*, London, Routledge & Kegan Paul, 1967, pp. 192–211.

Paul, R.W., "Teaching Critical Thinking in the 'Strong' Sense: A Focus on Self-Deception, World Views, and a Dialectical Mode of Analysis," *Informal Logic Newletter,* 4, no. 2, 1982, pp. 2–7.

Paul, R.W., "An Agenda Item for the Informal Logic/Critical Thinking Movement," *Informal Logic Newsletter*, 5, no. 2, 1983, pp. 23–4.

Paul, R.W., "Critical Thinking: Fundamental to Education for a Free Society," *Educational Leadership*, September, 1984, pp. 4–14.

Paul, R.W., "Critical Thought Essential to the Acquisition of Rational Knowledge and Passions," paper presented at the Connecticut Conference on Thinking, Sponsored by the Connecticut State Department of Education, 1984.

Paul, R.W., "McPeck's Mistakes," Review of John E. McPeck, *Critical Thinking and Education, Informal Logic*, 7, no. 1, Winter, 1985, pp. 35–43.

Perkins D.N., "Post-primary Education has Little Impact on Informal Reasoning," *Journal of Educational Psychology*, 77, no. 5, 1985, pp. 562–71.

Perkins, D.N., "The Nature of Shortcomings in Everyday Reasoning," unpublished manuscript.

Peters, R.S., "Reason and Habit: The Paradox of Moral Education," in Scheffler, ed., *Philosophy and Education*, pp. 245–62.

Peters, R.S., "Reason and Passion," in G. Vesey, ed., *The Proper Study*, Royal Institute of Philosophy Lectures, vol. 4, London, Macmillan, 1971.

Peters, R.S., "Education as Initiation," in R.D. Archambault, ed., *Philosophical Analysis and Education*, New York, Humanities Press, 1972, pp. 87–111.

Peters, R.S., "Aims of Education—A Conceptual Inquiry," in Peters, ed., *Philosophy of Education*, Oxford, Oxford University Press, 1973, pp. 11–57.

Peters, R.S., *Reason and Compassion*, London, Routledge & Kegan Paul, 1973.

Peters, R.S., *Education and the Education of Teachers*, London, Routledge & Kegan Paul, 1977.

Phillips, D.C., "The Anatomy of Autonomy," *Educational Philosophy and Theory*, 7, no. 2, 1975, pp. 1–12.

Phillips, D.C., "Can Scientific Method Be Taught?" *Journal of College Science Teaching*, 15, no. 2, November, 1985, pp. 95–101.

Pincoffs, E.L., "On Avoiding Moral Indoctrination," in Doyle, ed., *Educational Judgments*, pp. 59–73.

Pipho, C., "Minimum Competency Testing in 1978: A Look at State Standards," *Phi Delta Kappan*, 59, May, 1978, pp. 585–7.

Popham, W. J., "As Always, Provocative," *Journal of Educational Measurement*, 15, no. 4, Winter, 1978, pp. 297–300.

Popham, W. J., *Criterion-Referenced Measurement*, Englewood Cliffs, NJ, Prentice-Hall, 1978.

Popham, W. J., "Curriculum and Minimum Competency: A Reaction to the Remarks of H. S. Broudy," in Jaeger and Tittle, eds, pp. 121–3.

Popper, K. R., *The Open Society and Its Enemies*, vol. 2, Princeton, Princeton University Press, 1962.

Popper, K. R., "Normal Science and Its Dangers," in Lakatos and Musgrave, eds, pp. 51–8.

Proefriedt, W., "Socialist Criticisms of Education in the United States: Problems and Possibilities," *Harvard Educational Review*, 50, no. 4, November, 1980, pp. 467–80.

Resnick, L. B., "Education and Learning to Think," a draft report prepared for the Commision on Behavioral and Social Sciences and Education, National Research Council, September, 1985.

Robertson, E. E., "Practical Reasons, Authority, and Education," in R. E. Roemer, ed., *Philosophy of Education 1983: Proceedings of the Thirty-Ninth Annual Meeting of the Philosophy of Education Society*, Normal, Illinois, Philosophy of Education Society, 1984, pp. 61–75.

Roemer, R. E., "Pedagogy and Rationality," *Educational Theory*, 33, nos. 3–4, Summer–Fall, 1983, pp. 167–77.

Rohatyn, D., *Naturalism and Deontology*, The Hague, Mouton, 1975.

Russell, B., *A History of Western Philosophy*, New York, Simon & Schuster, 1945.

Ryle, G., *The Concept of Mind*, New York, Barnes & Noble, 1949.

Scheffler, I., *The Language of Education*, Springfield, Illinois, Charles C. Thomas, 1960.

Scheffler, I., *Conditions of Knowledge*, Chicago, Illinois, Scott Foresman, 1965.

Scheffler, I., ed., *Philosophy and Education*, second edition, Boston, Allyn & Bacon, 1966.

Scheffler, I., *Reason and Teaching*, New York, Bobbs-Merrill, 1973. First published in 1973 by Routledge & Kegan Paul.

Scheffler, I., "Philosophical Models of Teaching," in Scheffler, *Reason and Teaching*, pp. 67–81.

Scheffler, I., "Moral Education and the Democratic Ideal," in Scheffler, *Reason and Teaching*, pp. 136–45.

Scheffler, I., "Philosophies-of and the Curriculum," in Doyle, ed., *Educational Judgments*, pp. 209–18.

Scheffler, I., *Science and Subjectivity*, second edition, enlarged, Indianapolis, Indiana, Hackett, 1982.

Scheffler, I., "In Praise of the Cognitive Emotions," reprinted as Appendix B in Scheffler, *Science and Subjectivity*, pp. 139–57. Originally published in *Teachers College Record*, vol. 1977, pp. 171–86.

Scheffler, I., *Of Human Potential*, London, Routledge & Kegan Paul, 1985.

Schwab, J.J., *The Teaching of Science as Enquiry*, Cambridge, MA, Harvard University Press, 1962.

Scriven, M., "Cognitive Moral Education," *Phi Delta Kappan*, 57, 1975, pp. 689–94.

Scriven, M., "How to Anchor Standards," *Journal of Educational Measurement*, 15, no. 4, Winter, 1978, pp. 273–5.

Scriven, M., "Summative Teacher Evaluation," in J. Millman, ed., *Handbook of Teacher Evaluation*, Beverly Hills, California, Sage, 1981, pp. 244–71.

Searle, J., "The World Turned Upside Down," *New York Review of Books*, October 27, 1983, pp. 74–9.

Siegel, H., "Kuhn and Critical Thought," in I. Steinberg, ed., *Philosophy of Education 1977: Proceedings of the Thirty-Third Annual Meeting of the Philosophy of Education Society*, Urbana, Illinois, Philosophy of Education Society, 1978, pp. 173–9.

Siegel, H., "Kuhn and Schwab on Science Texts and the Goals of Science Education," *Educational Theory*, 28, no. 4, Fall, 1978, pp. 302–9.

Siegel, H., "Is It Irrational to Be Immoral? A Response to Freeman," *Educational Philosophy and Theory*, 10, no. 2, October, 1978, pp. 51–61.

Siegel, H., "On the Distortion of the History of Science in Science Education," *Science Education*, 63, no. 1, 1979, pp. 111–18.

Siegel, H., "Justification, Discovery and the Naturalizing of Epistemology," *Philosophy of Science*, 47, no. 2, 1980, pp. 297–321.

Siegel, H., "Objectivity, Rationality, Incommensurability, and More," *British Journal for the Philosophy of Science*, 31, no. 4, 1980, pp. 359–75.

Siegel, H., "Critical Thinking As An Educational Ideal," *Educational Forum*, 45, no. 1, 1980, pp. 7–23.

Siegel, H., "Rationality, Talking Dogs, and Forms of Life," *Educational Theory*, 30, no. 2, Spring, 1980, pp. 135–48.

Siegel, H., "Rationality, Morality, and Rational Moral Education: Further Response to Freeman," *Educational Philosophy and Theory*, 12, no. 1, March, 1980, pp. 37–47.

Siegel, H., "Creationism, Evolution, and Education: The California Fiasco," *Phi Delta Kappan*, 63, no. 2, 1981, pp. 95–101.

Siegel, H., "How 'Practical' Should Philosophy of Education Be?" *Educational Studies*, 12, no. 2, Summer, 1981, pp. 125–34.

Siegel, H., "The Future and Purpose of Philosophy of Education," *Educational Theory*, 31, no. 1, Winter, 1981, pp. 11–15.

Siegel, H., "Rationality, Critical Thinking, and Moral Education," unpublished paper presented at the First International Conference on Critical Thinking, Moral Education, and Rationality, Sonoma State

University, May, 1981.

Siegel, H., "Truth, Problem Solving and the Rationality of Science," *Studies in History and Philosophy of Science*, 14, no. 2, 1983, pp. 89–112.

Siegel, H., "Brown on Epistemology and the New Philosophy of Science," *Synthese*, 56, no. 1, 1983, pp. 61–89.

Siegel, H., "Educational Ideals and Educational Practice: The Case of Minimum Competency Testing," *Issues in Education*, 1, nos. 2–3, 1983, pp. 154–70.

Siegel, H., "Genderized Cognitive Perspectives and the Redefinition of Philosophy of Education," *Teachers College Record*, 85, no. 1, 1983, pp. 100–19.

Siegel, H., "Critical Literacy and Minimum Competency Testing," in E. Grossen, ed., *Proceedings of the Fourteenth Annual Meeting of the Far West Philosophy of Education Society*, 1983, pp. 46–64.

Siegel, H., "Empirical Psychology, Naturalized Epistemology, and First Philosophy," *Philosophy of Science*, 51, no. 4, 1984, pp. 667–76.

Siegel, H., "Goodmanian Relativism," *Monist*, 67, no. 3, July, 1984, pp. 359–75.

Siegel, H., "The Response to Creationism," *Educational Studies*, 15, no. 4, 1984, pp. 349–64.

Siegel, H., "What Is the Question Concerning the Rationality of Science?" *Philosophy of Science*, 52, no. 4, December, 1985, pp. 517–37.

Siegel, H., "Educating Reason: Critical Thinking, Informal Logic, and the Philosophy of Education. Part One: A Critique of McPeck and a Sketch of an Alternative View," *American Philosophical Association Newsletter on Teaching Philosophy*, Spring-Summer, 1985, pp. 10–13.

Siegel, H., "Educating Reason: Critical Thinking, Informal Logic, and the Philosophy of Education. Part Two: Philosophical Questions Underlying Education for Critical Thinking," *Informal Logic*, 7, nos. 2–3, Spring–Fall, 1985, pp. 69–81.

Siegel, H., "Relativism, Rationality, and Science Education," *Journal of College Science Teaching*, 15, no. 2, November, 1985, pp. 102–5.

Siegel, H., "McPeck, Informal Logic, and the Nature of Critical Thinking," in D. Nyberg, ed., *Philosophy of Education 1985: Proceedings of the Forty-First Annual Meeting of the Philosophy of Education Society*, Normal, Illinois, Philosophy of Education Society, 1986, pp. 61–72.

Siegel, H., "Relativism, Truth and Incoherence," *Synthese*, 68, no. 2, August, 1986, pp. 225–59.

Siegel, H., *Relativism Refuted: A Critique of Contemporary Epistemological Relativism*, Dordrecht, D. Reidel, (Sunthese Library, vol. 189), 1987.

Siegel, H., "Rationality and Ideology," *Educational Theory*, 37, no. 2, Spring, 1987, pp. 153–67.

Simon, R. I., "Signposts for a Critical Pedagogy: A Review of Henry

Giroux's *Theory and Resistance in Education*," *Educational Theory*, 34, no. 4, Fall, 1984, pp. 379–88.

Small, R., "Knowledge and Ideology in the Marxist Philosophy of Education," *Educational Philosophy and Theory*, 15, no. 2, October, 1983, pp. 15–37.

Smart, P., "The Concept of Indoctrination," in G. Langford and D.J. O'Connor, eds, *New Essays in the Philosophy of Education*, London, Routledge & Kegan Paul, 1973, pp. 33–46.

Snook, I.A., *Indoctrination and Education*, London, Routledge & Kegan Paul, 1972.

Snook, I.A., ed., *Concepts of Indoctrination*, London, Routledge & Kegan Paul, 1972.

Snook, I.A., "'Ideology' in Educational Theory," *Access*, 1, no. 1, 1982, pp. 12–20.

Stigliano, T., "Remarks on C.A. Bowers's 'Curriculum as Cultural Reproduction: An Examination of Metaphor as a Carrier of Ideology,'" *Teachers College Record*, 83, no. 2, Winter, 1981, pp. 285–91.

Suttle, B.B., "The Need For and Inevitability of Moral Indoctrination," *Educational Studies*, 12, no. 2, 1981, pp. 151–61.

Thagard, P., and R.E. Nisbett, "Rationality and Charity," *Philosophy of Science*, 50, no. 2, June, 1983, pp. 250–67.

Toulmin, S., *Human Understanding*, Volume I, Princeton, NJ, Princeton University Press, 1972.

Trigg, R., *Reason and Commitment*, Cambridge, Cambridge University Press, 1973.

Wagner, P., "Moral Education, Indoctrination, and the Principle of Minimizing Substantive Moral Error," in D.R. DeNicola, ed., *Philosophy of Education 1981: Proceedings of the Thirty-Seventh Annual Meeting of the Philosophy of Education Society*, Normal, Illinois, Philosophy of Education Society, 1982, pp. 191–8.

Waks, L.J., "Knowledge and Understanding as Educational Aims," *Monist*, 52, 1968, pp. 105–19.

Watkins, J.W.N., "Against 'Normal Science,'" Lakatos and Musgrave, eds, pp. 25–38.

Weddle, P., Review of John E. McPeck, *Critical Thinking and Education*, *Informal Logic*, 6, no. 2, 1984, pp. 23–5.

Wilson, J., "Indoctrination and Rationality," in Snook, ed., *Concepts of Indoctrination*, pp. 17–24.

Wise, A.E., "Minimum Competency Testing: Another Case of Hyper-Rationalization," *Phi Delta Kappan*, 59, May, 1978, pp. 596–8.

Index

absolutism 144n; in science education, 107–8
accountability in education, and minimum competency testing, 116, 117
action, rational, 41, 128
adulthood, and critical thinking in education, 54–5, 57–8
Alderman, H., 152–3n
Apple, M. W., 64
argument networks, 12–13
assessment, 6–7, 9, 10, 14, 25–6, 35–6, 44; needs, in testing, 121–3, 124; *see also* reasons conception, reason assessment
assumptions, identification of, 20–2
atomism, 11–13, 15
attitude, critical, *see* spirit, critical
autonomy, as mark of critical thinker, 54–5, 79, 88, 106–7, 122, 125–6

Bailin, S., 152n.
belief, personal, and critical thinking, 11–13, 15–17, 78–80; evidential style, 83–5, 87, 88, 89–90; non-evidential/non-critical, 80–1, 84–5, 87–9; *see also* indoctrination
Binkley, R. W., 39, 147n., 151n.
Black, M., 140n.
Blair, J. A., 51, 138n., 139n.
Blair, J. A., and Johnson, R., 139n.
Bowers, C. A., 64, 67, 74–5, 76
Bowles, S., 67, 73, 76
Broudy, H., 124
Burbules, N. C., 32, 64, 73, 76, 159n.

careerism in science, 91, 111–12
character traits, 2, 7–8, 18, 39–41, 46–7, 79, 125, 131
Chesterton, G. K., 48
cognition and affect, 40–1
Cohen, M., 155n.
competency, and critical thinking, 8
competency testing, *see* testing, minimum competency
conceptual analysis, in philosophy of education, ix; *see also* ordinary language analysis
consciousness, see ideology
consistency and rationality, 33–4
context, of education, 115
Cornell Critical Thinking Tests, 8
creationism and education, 48, 168n., 172n.
creativity and critical thinking, 152n.
critical thinking, criteria for, 9, 36–7, 44–5; definitions, 5, 6, 22–3, 141–2n.; as dialectical, 13–14; as educational cognate of rationality, 30, 32, 90, 127–8, 140–1n.; as generalizable, 18–24, 44, 46; 'pure skills' view, 6–7, 8, 13, 18; as regulative ideal, 46–7; 'skills plus tendencies' view, 7–8, 18, 139–50n.; strong sense, 11, 12–18; as subject-specific, 19–21, 22–3, 25, 27–8, 34–5; theory of, 15, 127, 131, 135–6; value of, 9–10, 14; weak sense, 11–12, 17; *see also* philosophy; rationality; reasons conception
critical thinking, justification of, 3, 9, 31, 168n.;

pragmatic/philosophical, 51–2;
transcendental argument, 155n.;
see also ideal, educational
curriculum, inclusion of reasoning,
ix, 1, 43, 114–15; and science
education, 3, 111, 113, 114

decision-making, rational, 4, 128,
141–2n.
deconstructionism, 49
democracy, 60–1, 70
Derrida, J., 49
determinism, ideological, 68–9,
71–3
Dewey, J., xi, 77, 126, 172n.
dialectical analysis, 13–15
dispositions, 2, 7–10, 23, 30, 32, 39–
41, 46–7, 79, 125, *see also*
tendencies
dogmatism, 93, 96, 102, 107–9, 111
Dostoevsky, F., 49–50
Dray, W., 155n.

education, aims, ix, 31, 46–7, 50,
110, 114–15, 116–17, 122, 125–6;
content, 44–5; epistemology,
43–4; ethics, 42–3; manner, 42,
45–6, 47, 55–7; philosophy, 2,
3–4, 128; as political, 66–8, 69–71
education, and critical thinking, 2,
13, 17–18, 19–21, 24–5, 28, 42–7;
challenges to, 48–9
efficiency, and rationality, 129–31
emotion and reason, 40–1, 49–50
empathy and morality, 43
Ennis, R., 2, 5, 6–10, 18, 30–1, 35,
148n.
enquiry, fluid/stable, 3, 100–4,
109–11
epistemology, and critical thinking,
24–5, 27, 29–30, 142n.; and
ideology, 66; and reason
assessment, 35–8, 128; *see also*
education; justification; reasons;
relativism
ethics, *see* education; morality
evaluation, in education *see* testing,
minimum competency
evaluation, *see* assessment

evidence, and rationality, 9, 39, 43–
5, 110–11, 112, 279; theory of,
142n.
evolution and universality, 134–5

faith and reason, 128
fallacies, recognition of, 11, 12, 14,
20, 25–6
fallibilism, 144n.
falsificationism, 17, 112, 146n.
Falwell, J., 48
feminism and critical thinking, 49
Feyerabend, P., 49, 107, 109
Flew, A., 164–5n.
Floden, R., 153n.
Freire, P., 66–7, 70, 74, 76

Geertz, 64
Geuss, R., 159n.
Giarelli, J., 161n.
Gintis, H., 67, 73, 76
Giroux, H. A., 62, 65, 66–7, 73, 76,
159n.
Glass, G. V., 118–21, 123–4
Goodman, N., 117, 171n.
Govier, T., 147n.
Green, T. F., 80, 83–5, 153n.

Habermas, J., 161–2n.
habits, rational, 2, 7–8, 10, 39–41,
44, 86–7
Harris, K., 67, 68, 73
honesty, in education, 9, 45, 56–7,
110–11; intellectual, 39

ideal, educational, critical thinking
as, ix, 2, 10, 31, 110–11, 117, 122,
125, 127, 136–7
ideal, educational, critical thinking
as, justification, 3, 9, 48–61, 62,
133–4; as regulative, 46–7
ideals, educational, and ideology, 3,
66–8
ideology, and consciousness, 68–9,
71–2; definition, 64–5; and
liberation, 76–7; and objection to
critical thinking, 3, 62–77; and
rationality, 72–6
Illich, I., 67

impartiality, 34, 39, 43, 88, 110–11, 134–5
inculcation of beliefs 82–5, 87, 89–90, 97–9; *see also* indoctrination
indoctrination, 3, 48, 78–9, 89–90; avoidance, 87–9; definition, 79–81; inevitability, 81–5; justified, 81–5, 170n.; in science education, 93, 95–7, 109
inference, in education, 43
Informal Logic Movement, ix, 1–2, 24–5, 38
Informal Logic Movement, critique of, 19, 26–7, 35; and education, 5, 28
information, and logic, 8, 27–8
initiation, education as, 59–60, 96, 98, 111, 133–4

Johnson, R., 51, 139n.
judgment, competent, 58; grounded/capricious, 120–1; independent, 58; rational 38, 39, 44
justification, and epistemology, 35, 36–8, 39, 45, 128

Kant, I., 56, 70, 116
Katz, M. B., 67
Katz, M. S. 157n.
Kozol, J., 67, 76, 160n.
Kuhn, T. S., critique of, 99–115; on science, 3, 91–9

Laudan, L., 30, 32
legitimation, 159n.
liberation, and education, 76–7
literacy, functional, 117, 123, 124–5, 126
logic, formal, 1, 24–6; informal, and critical thinking, 2, 5, 140–1n., 24–7; *see also* Informal Logic Movement

Macmillan, C. J. B., 156n.
McPeck, J. E., 2, 5, 18–31, 35; critique of, 24–30, 152n.; and epistemology, 36–8, 113, 114; and

justification of critical thinking, 52–4, 157n.
Mannheim, K., 68, 160–1n.
Martin, M., 109–10
Marx, K., on ideology, 65, 160–1n.
Marxism, on critical thinking, 49
Matthews, M., 159n.
Mooney, E., 152n.
morality, and education, 42–3, 71, 86; and rationality, 4, 10, 16, 128, 129–30, 151n.

neutrality, in education, 3, 66–8, 70–1; and rationality, 11, 13–14, 74
Newcomb's problem, 4, 128
Noddings, N., 142n.

objectivity, and critical spirit, 39; in education, 110–11
ordinary language analysis, 166n.; *see also* conceptual analysis

paradigms, scientific, 92–3, 94–5, 96–7, 99, 100–1, 104–6, 107, 111
paradox, 4, 128
passions, rational, 40–1
Passmore, J., 147n.
paternalism, and rationality, 167n.
Paul, R., 1–2, 5, 10–18, 30–1, 40, 138n.; on education, 158n.
persons, respect for, 55–7, 70–1, 106–7
Peters, R. S., 33, 40–1, 59, 149n.; on indoctrination, 86
Phillips, D., 152n., 166n., 172n., 174n.
philosophy, and critical thinking, 4, 112–13, 114, 157n.
pluralism, in science education, 108–10, 111–12
policy, education, 116–17, 126
Popham, W. J., 120–1, 124
Popper, K., 94
premise and conclusion, 20, 26, 43–4
principles, 33–4; alterability, 59, 133–5; subject-neutral, 34–5, 38, 40; subject-specific, 34–5, 36–8

prisoner's dilemma, paradox of, 4, 128
proficiencies: for critical thinking, 6–7, 9–10, 35; testing for, 8
propaganda, *see* indoctrination
psychology of education, 115

Quine, W. van O., 146n.

rationalism, enlightened, 74–5
rationality, criteria for, 9–10; and critical thinking, 2, 28–30, 32–4, 127–8, 140–1n., 143n.; definition, 33; in education, 8; enhancement, 81, 84, 85, 86–7, 89–90; justification, 132, 135, 142n., 155n.; limits, 132–3, 135, 155n.; means-ends, 129–31, 135; nature, 4, 128–9; as self-justifying, 132, 167n.; theory, 15, 127–37; *see also* morality; neutrality; paternalism; science
reason assessment, 23–4, 26–8, 29–30, 34–8, 39, 44; alterability of principles, 133–5; in education 59–60
reasoning, development, neglect of, 1; 'everyday', 1; theoretical/practical, 140n.
reasons, epistemology of, 128–31, 135; good, 27, 28–30, 36–7, 142n., 145n., 149.; nature of, 4, 26, 29, 37–8, 127, 131; in science, 112–13, 114
reasons conception, 2, 8–9, 23–4, 30–1, 32–47; and education, 42–7
reciprocity, concept of, 145n
relativism, 143n., 160–1n.; epistemological, 14–15, 49, 107, 162n; inscience education, 107–10; scientific, 95
religion, reason and faith, 128
Robertson, E., 149n., 153n
Roemer, R., 175n
Rohatyn, D., 64, 164n., 167n
rote memorization, move away from, ix, 1
Russell, B., 78, 91
Ryle, G., 44

Scheffler, I., ix, 1; on democracy 60–1, 138n.; on education, 45–6, 58, 59, 139n., 151n; on rationality, 30, 32, 33, 48, 62, 127, 134, 149–50n
schools, structure, 115
Schrag, F., 152n.
Schwab, J. J., 3, 100–3, 105, 107, 108–9
science and critical thinking, 91–3, 111–13; history, 93, 97–9, 105–6, 109; normal, 92, 93–4, 97–8, 100–1, 103–6, 111; philosophy, 112–13, 114, 127; and pseudo-science, 113, 114
    as rational, 130–1; revolutionary, 92, 94–5, 101, 103–4; *see also* relativism
science education, 3, 59, 91–111; dogmatic, 107–9, 111; goal of, 48, 99–100, 102–3, 104–6, 110–12, 113–14; Kuhn on, 92–3, 95–9, critique of, 99–115; morality of, 106–7; reasons in, 112–13; *see also* indoctrination; pluralism; relativism
Scriven, M., 51, 120–2, 124, 172n.
self-deception, 11–13, 15–17
self-interest and impartiality, 15–17, 39, 43, 60
self-sufficiency, 54–5, 57–8, 122, 126
Simon, R., 64
skepticism, reflective, 12, 22–4
skills, life, testing for, 117, 121–3, 125
skills, view *see* critical thinking, 'pure skills' view *and* 'skills plus tendencies' view
Smart, P., 167n.
Snook, I. A., 64, 164n.
spirit, critical, and critical thinking, 23–4, 30, 39–42, 44, 110, 156n.
Spring, J., 67
standards and rationality, 34
statement assessment, 6–7, 141n.
Sumner, C., 158n.
Suttle, B. B., 86, 165n., 166n.

teaching, manner of, 45–6, 56–7

tendencies, for critical thinking, 6–7, 8–10; testing for, 8; under attention, 7, 8, 9, 10

testing, criterion-referenced, 119–20; for critical thinking, 1, 7–8, 10, 148n., 174n.; minimum competency, 3, 116–26, as arbitrary, 117, 118–24, defined, 117–18, needs assessment approach, 121–3, 124; norm-referenced, 119

theories, proliferation of, 109–10

theory choice in science, 4, 94–5, 112, 127, 130–1

thinker, critical 9–10, 11, 13, 18, 23, 38, 41–2

Toulmin, S., 150n.

tradition and rationality, 59–60, 133–5

training, education as, 99, 121–3, 124

truth, and reason, 9, 128, 153n.; and science, 170n.

universities, critical thinking in, 1

value, of critical thinking, 9–10, 14

values, of critical thinker, 39, 131

Wagner, P., 82, 166n.

warrant and epistemology, 35, 36–8, 59n., 66

Watkins, J., 94

Weddle, P., 140n.

Wilson, J., 78, 81, 84, 164n., 165n., 168n.

Wirth, L., 65

world views, 16–17